Postcard History Series

North Dakota Postcards 1900–1930

POSTCARD HISTORY SERIES

North Dakota Postcards 1900–1930

Larry Aasen

ARCADIA PUBLISHING

ISBN 978-0-7385-0161-1

Published by Arcadia Publishing
Charleston, South Carolina

Printed in the United States of America

Library of Congress Catalog Card Number: 99-63797

For all general information contact Arcadia Publishing at:
Telephone 843-853-2070
Fax 843-853-0044
E-Mail sales@arcadiapublishing.com
For customer service and orders:
Toll-Free 1-888-313-2665

Visit us on the Internet at www.arcadiapublishing.com

Contents

INTRODUCTION

Life in North Dakota from 1900 to 1930 was a world different from today. We get a glimpse of that world in this book because my mother, Clara (Brenden) Aasen, saved 488 postcards in a big leather album where they remained protected.

She saved these postcards because they were a part of her life. In those days, postcards were a very important method of communication. My mother, who lived on a farm five miles from Hillsboro, North Dakota, used postcards to keep in touch with her boyfriend, her relatives, and friends. And they sent postcards back to her with the same intentions.

There was no e-mail in those days and not everybody had telephones. In fact, during the Depression of the late 1920s and early 1930s, many North Dakotans discontinued telephone service.

These cards tell tales of flirting, parties, barn dances, crop and weather reports, politics, and so on. Many cards were sent just to give somebody a laugh. The cards show fashions of the day, the buildings, and streets, as well as revealing a lot about the culture of the time.

Postcards were also a very cheap way to communicate. The cards probably cost about a nickel and you could mail them for one penny—up until 1917 when the price was doubled to 2¢. The post office department said the increase would help pay for the war effort. After the war ended in 1919, the price dropped back to 1¢.

Many of my mother's cards were sent to and from her boyfriend Theodore Aasen, my dad, whom she married in 1914. Some of the cards contain rather personal comments, which I am sure the rural delivery mailman read and enjoyed.

In my imagination, I can see my mother at age 19, walking a half a mile up to our mailbox in the middle of a North Dakota snowstorm. I can see her open the mailbox, and there is a colorful postcard from her boyfriend Ted. She turns the card over and it says, "What are you doing Saturday night?"

Love by postcard! And I have that postcard.
This book is dedicated to my mother, Clara Brenden Aasen.

—Larry Aasen

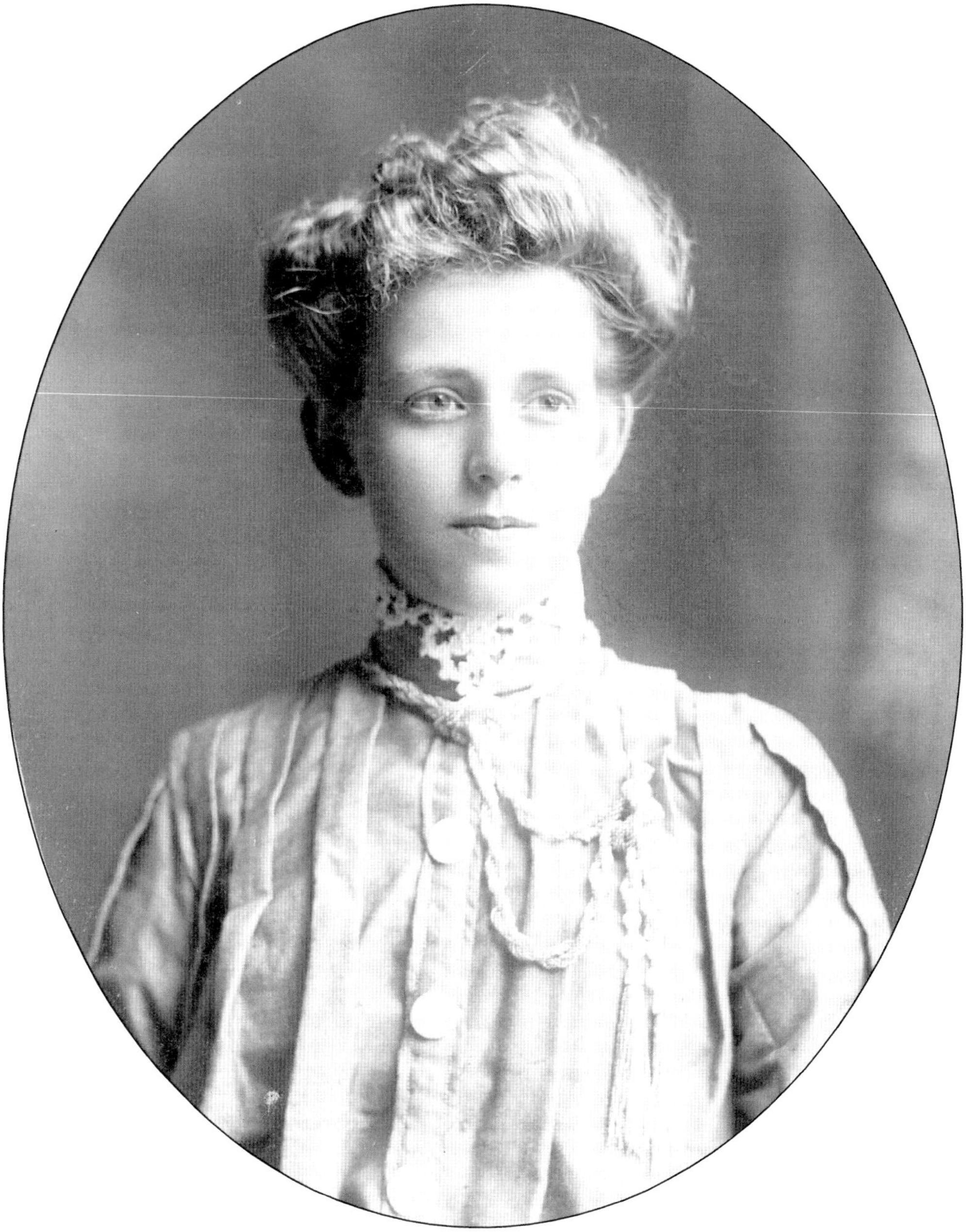

I dedicate this book to my mother,
Clara Brenden Aasen, who saved all the postcards.

One

North Dakota Cities

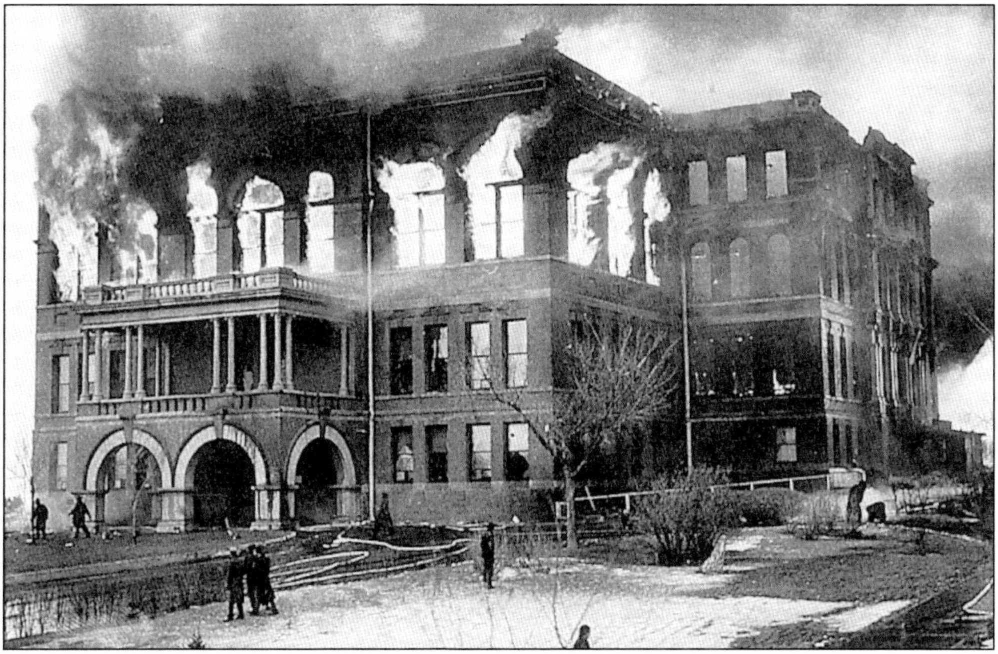

This rare postcard shows North Dakota's first capitol building being destroyed by fire on December 28, 1930.

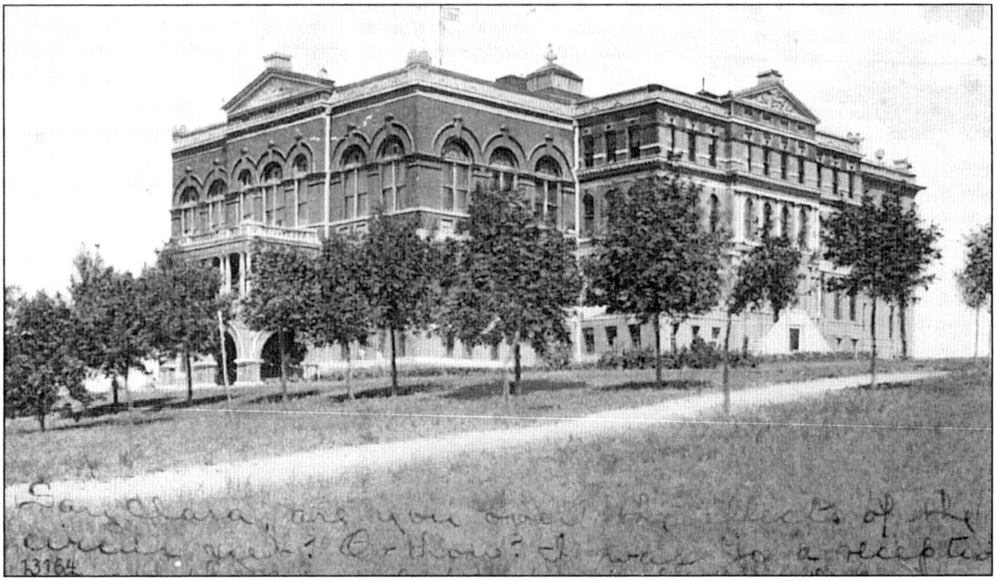

Before the fire, the capitol looked like this. Vice President Charles M. Curtis dedicated the cornerstone for the new $2 million capitol. It was constructed like a skyscraper (see below), and many North Dakotans wondered why they had to build the capitol up in the air when there was so much space on the ground.

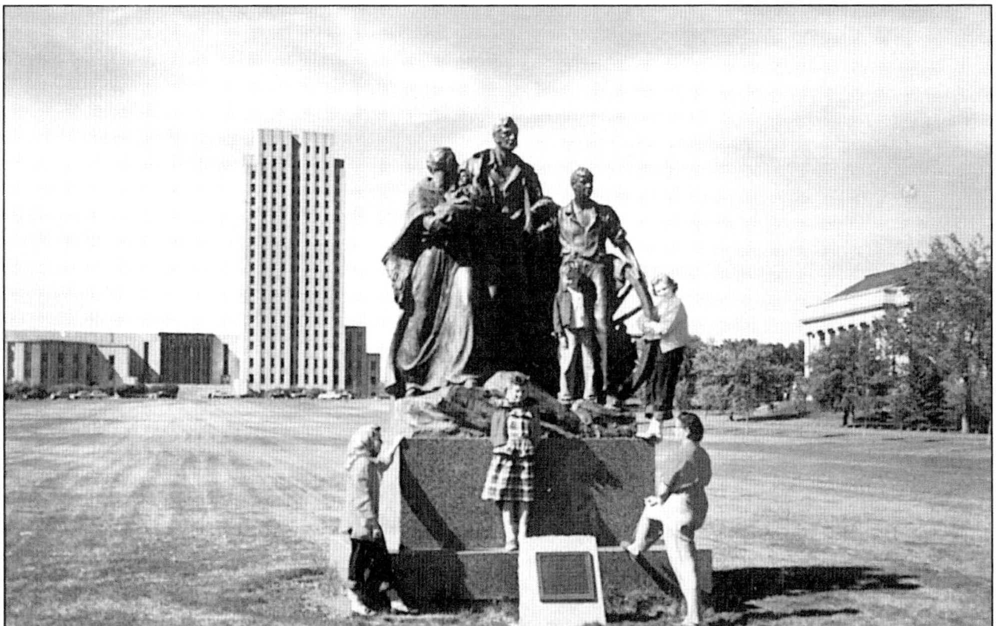

The new skyscraper capitol (seen above) is the only tall building in North Dakota. Since the state constructed the building during the Depression, they got a beautiful building at bargain prices; it was one of the best financial deals ever made.

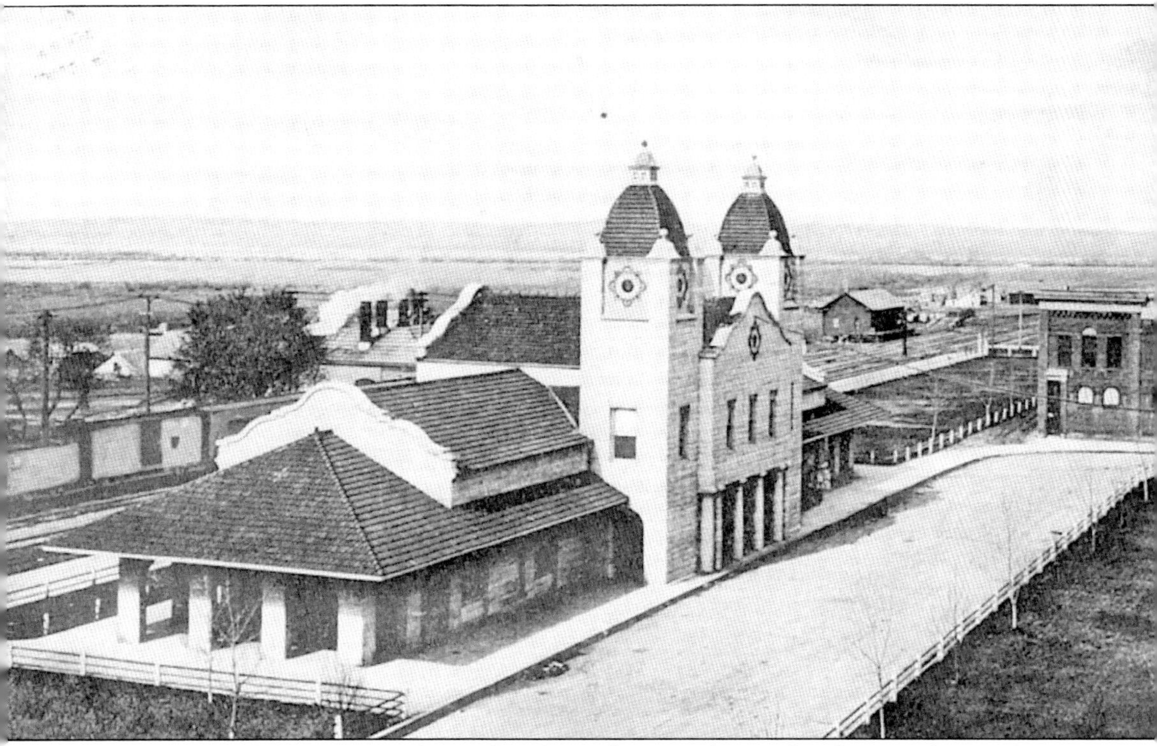

This 1908 postcard shows Bismarck, North Dakota, the capitol city. The photograph was taken from the top of the old Northwest Hotel.

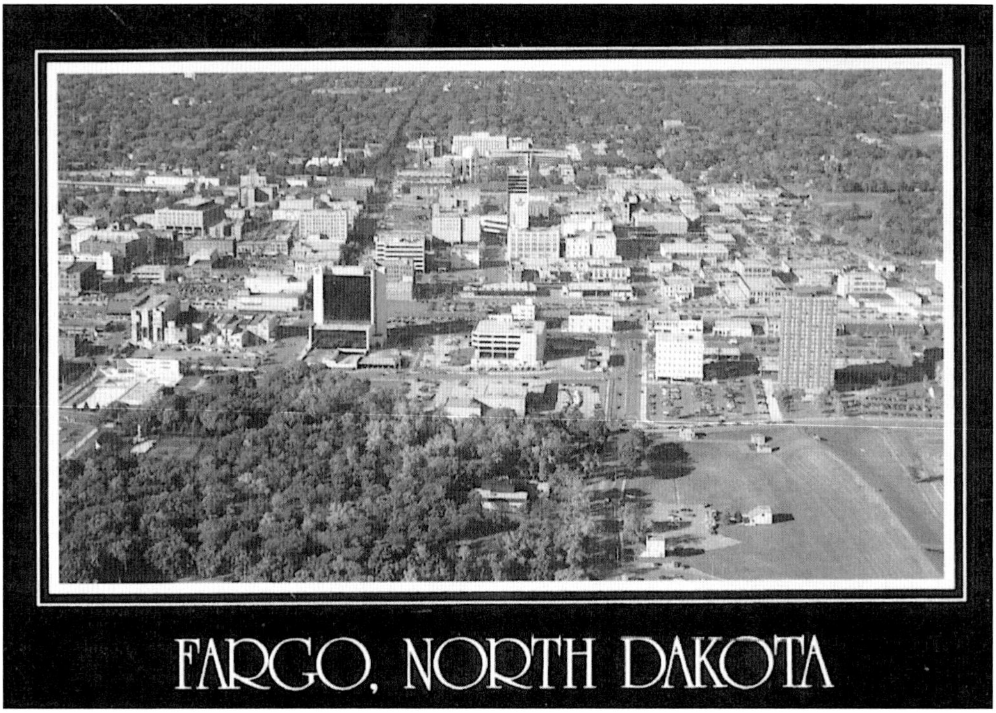

In 1890, Fargo had only 5,664 people, but it had three newspapers. Fargo also had stockyards, a rolling mill, a foundry, and carriage shops. By 1910, Fargo had a population of 14,331. Today, Fargo, the largest city in North Dakota, has 74,111 people. Grand Forks and Bismarck are in a tight race for second and third place. This aerial view of Fargo was taken in the 1990s.

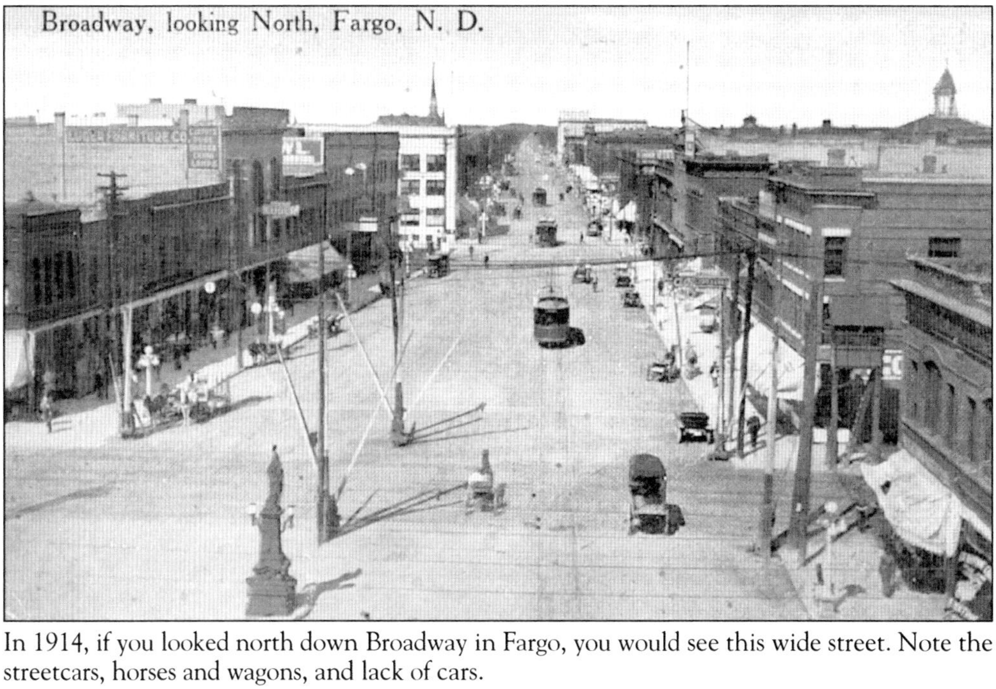

In 1914, if you looked north down Broadway in Fargo, you would see this wide street. Note the streetcars, horses and wagons, and lack of cars.

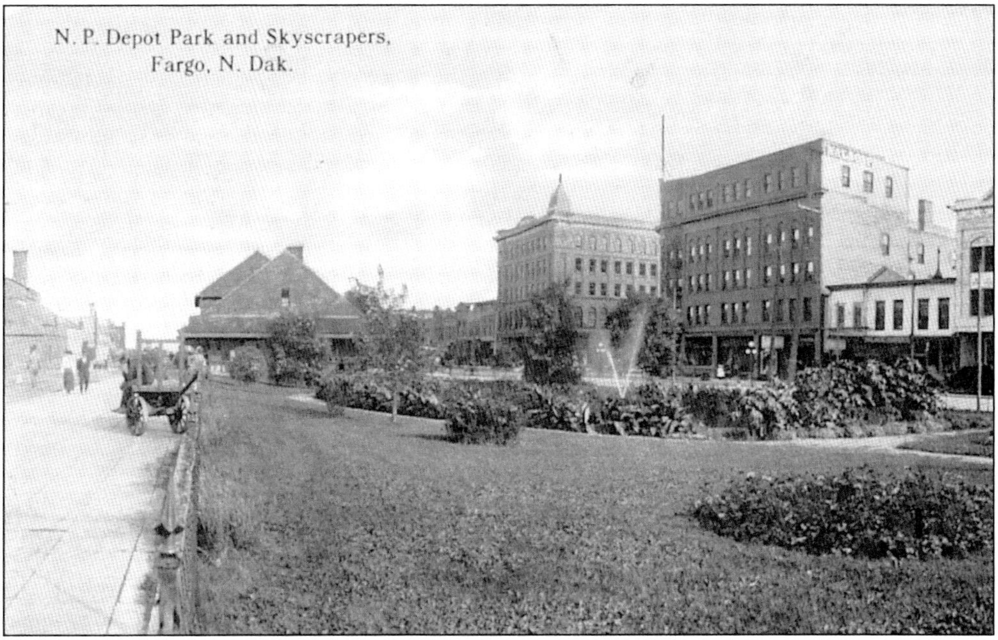

The caption on this postcard from Fargo, North Dakota, reads, "N.P. Depot and Skyscrapers." N.P. refers to the Northern Pacific, but the skyscrapers are not visible! The railroad helped to bring settlers to North Dakota, for which they were handsomely rewarded. The Northern Pacific was given 10 million acres of land or 23.7 percent—nearly a fourth—of the state!

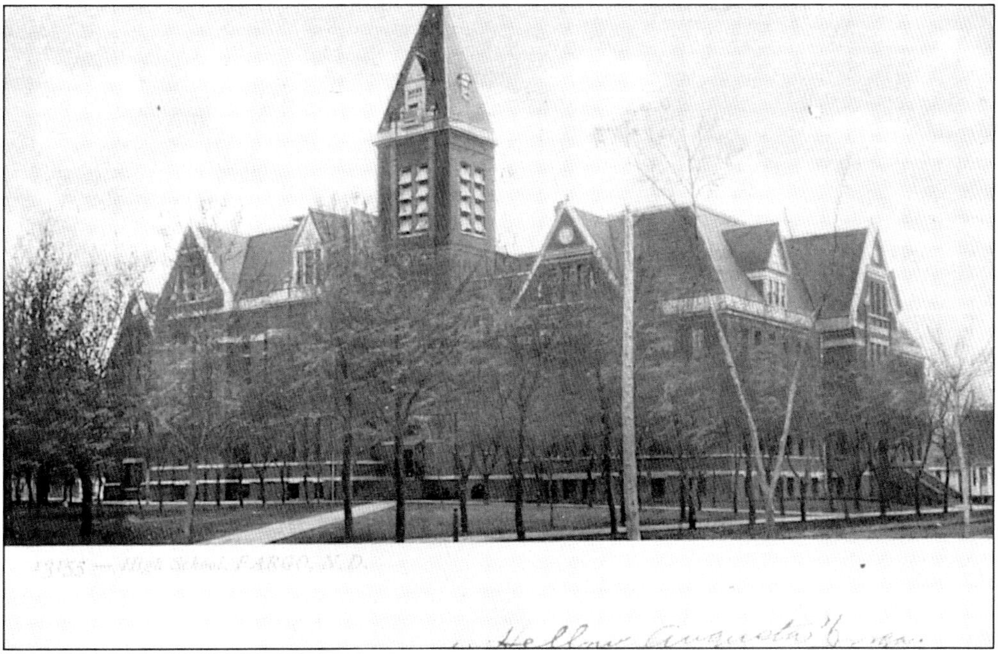

Here is the Fargo High School, *c.* 1907. Now there are three public high schools in Fargo.

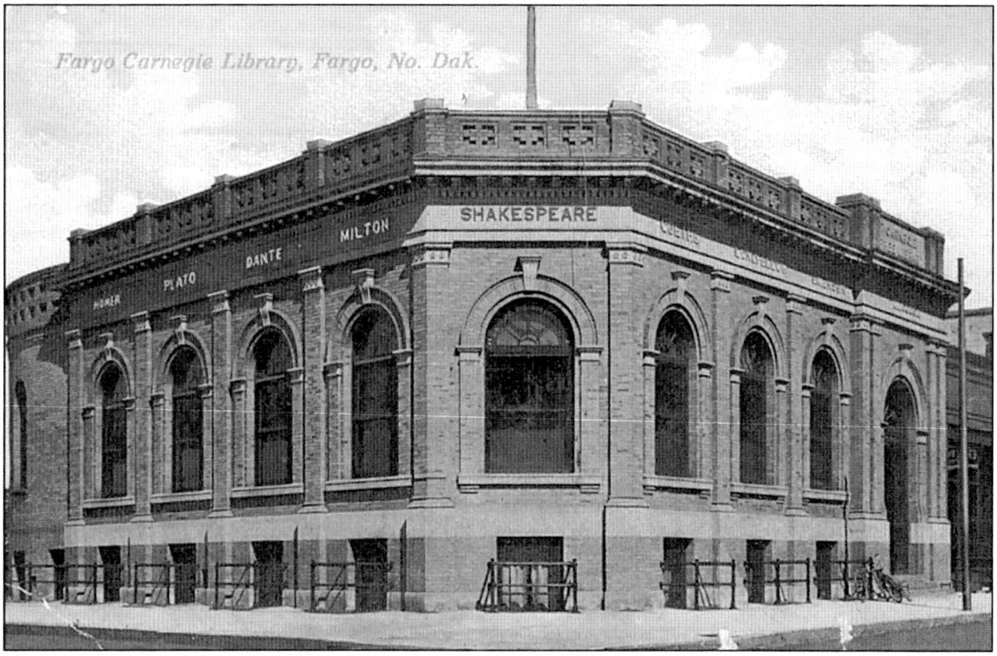

This 1915 postcard shows the new Fargo Carnegie Library. In a custom of the day, famous writers got their names on the buildings.

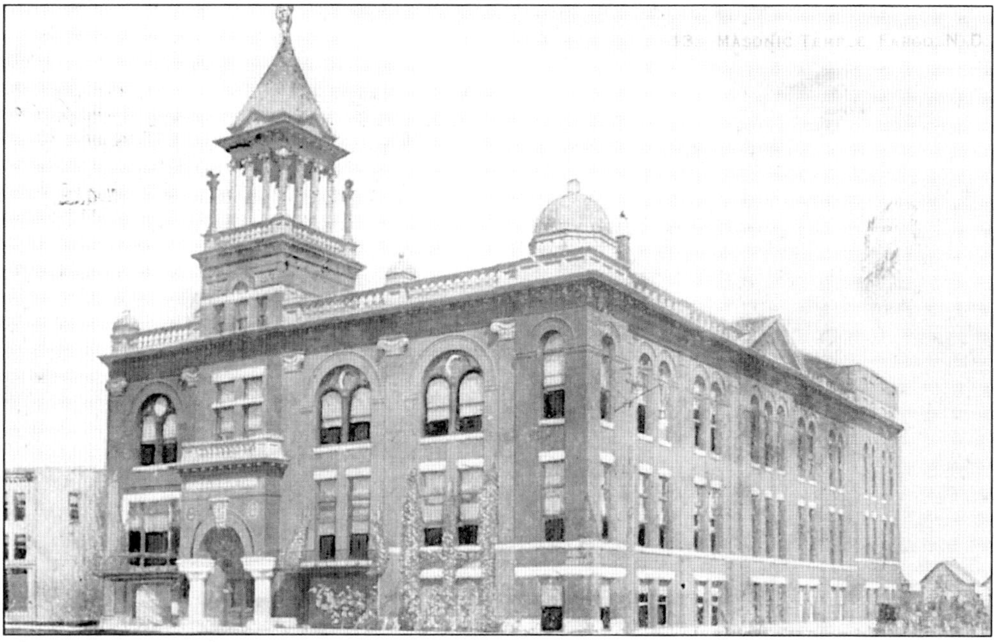

The Masonic Temple in Fargo was a very impressive building, *c. 1910*.

This 1908 postcard shows the Norwegian Lutheran Church in Fargo. According to the North Dakota Conference of Churches, North Dakota has about an equal number of Lutherans and Catholics.

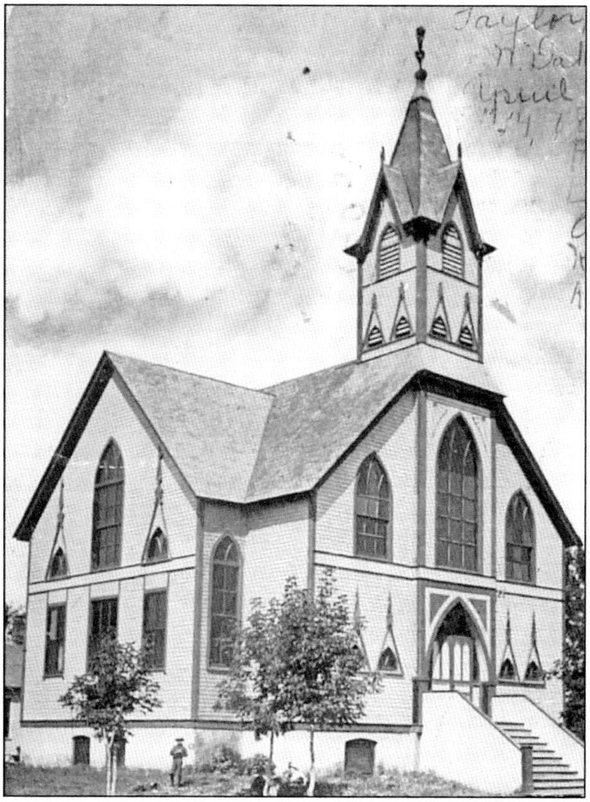

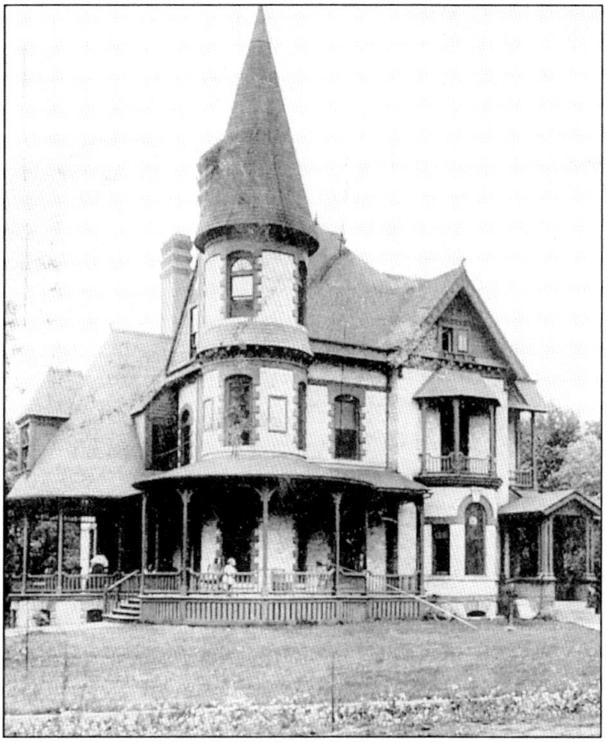

The Oak Grove Seminary in Fargo, *c.* 1908, was a high school for Lutheran girls. One of the goals of the seminary was to "teach social graces." This beautiful building was torn down. Today, with more interest in the past, the building probably would have been saved.

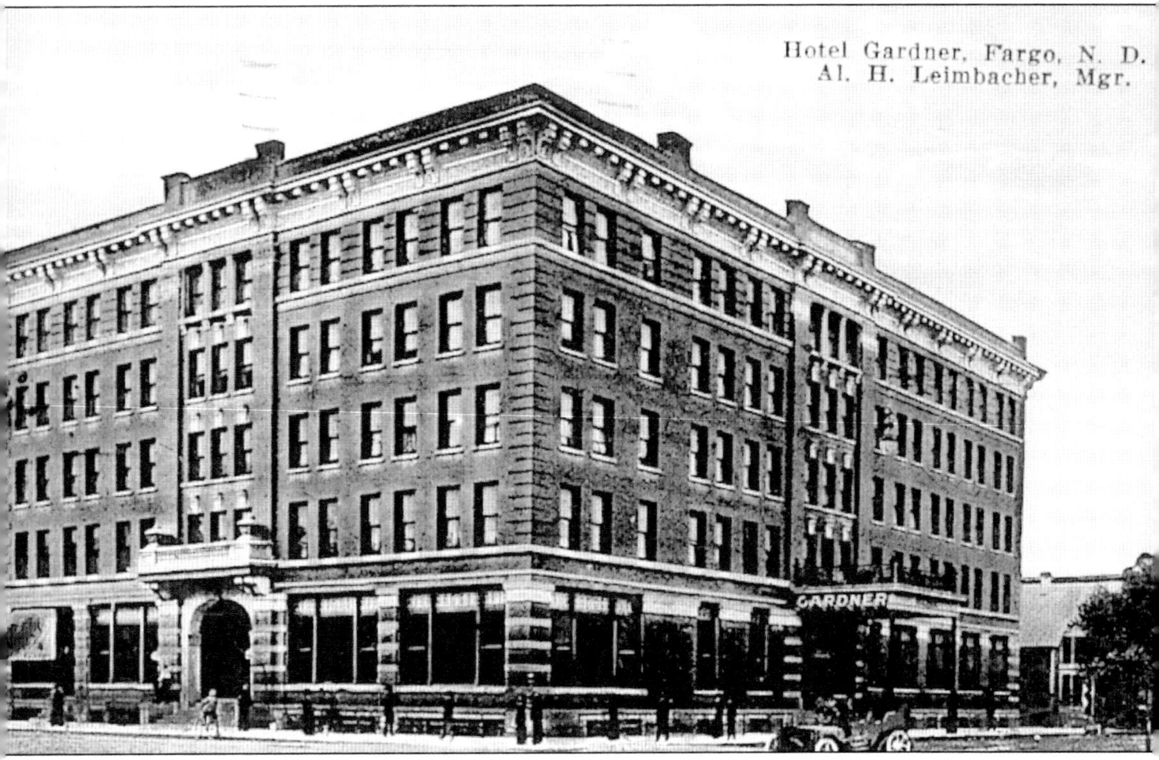

In the early 20th century, the Hotel Gardner in Fargo, North Dakota, was one of the finest hotels in the state. By 1890, it is strange to find out that Fargo had become a "divorce mill" to many eastern society women, Broadway actresses, millionaires, merchant princes, and even British aristocrats who lived in Fargo hotels while establishing the necessary residence requirements. Elwyn B. Robinson's great book *History of North Dakota* states that the wife of world heavyweight champion prize fighter James J. Corbett was among those congregating.

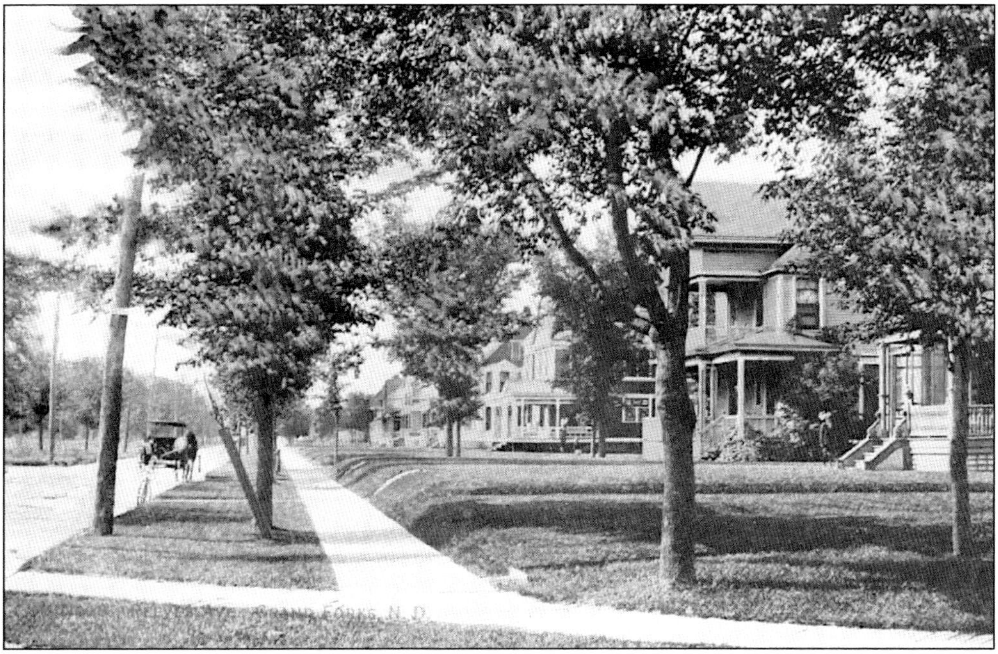

In the early 1900s, Reeves Avenue in Grand Forks, North Dakota, looked like a very quiet street. Only one buggy can be seen. This street was badly flooded in the terrible flood of 1997.

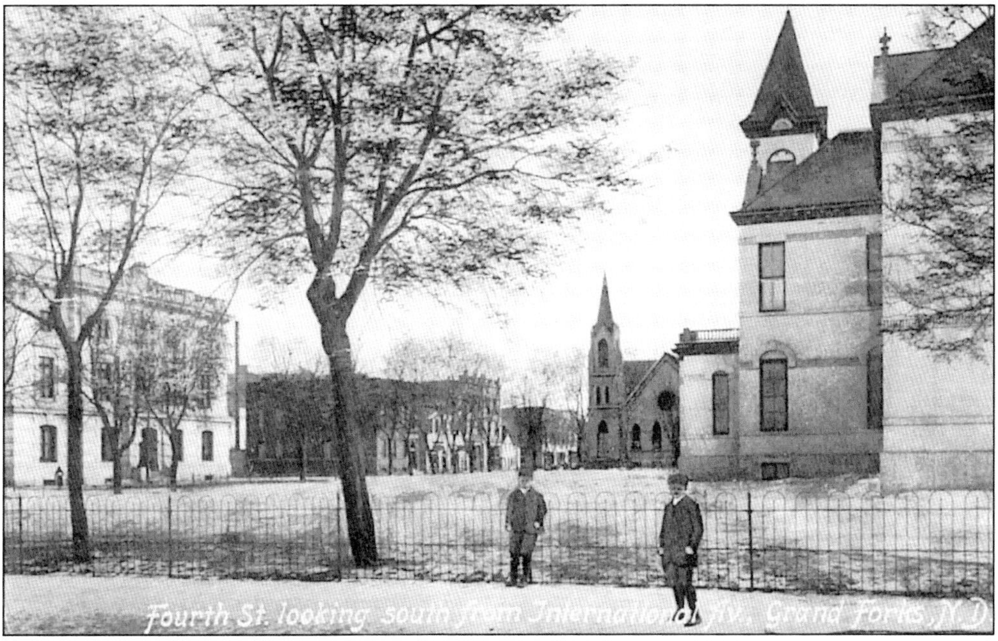

Here is a view of Fourth Street in Grand Forks, North Dakota, c. 1914.

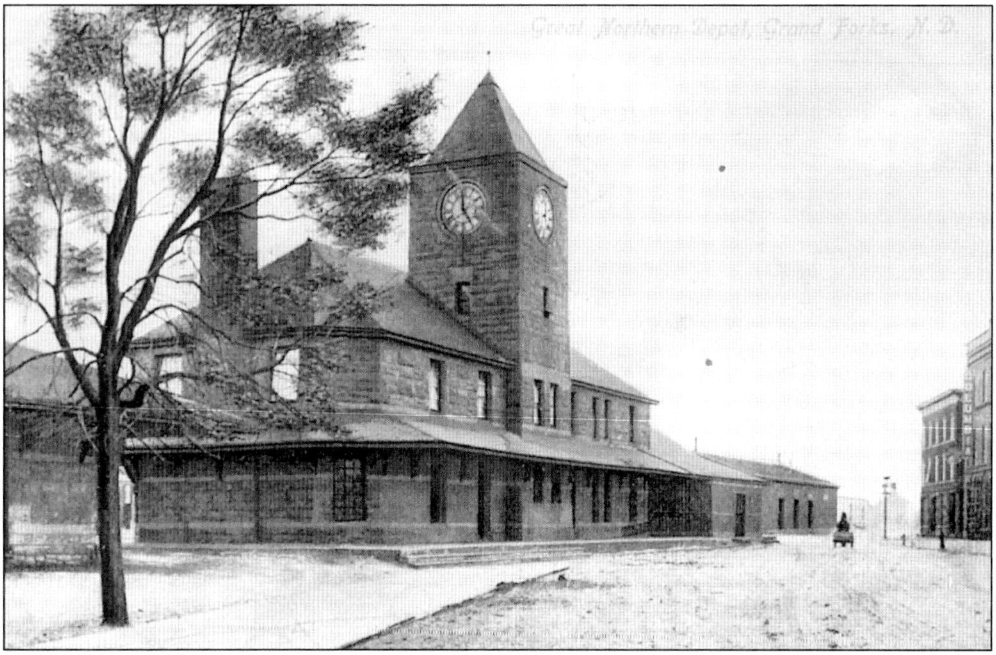

Pictured here is the Great Northern Depot in Grand Forks, North Dakota, in 1909.

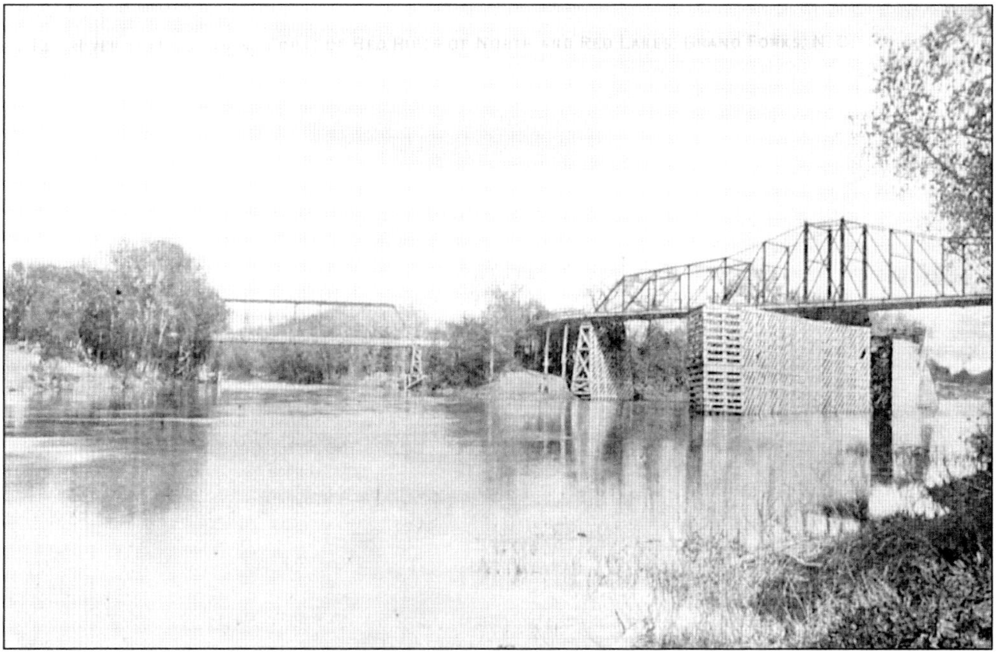

Here is an early postcard showing the Red River of the North and Red Lake in Grand Forks, North Dakota. In 1997, this area had its worst flood in the state's history.

Some towns, instead of showing their main street, printed beautiful colored cards showing flowers or children. This card is from Buxton, North Dakota, in eastern North Dakota.

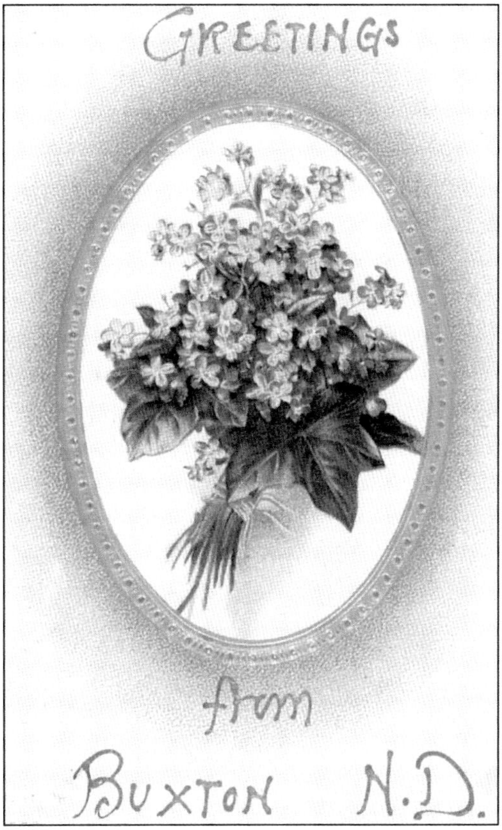

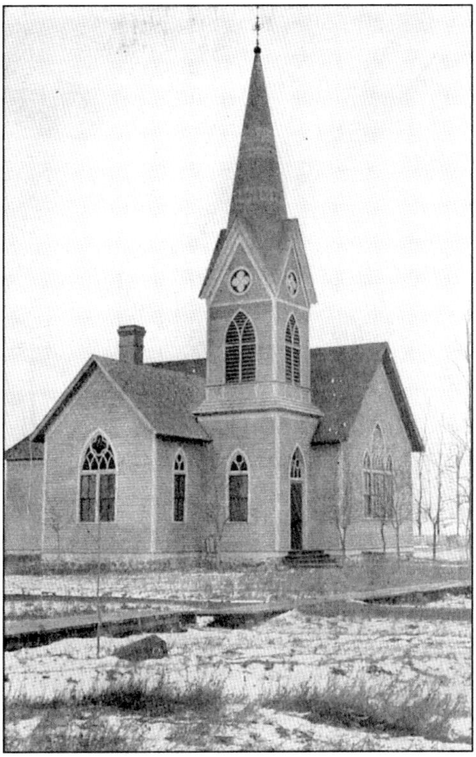

This 1909 photograph was taken of the Norwegian Lutheran Church in Buxton, North Dakota. From *c.* 1880 to *c.* 1920s, all sermons in Norwegian Lutheran churches were spoken in Norwegian. Later on, every third sermon would be in Norwegian. Finally, most Norwegian sermons were dropped because the younger people had not learned the language.

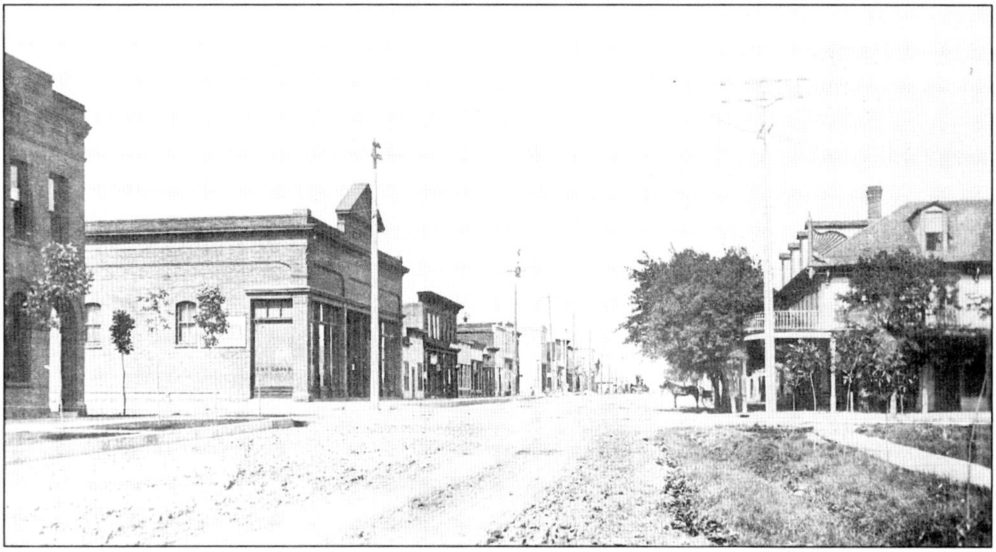

Cooperstown's Main Street was not paved in the 1900s. Gerald P. Nye, a famous U.S. senator, was the editor of the Griggs County *Sentinel-Courier* in Cooperstown in the 1920s. Other famous North Dakota politicians of this period included Fred G. Aandahl, Otto Krueger, Usher L. Burdick, William Langer, Milton R. Young, and John Burke. Of course, there were many others. On November 2, 1920, the women of North Dakota had the full right to vote for the first time.

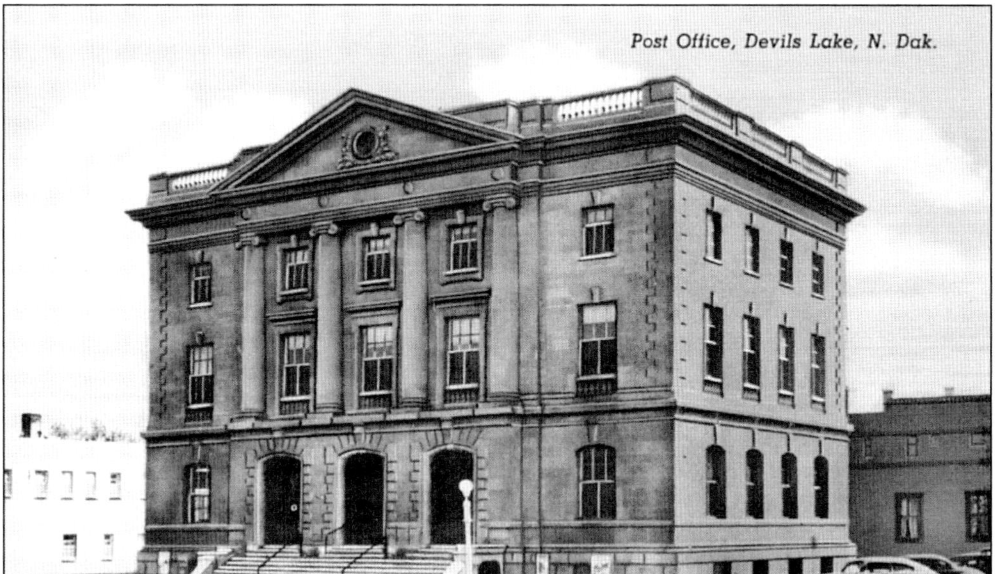

The post office in Devils Lake was featured in this late 1930s postcard. Devils Lake is one of the areas of North Dakota that has suffered from floods.

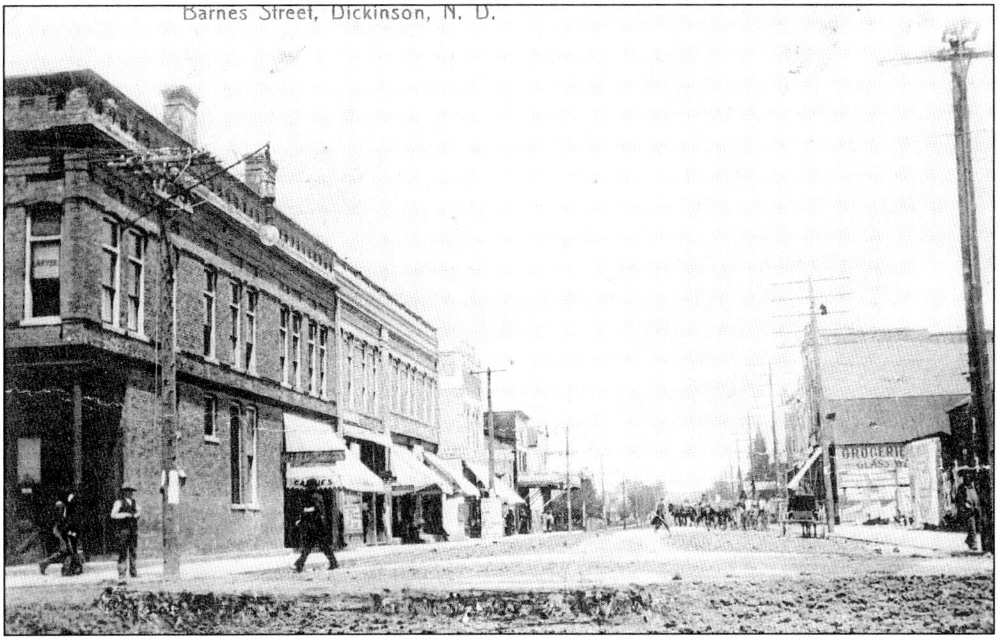

In 1909, this Barnes Street scene in Dickinson, North Dakota, shows one buggy, but no cars. The postcard was printed in Germany.

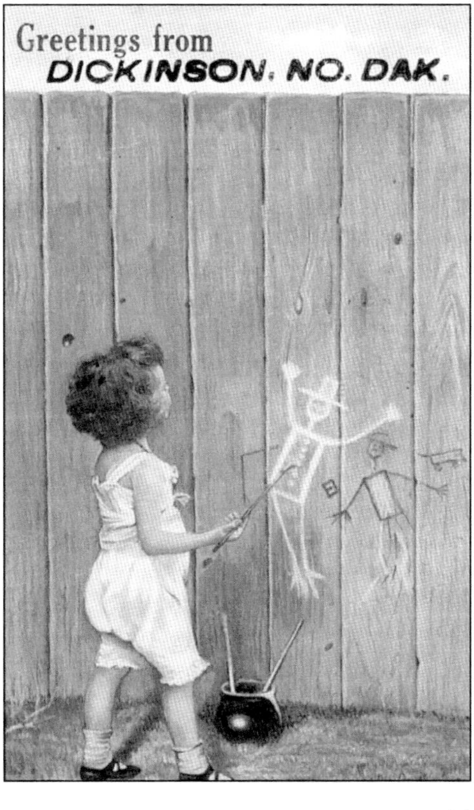

This postcard printer in Dickinson, North Dakota, knew that an attractive child would help sales.

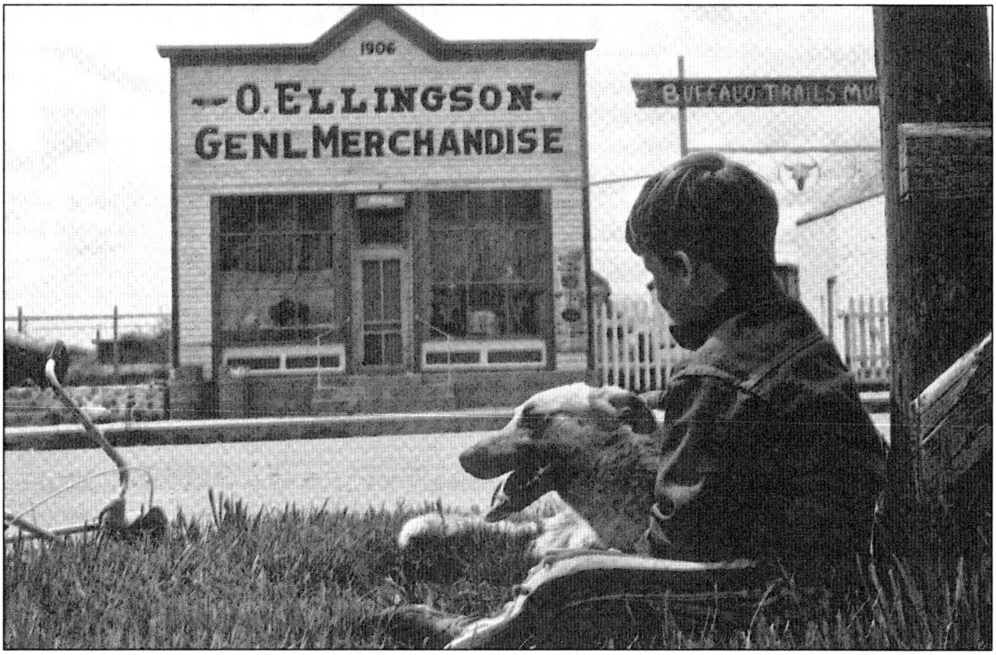

This structure is the main building for the Buffalo Trails Museum located at Epping in northwestern North Dakota. The museum tells the story of the history in the region.

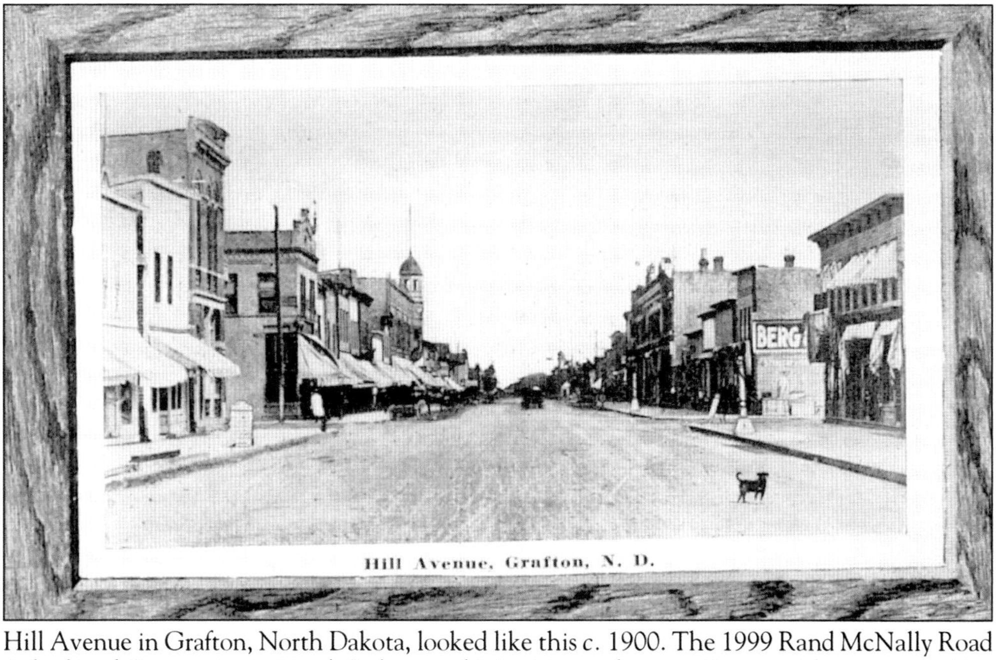

Hill Avenue in Grafton, North Dakota, looked like this c. 1900. The 1999 Rand McNally Road Atlas listed 53 counties in North Dakota and 141 cities and towns. Towns without a post office are not listed.

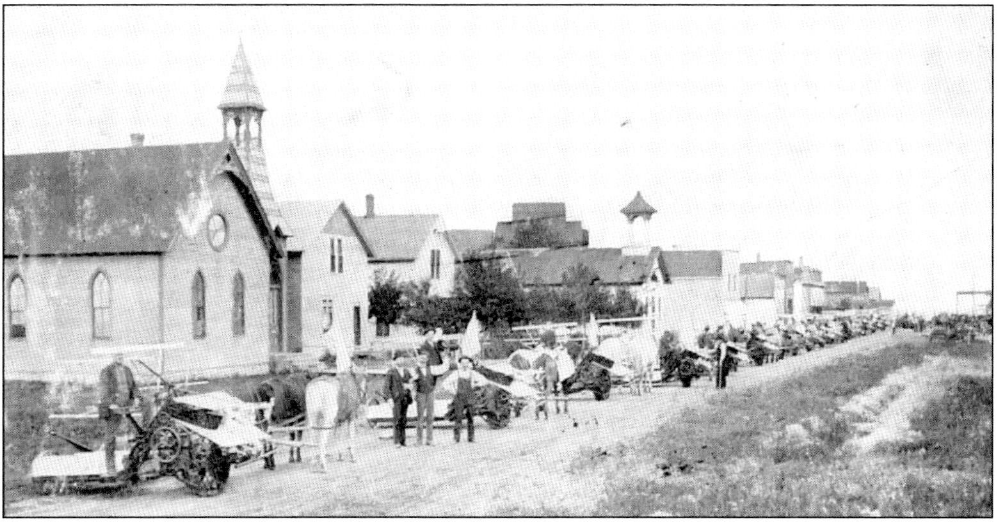

This historic postcard shows at least 40 "binders" lined up on the main street of Grandin, North Dakota. Binders were pulled by horses; they cut and tied the grain in bundles. The binders probably belonged to a bonanza (large) farmer in the area. Soon after this postcard was photographed, combines replaced the binders. Bonanza farmers left North Dakota in the late 1920s. However, large farms are coming back. North Dakota had some 77,700 farms in 1920, and today, there are only about 30,500 in the state. The small farms have been disappearing for some time.

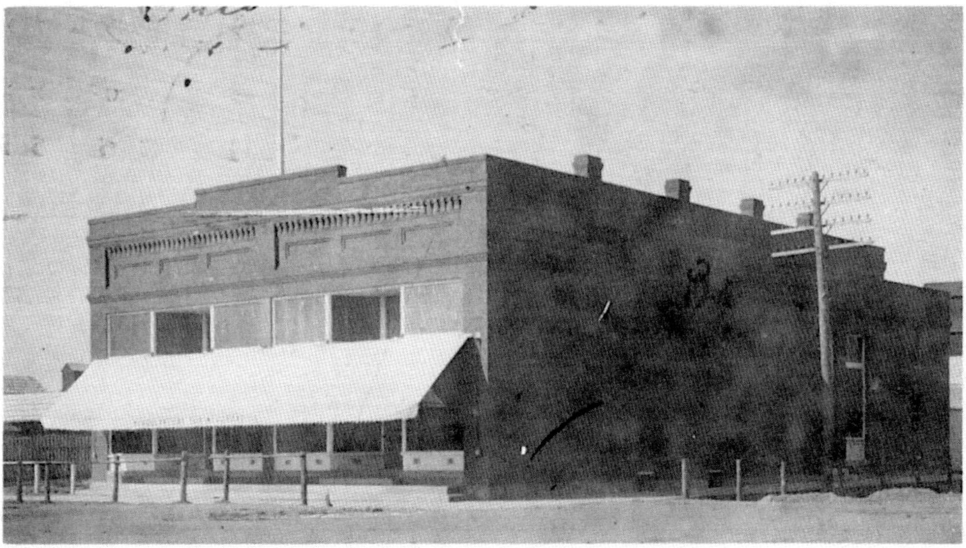

86/19 Bemis Department Store at Inkster, ND

To honor North Dakota's centennial in 1989, postcards like this one from Inkster, North Dakota, were reproduced.

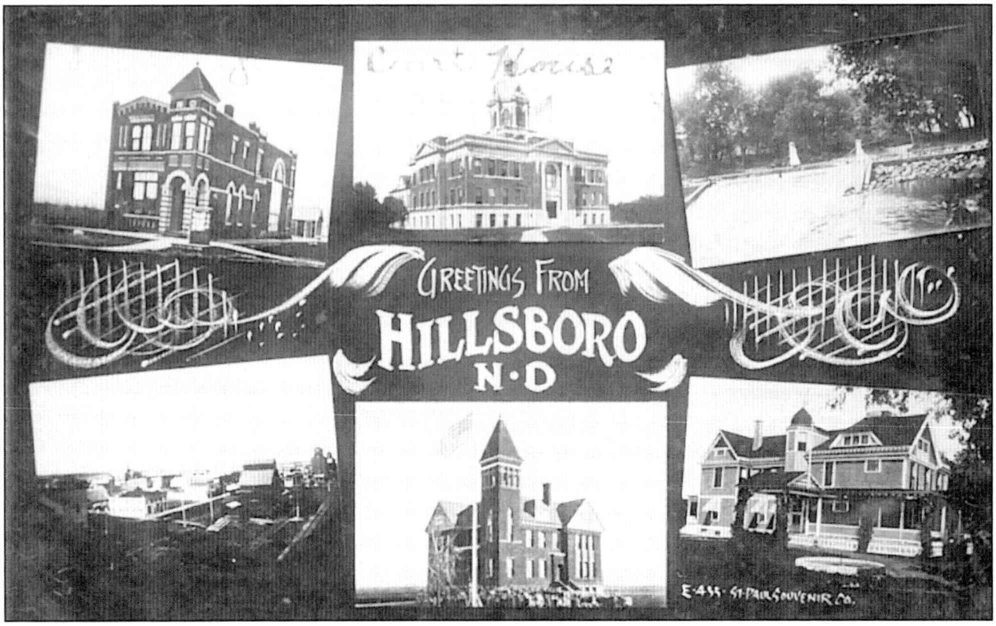

Even small towns, like my hometown of Hillsboro, North Dakota, with a population of about 1,000, printed up postcards like this one to brag about their hometown. My mother sent this card to her uncle in Spring Grove, Minnesota, in an attempt to persuade him to come and visit the relatives in Hillsboro.

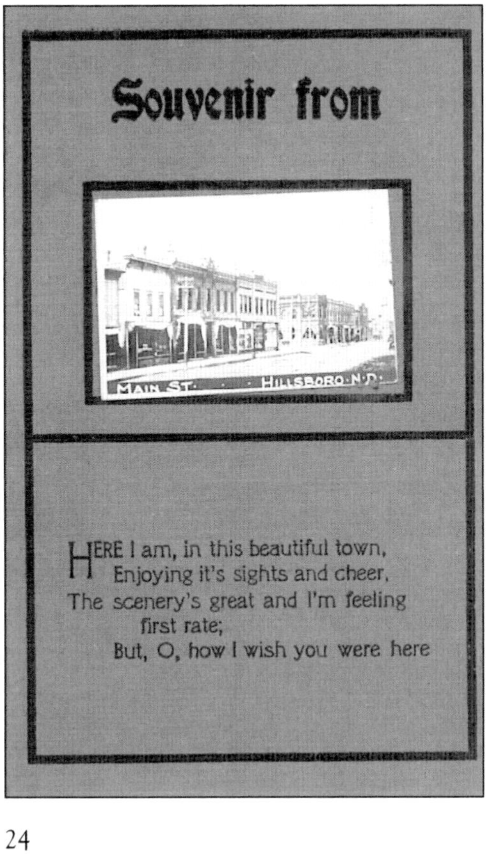

Hillsboro, North Dakota, resorted to poetry to brag about their town. The poem reads, "Here I am in this beautiful town, enjoying its sights and cheer. The scenery's great and I'm feeling first rate, But, O, how I wish you were here."

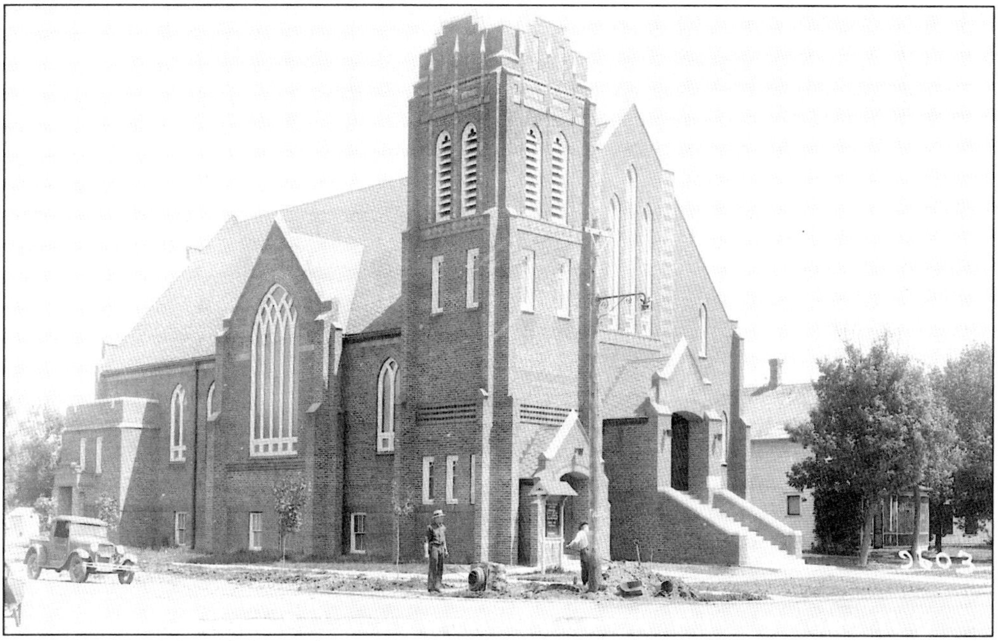

After the wood church burned in 1924, Our Savior's Church in Hillsboro built this structure in 1928. At first, all services were held in Norwegian, but by 1930, English language services were expanded and Norwegian ones were reduced. By 1938, only English was used.

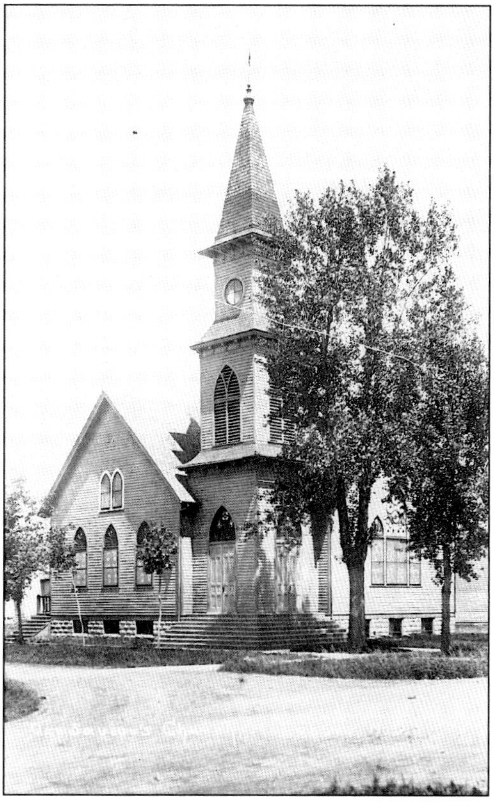

Many of the early churches in North Dakota were made of wood, like this one in Hillsboro. It burned and was replaced by a brick and cement church. Before the churches were built, the early settlers would meet in sod houses—their homes—and hear a sermon from a traveling minister or priest; these clergymen were called circuit riders.

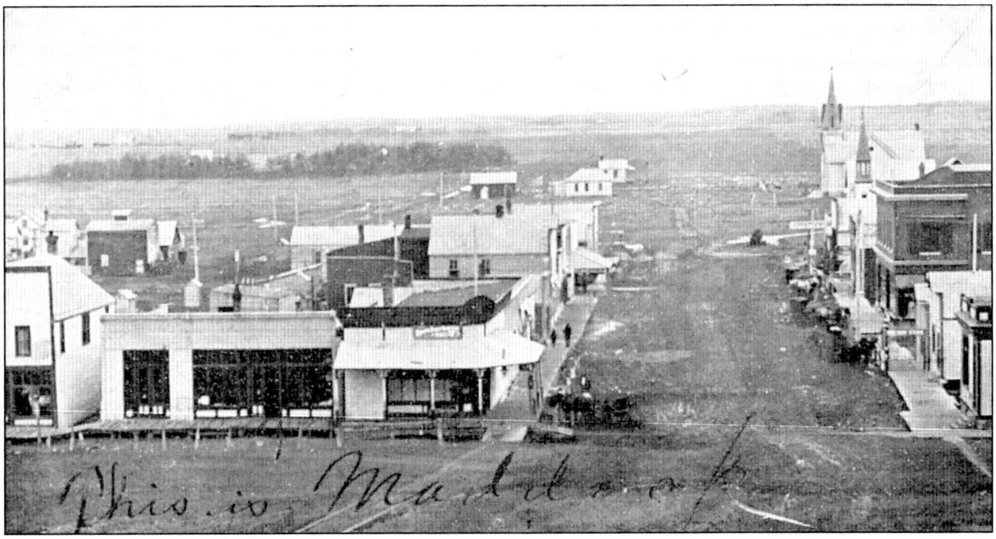

This is Maddock, North Dakota, *c.* 1908. Although the town appears to be small, it sustained the two churches on the right side. The wide street indicates they were getting ready for more traffic.

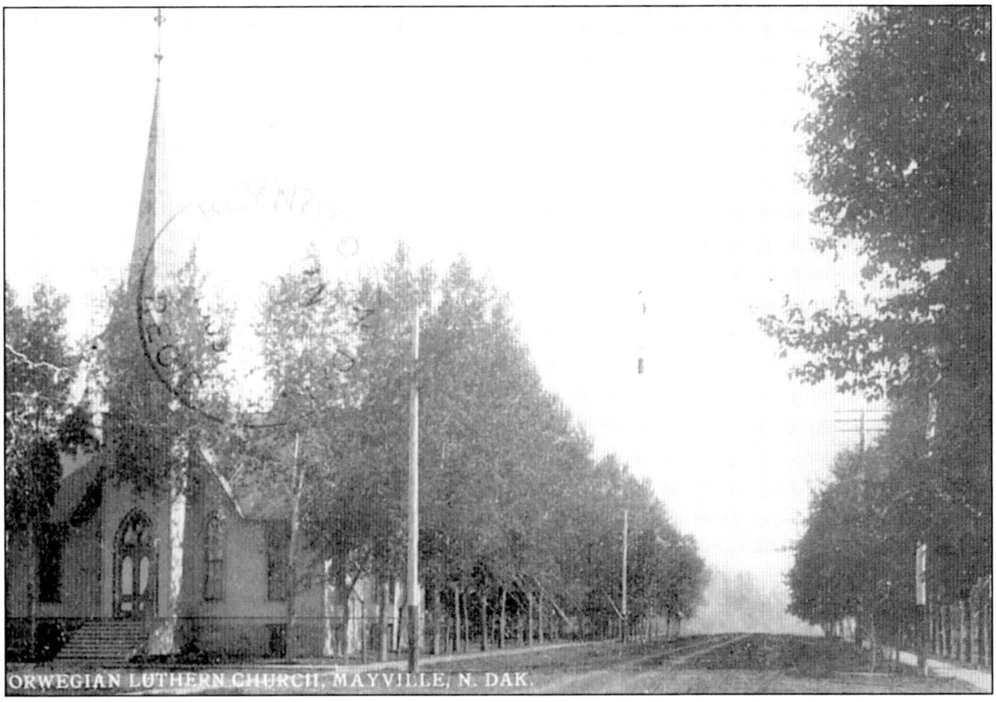

This postcard shows the Norwegian Lutheran Church in Mayville, North Dakota, *c.* 1908. Mayville and Hillsboro are in eastern North Dakota and have been traditional rivals in all sports for many years.

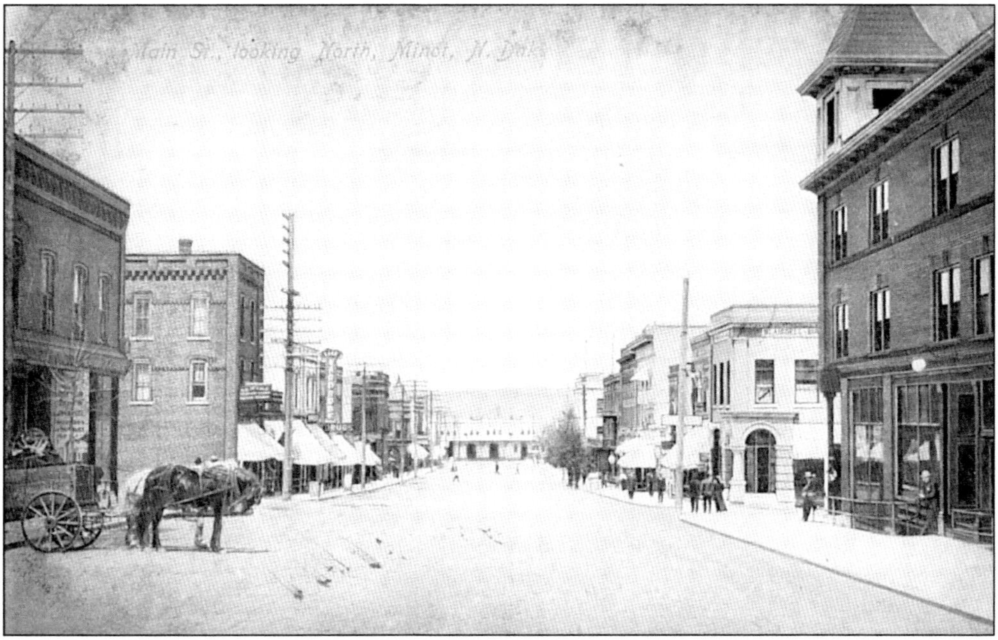

Printed in Germany, this postcard looks north down Main Street in Minot, North Dakota. Minot is famous for its Norsk Hostfest, which draws thousands of visitors from all over the U.S., its air base, and Minot State University.

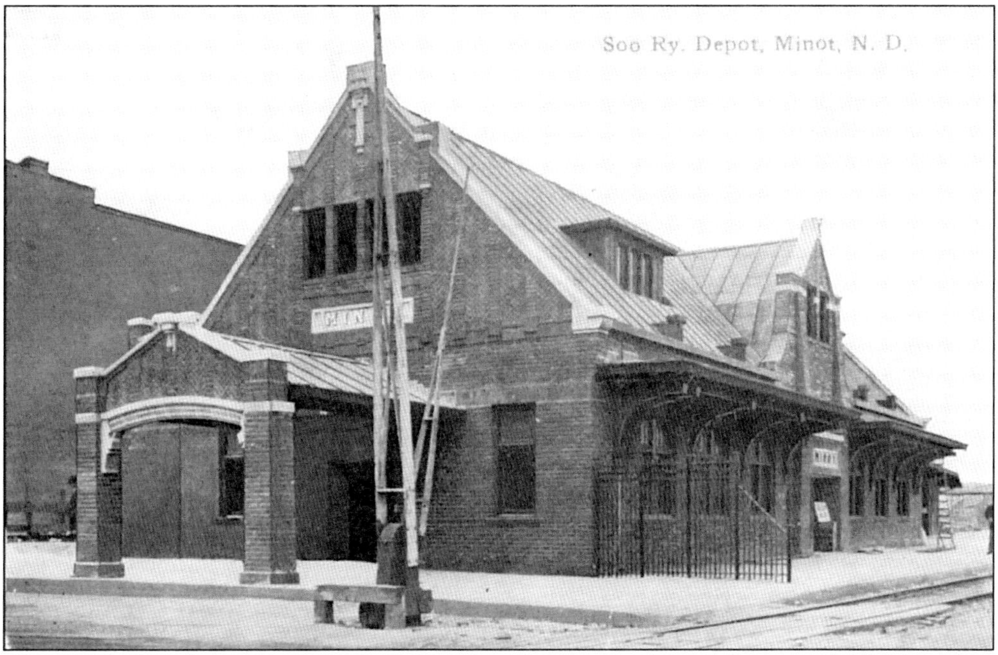

The Soo Railroad in Minot, North Dakota, can be seen in this 1915 postcard. Unlike today, railroad depots were in the heart of the action in this period. However, cars and airplanes stole their thunder. As fewer trains now stop in North Dakota cities, many railroad depots have been closed.

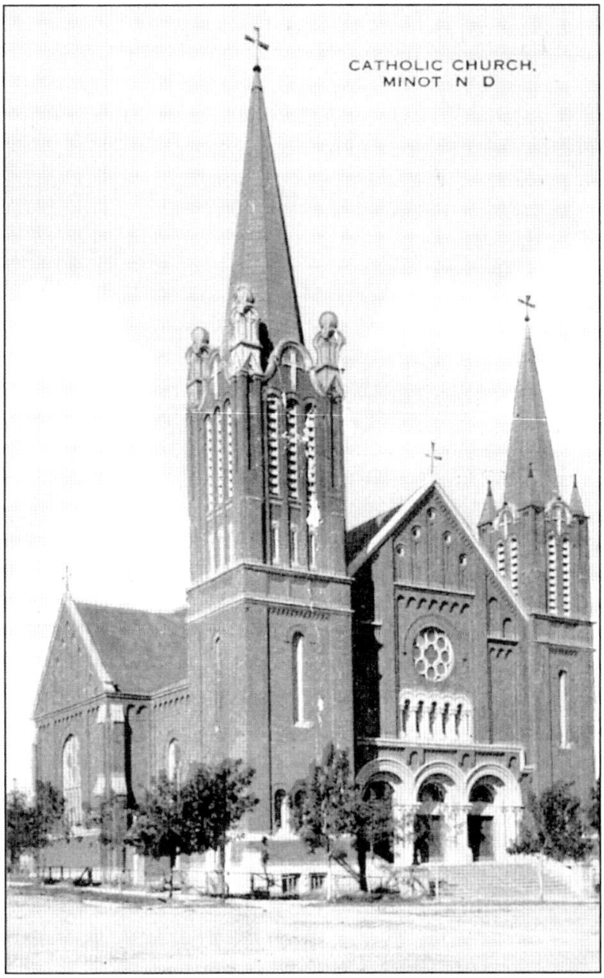

In 1924, this photograph was taken of the Catholic church in Minot, North Dakota. North Dakota has two Catholic bishops—one in Bismarck and the other in Fargo.

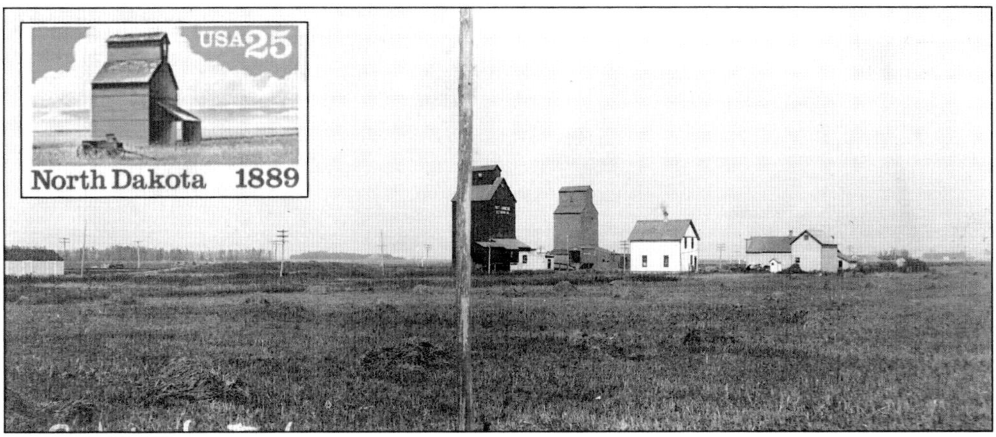

One family lived in Taft, but it was called a "city" anyway. The Aasen Farm is a half-mile from Taft, near Hillsboro, North Dakota. North Dakota's famous stamp (shown in the inset) looked a lot like Taft, North Dakota.

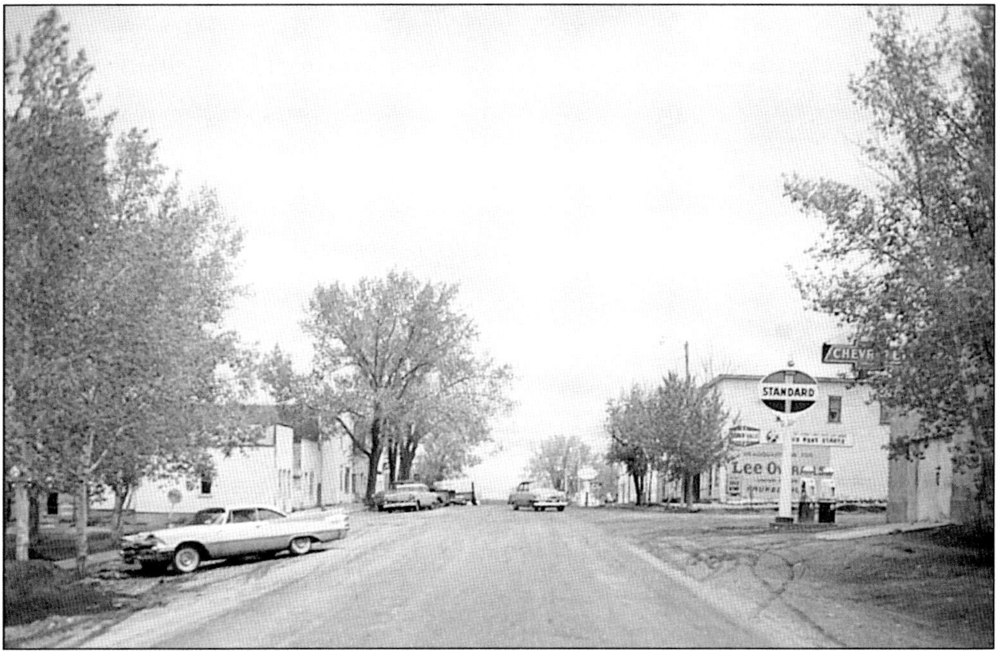

Wildrose, North Dakota, is located north of Williston. Wildrose is typical of many small towns in the state.

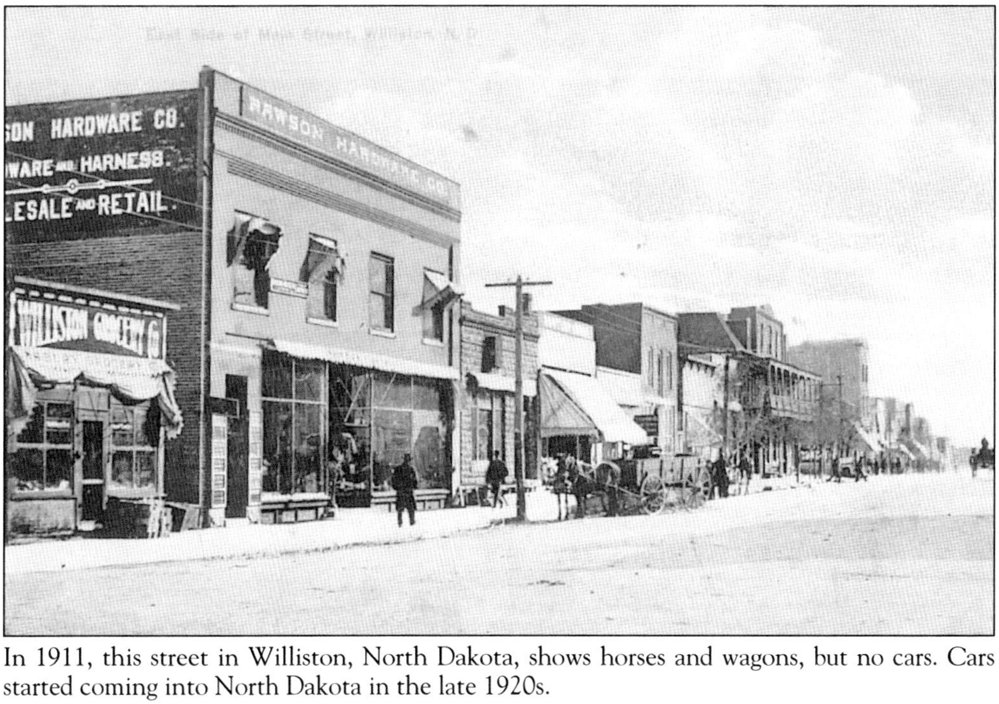

In 1911, this street in Williston, North Dakota, shows horses and wagons, but no cars. Cars started coming into North Dakota in the late 1920s.

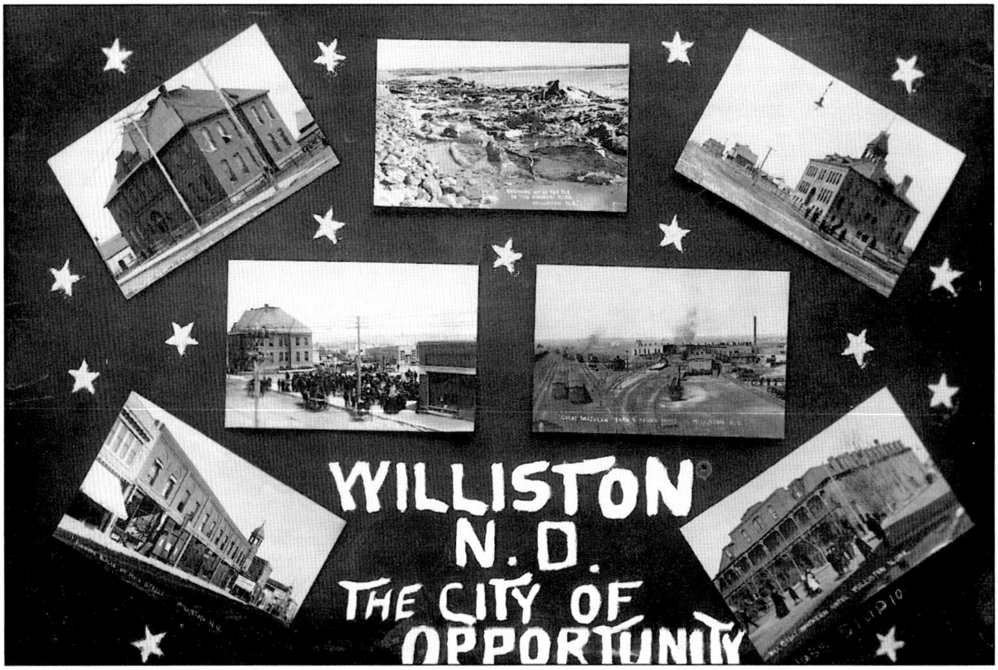

This postcard shows seven scenes of Williston, North Dakota, *c.* early 1900s.

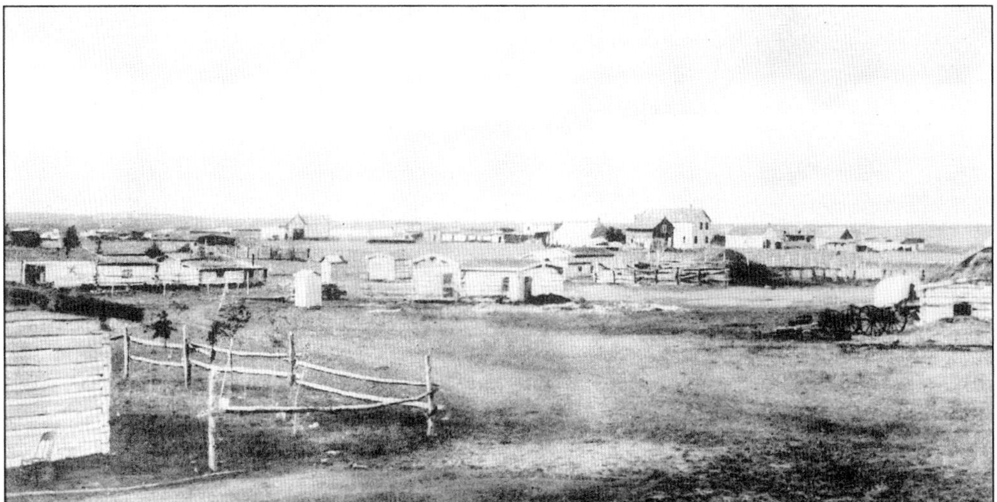

In 1889, Williston, North Dakota, looked like the above postcard. Today, Williston has 13,131 residents. Some of these postcards are from the collections of Dean Winkjer of Williston, J.B. Lyon Jr. of Williston, and Andrea Winkjer Collin of Bismarck.

Two

COLLEGES

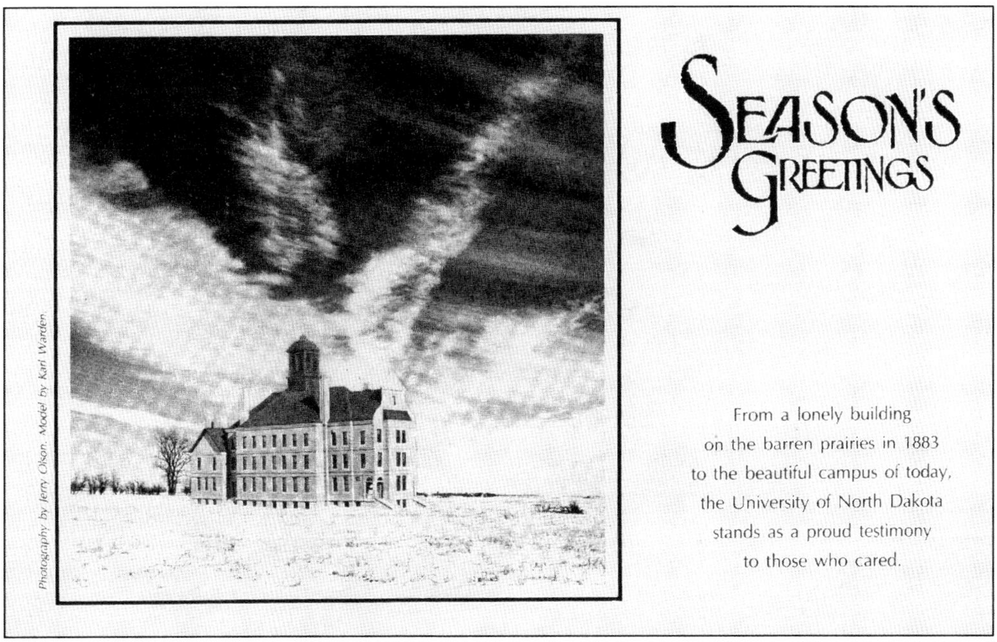

This University of North Dakota (UND) Christmas card shows the first building, which stood all alone on the prairie 5 miles west of Grand Forks. UND in Grand Forks, North Dakota, was founded in 1883—six years before North Dakota became a state in 1889. In 1900, tuition, board, and room only cost $118 for nine months of college! In 1913, UND had 679 students. Today, it has over 11,000. UND has witnessed many historical moments since 1883, including many visits by famous Americans, the tornado in 1887, the terrible flood of 1996-1997, and a time when John C. West served as president of both UND and North Dakota State University in Fargo. In 1919, an event happened that indicated what was going on in America. The UND president turned in his horse and buggy for a Dodge automobile!

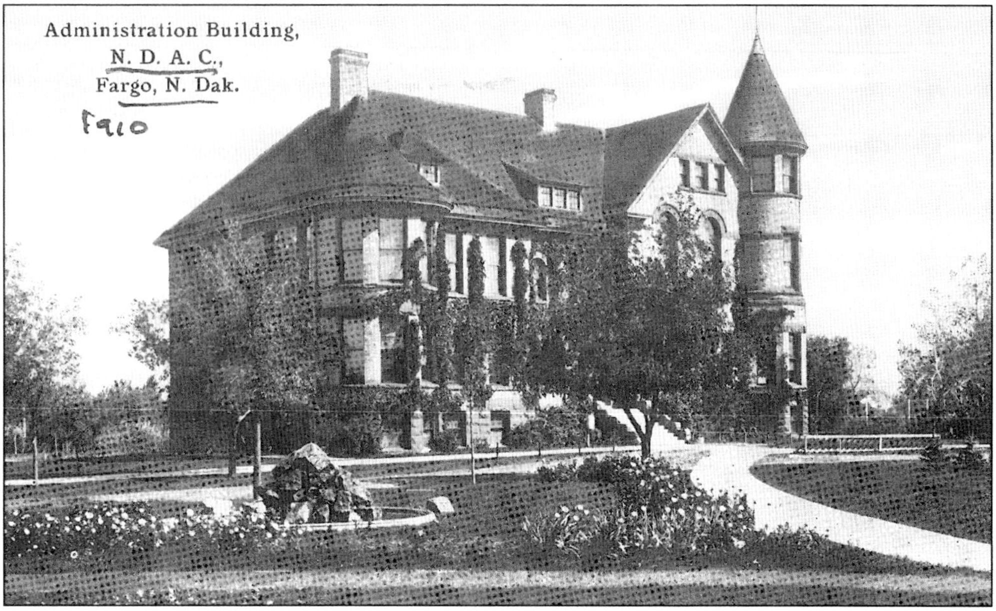

North Dakota State University in Fargo was called North Dakota Agricultural College in 1910. The name was changed in 1960 by an active statewide political election.

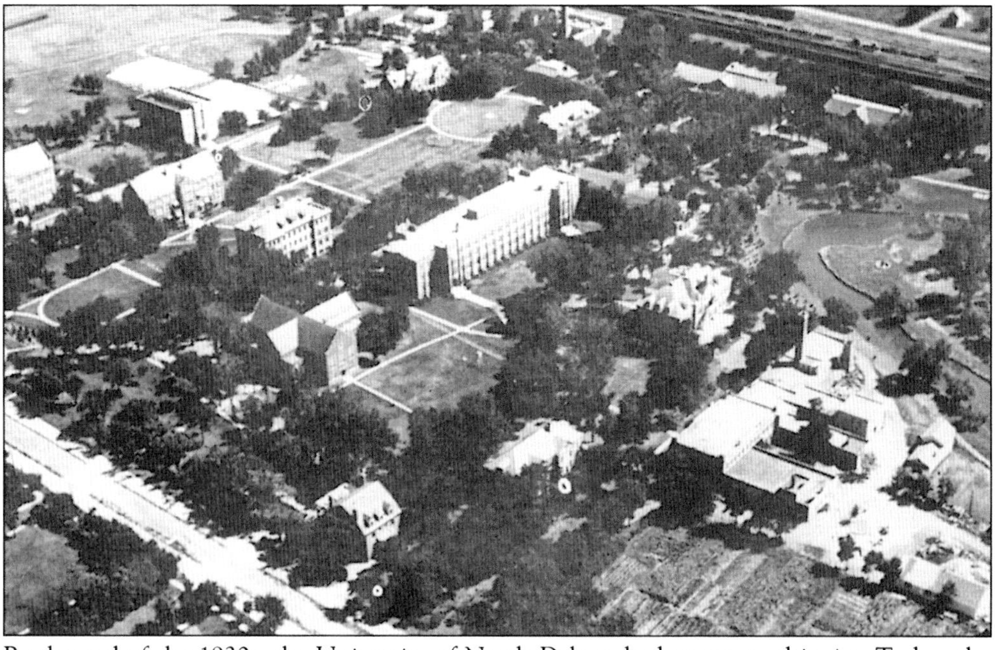

By the end of the 1930s, the University of North Dakota had grown to this size. Today, the campus is twice as large.

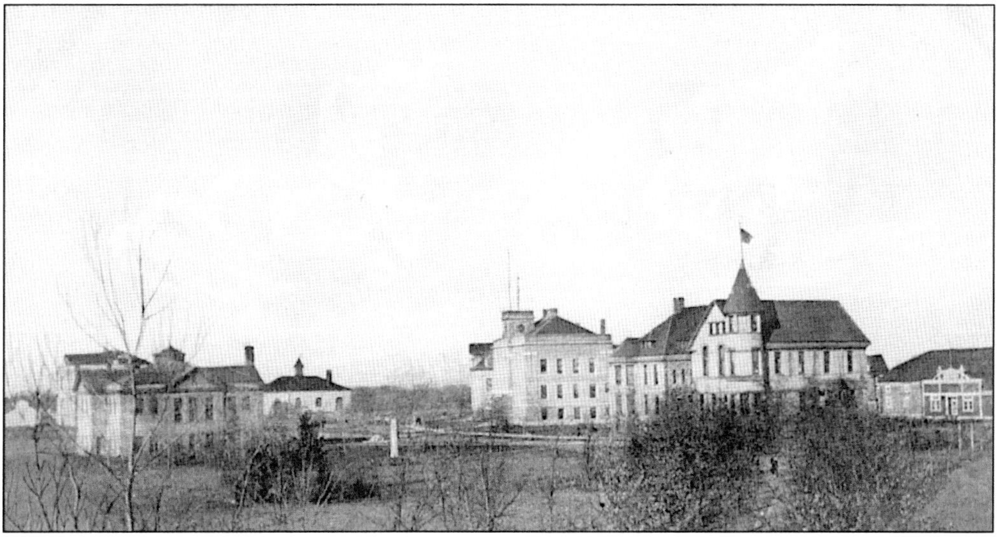

In 1907, North Dakota State University was referred to on this card as "Agricultural College."

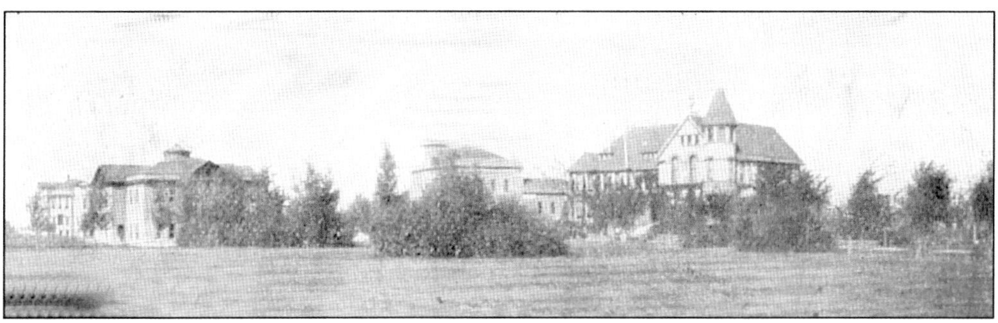

Graduates of North Dakota State University will be able to name some of these buildings.

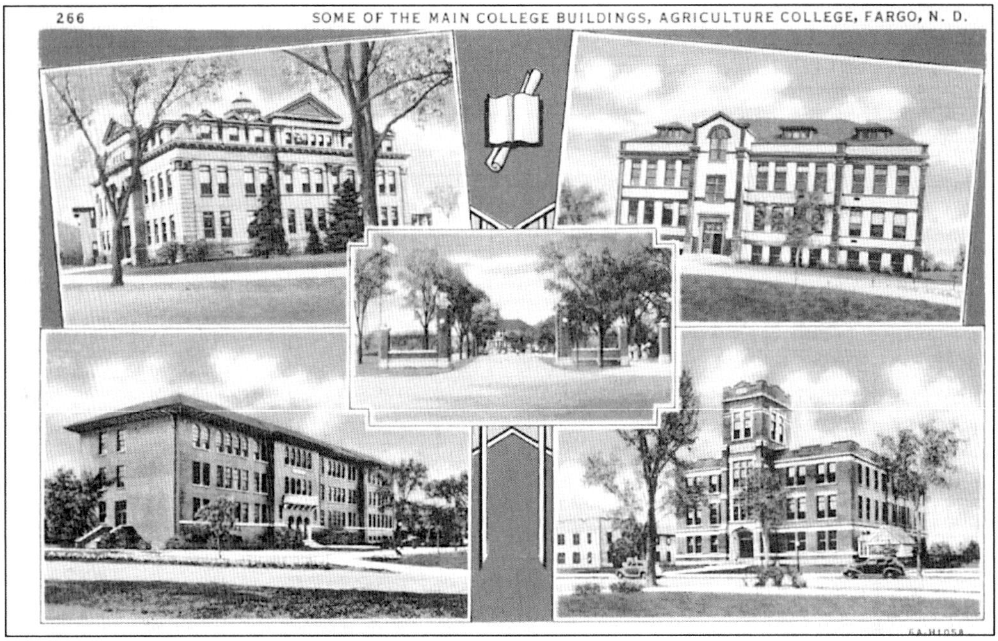

North Dakota State University was founded in 1890. The postcard above shows some of the main buildings at the university, c. 1910.

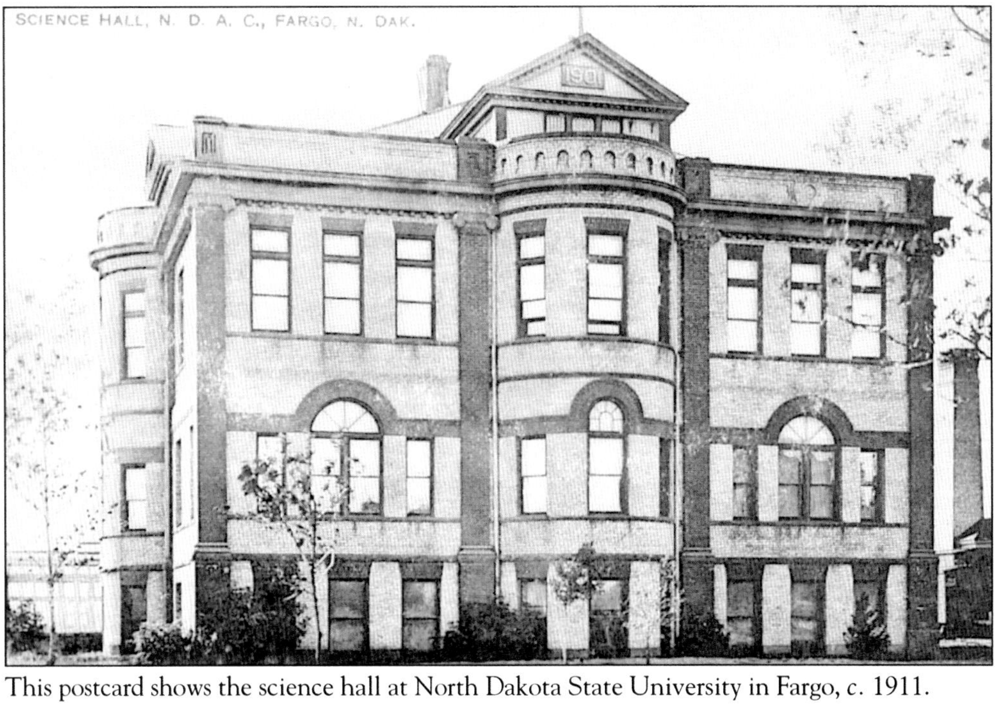

This postcard shows the science hall at North Dakota State University in Fargo, c. 1911.

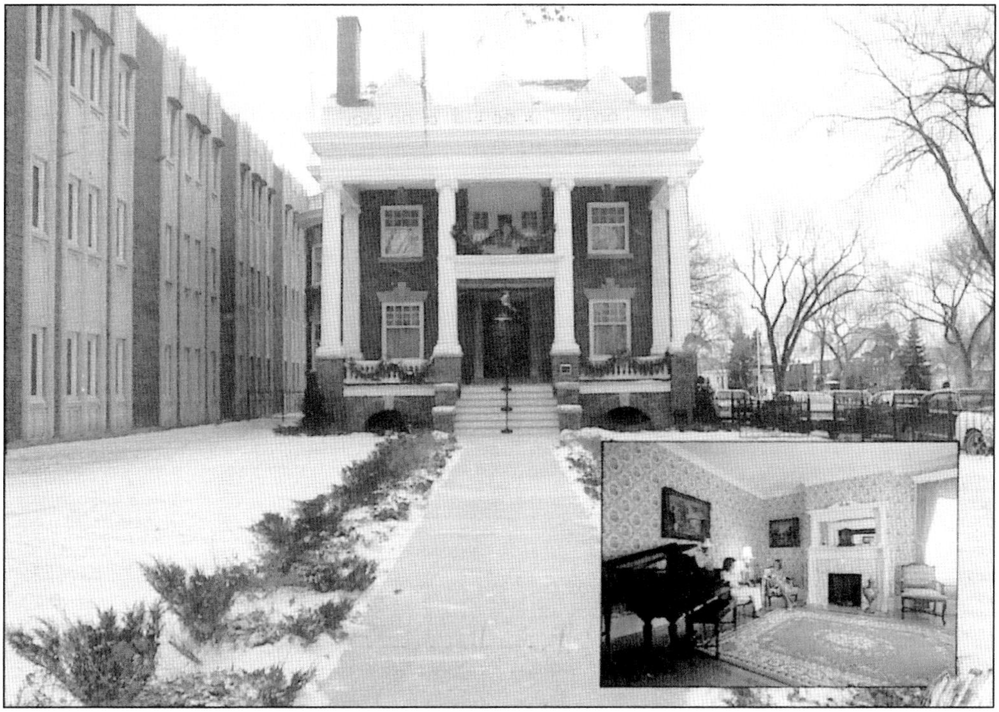

This turn-of-the-century mansion was once the home for the University of North Dakota presidents. It now serves as the J. Llyod Stone Alumni Center for the university.

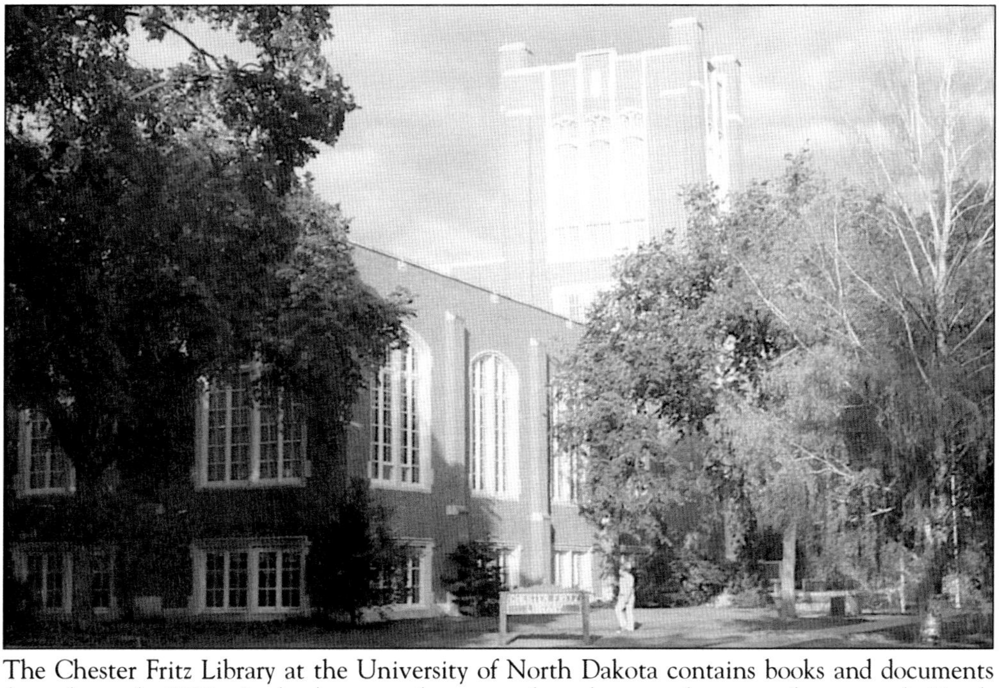

The Chester Fritz Library at the University of North Dakota contains books and documents from the early 1900s. It also has genealogy records and personal papers of many early North Dakota leaders.

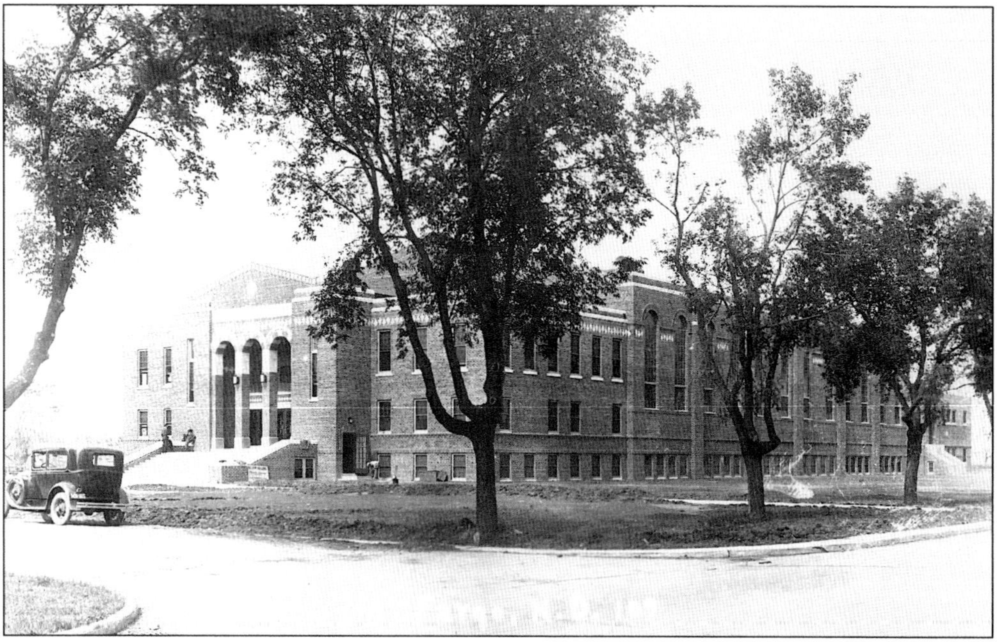

The gymnasium at North Dakota State University in Fargo has been the scene of many heated basketball games over the past 60 years. The most heated were probably when the North Dakota State University Bisons met their traditional rival—the Sioux from the University of North Dakota.

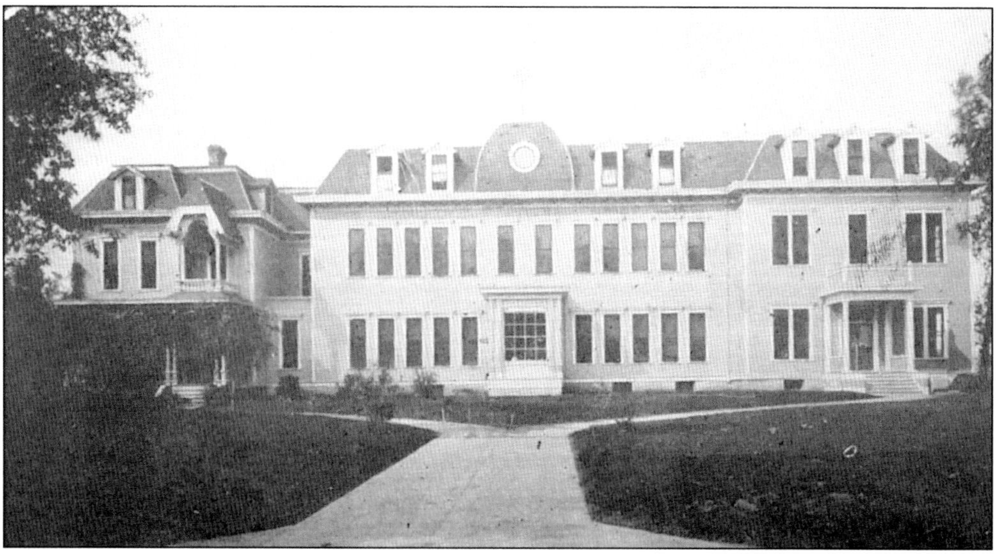

This postcard shows the Sacred Heart Academy in Fargo, North Dakota.

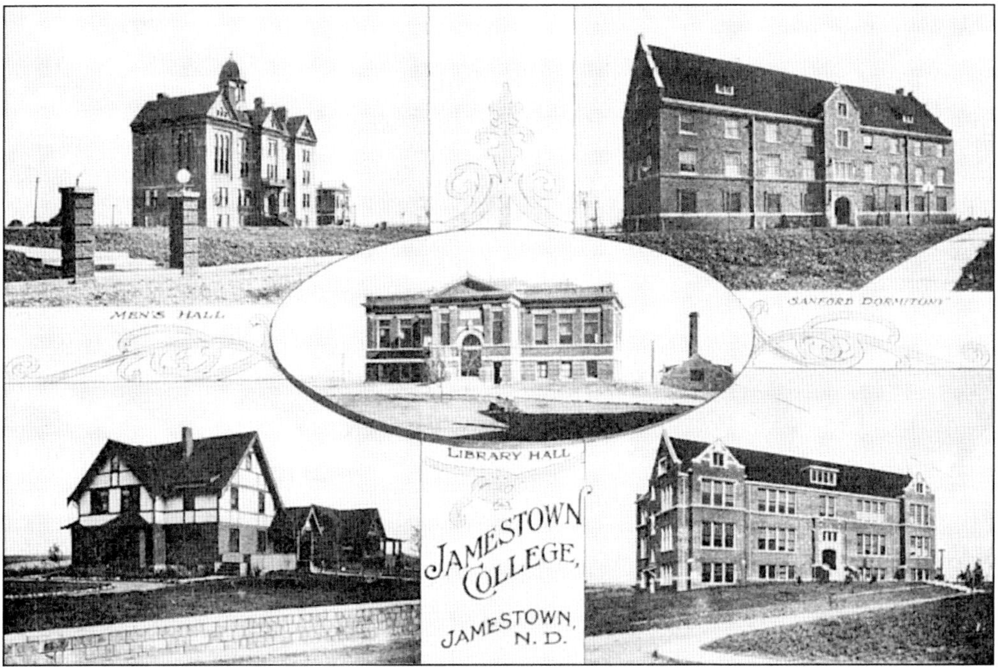

Jamestown College was chartered in 1884 under sponsorship of the Presbyterian Church (USA). The first classes began in 1886, three years before North Dakota achieved statehood. Early students had rough conditions. They studied by the light of oil lamps, and wood stoves provided heat. Today, the college has about 1,100 students.

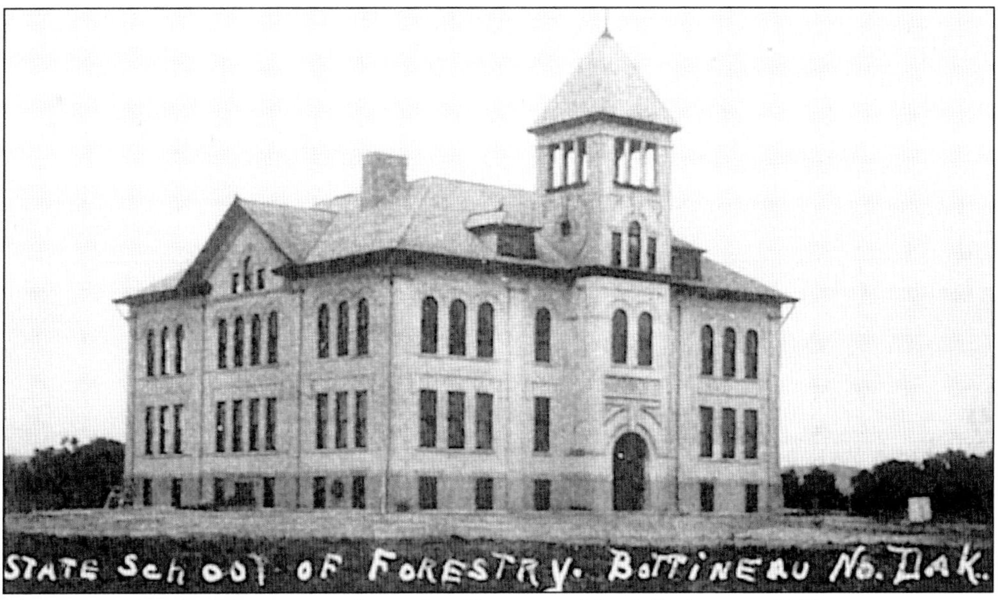

The State School of Forestry was located in Bottineau, North Dakota, in 1908.

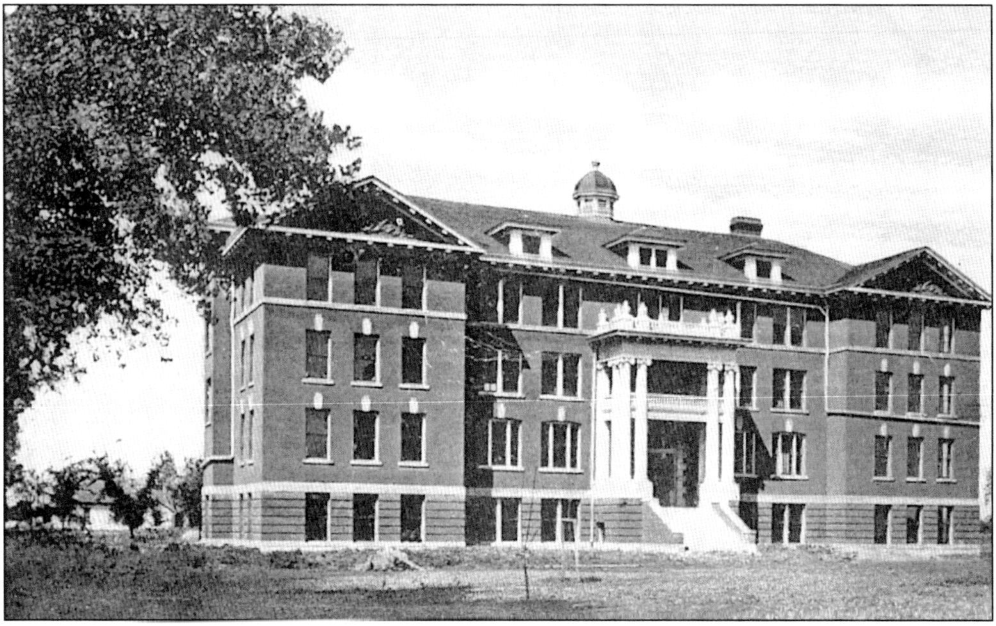

Many North Dakota teachers will remember this building. It is the Girls' Dormitory at the State Normal School in Mayville, North Dakota.

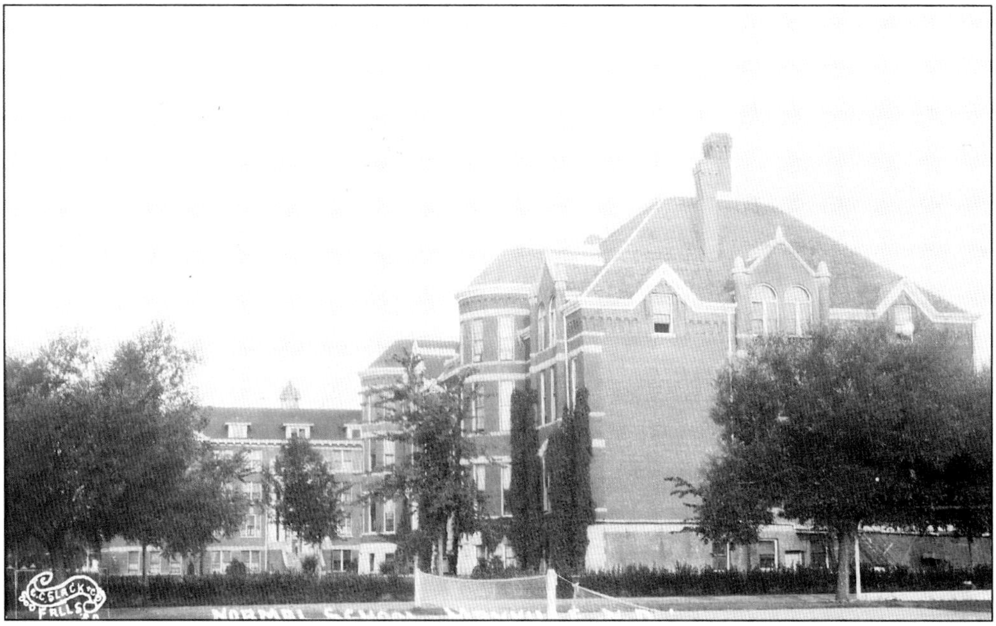

This picture shows another view of the "Normal School" in Mayville, North Dakota, *c.* 1900s. Now called Mayville State University, the first classes met on December 1, 1890, in the Mayville City Hall.

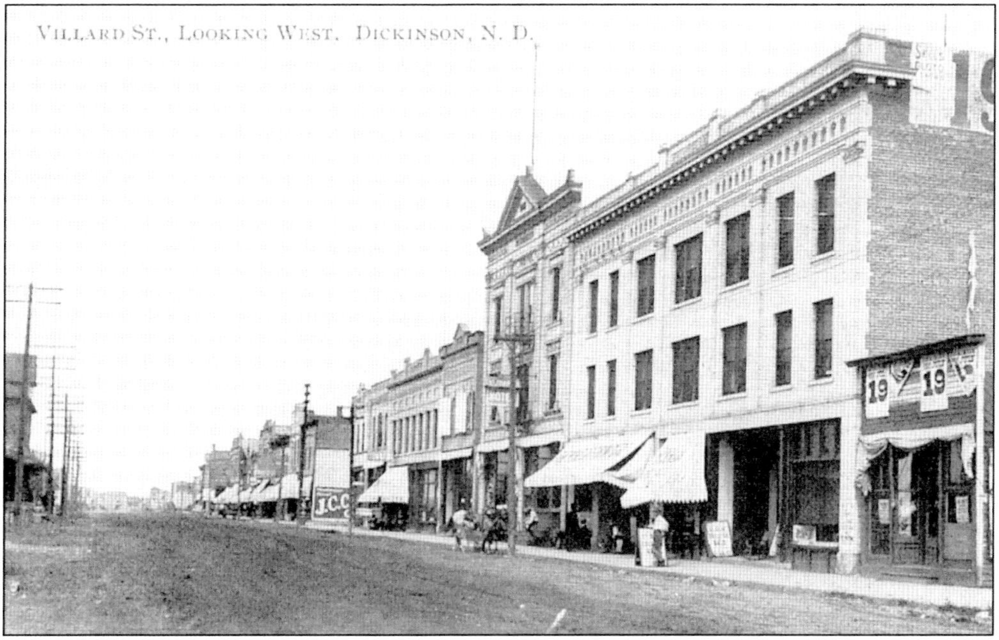

This is Villard Street looking west in Dickinson, North Dakota. Dickinson is proud of Dickinson State University, which was created by popular state vote in 1916.

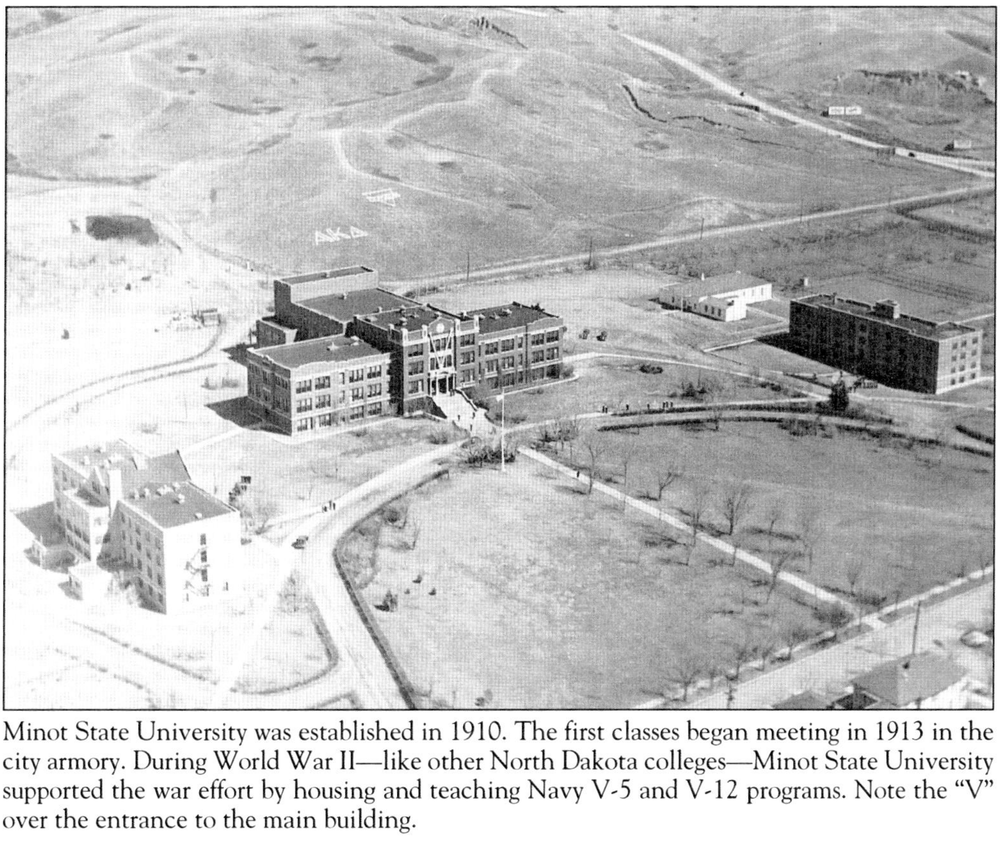

Minot State University was established in 1910. The first classes began meeting in 1913 in the city armory. During World War II—like other North Dakota colleges—Minot State University supported the war effort by housing and teaching Navy V-5 and V-12 programs. Note the "V" over the entrance to the main building.

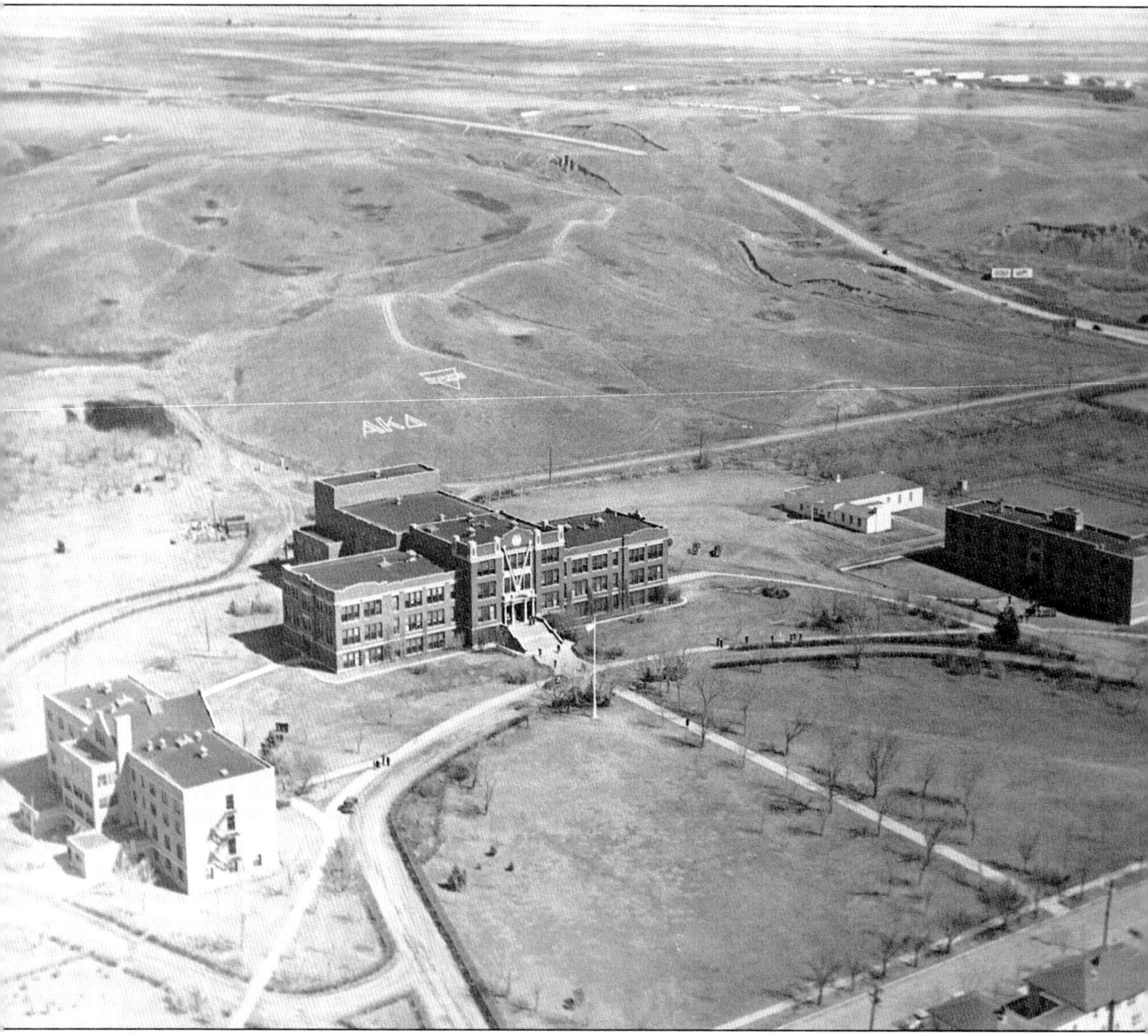

Minot State University campus is shown here in 1914. There were only two buildings and a small power house. The building on the right is "Old Main," and the one on the left is the first dormitory built to house women students. It is now called "Pioneer Hall."

Three

FARMING

Unless you lived near the railroad, early North Dakota farmers got some of their supplies from 10 or 12 horses pulling several wagons. How did you get land in North Dakota in the 1870s? There were three ways one could claim land: you lived on it for a year, you planted trees on your land, or you bought it from the Northern Pacific Railroad or the federal government. The price ranged from $2.50 an acre and up. When the settlers first arrived on their claim they might have slept under their wagon, in a tent, or in a cave like the author's grandfather did along the Red River.

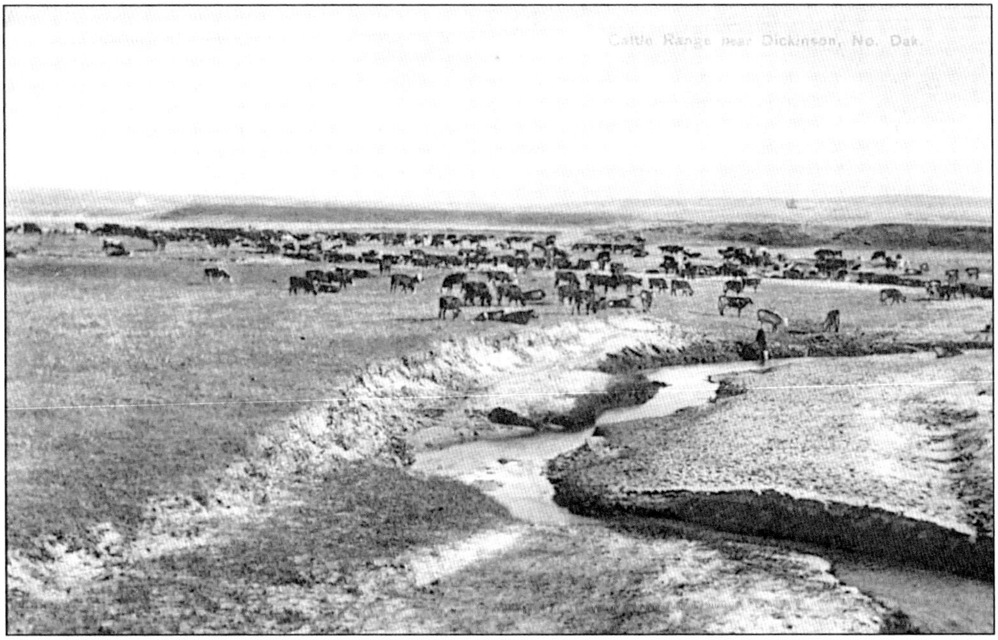

A cattle range near Dickinson, North Dakota, is shown on this postcard, which was mailed October 7, 1924. The card, mailed for 1¢, was printed in Germany.

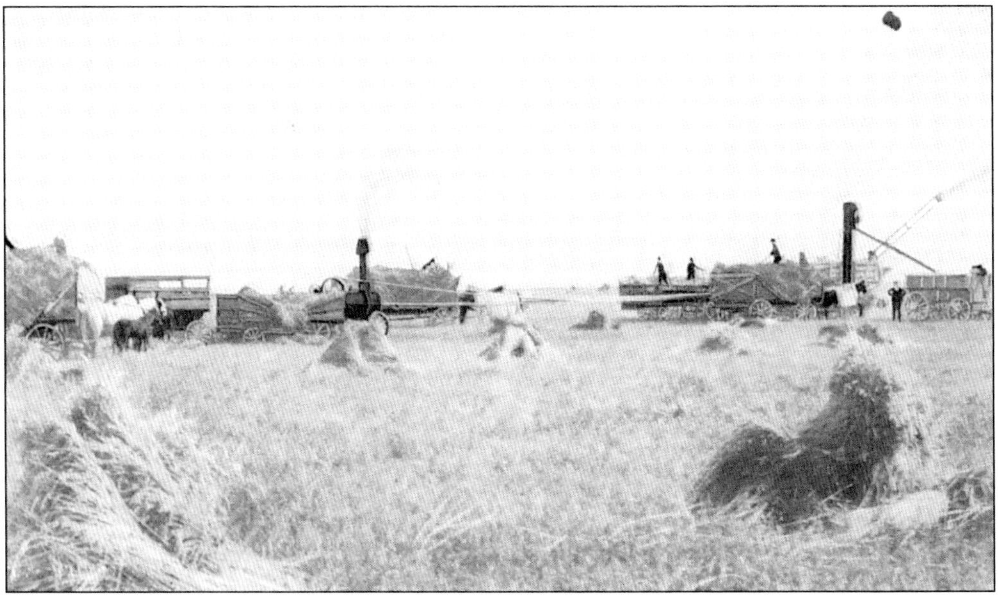

This threshing (harvesting) scene was taken near Fargo in 1910. The work was done by manpower, horsepower, and a large steam engine. Even the average farmer had to hire about 20 additional men to do the hand intensive work. Tractors started coming into North Dakota in the late 1920s. In 1932, the tractors started using rubber tires. The manufacturer of tractors actually started during World War I; some of the early tractors were an inspiration for army tanks.

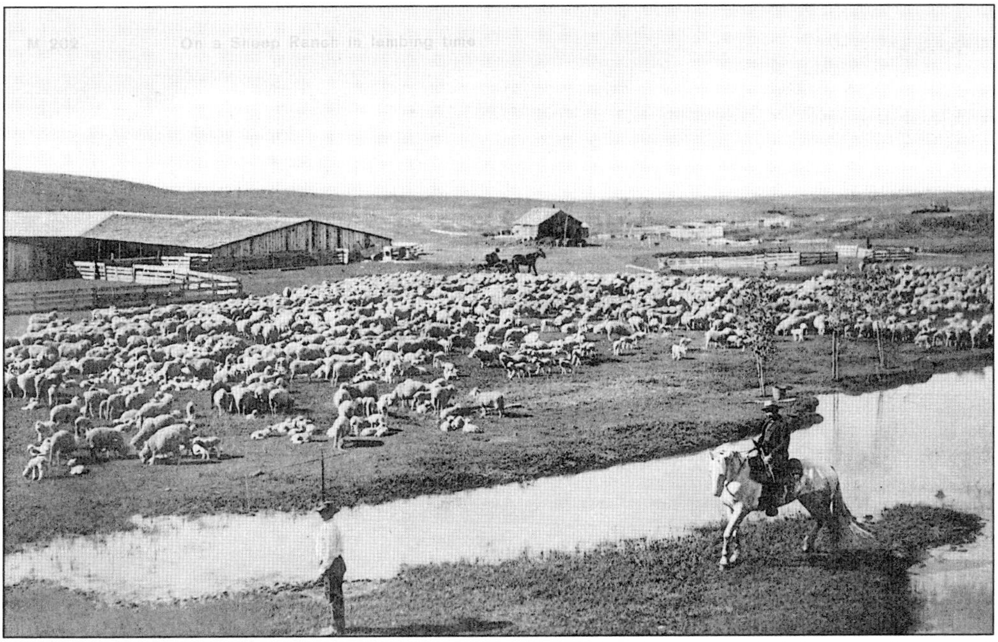

This photograph shows "lambing" time on a North Dakota sheep ranch. The term "lambing" refers to the time lambs are being born.

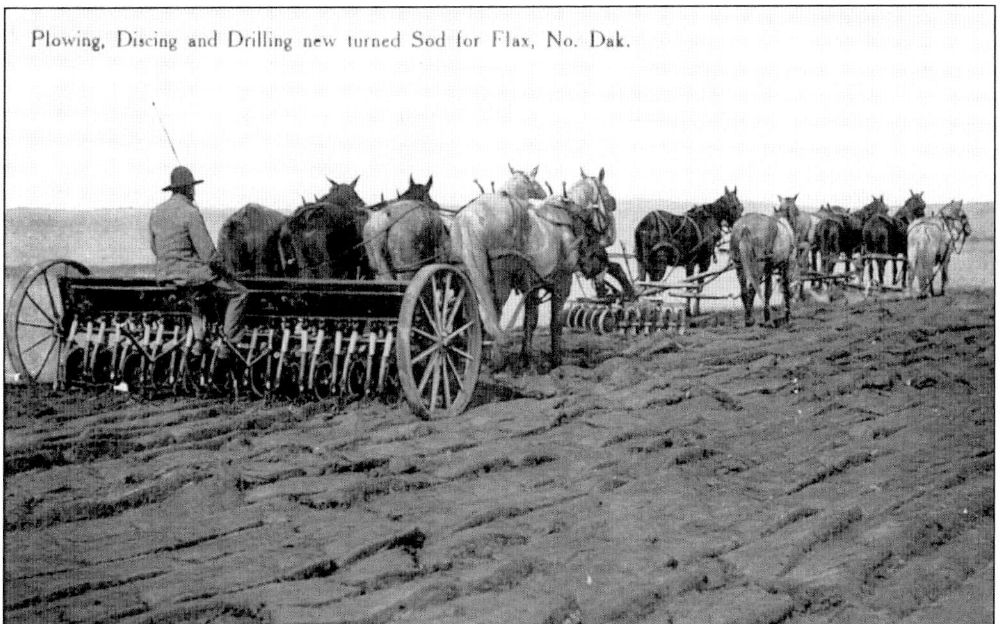

From 1900 to 1930, horses provided the muscle to plow, disk, and seed. It was estimated that farm horses walked about 20 miles a day. The biggest frustration for the early farmers was that they had to sell their wheat in outside markets where they could not control its grading or price.

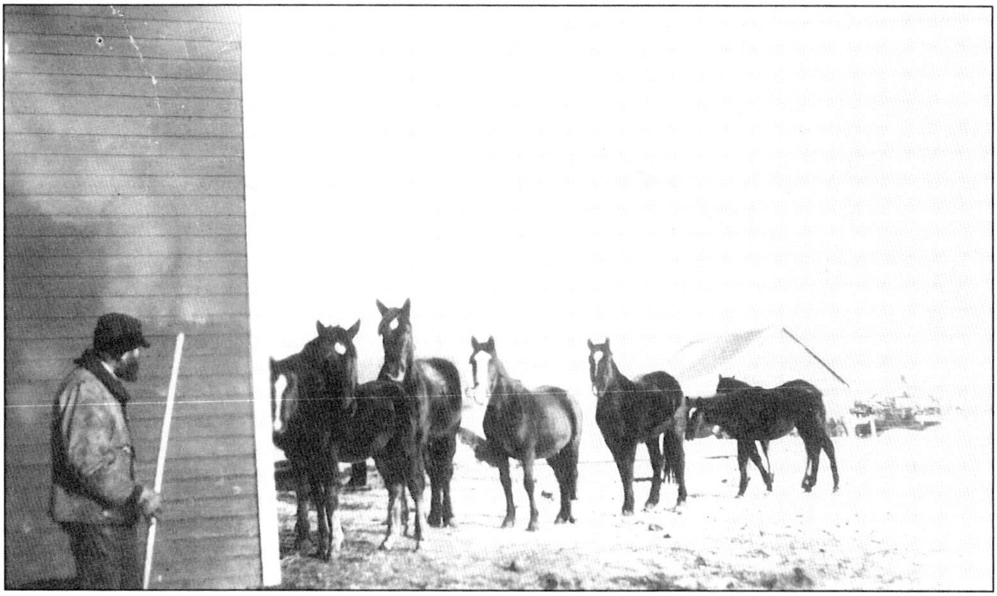

Even the average farmer would have eight horses in the early 20th century. When the tractors started to come into the state, farmers either sold their horses or kept them around the farm for sentimental reasons. Each horse had a name, and most responded to it.

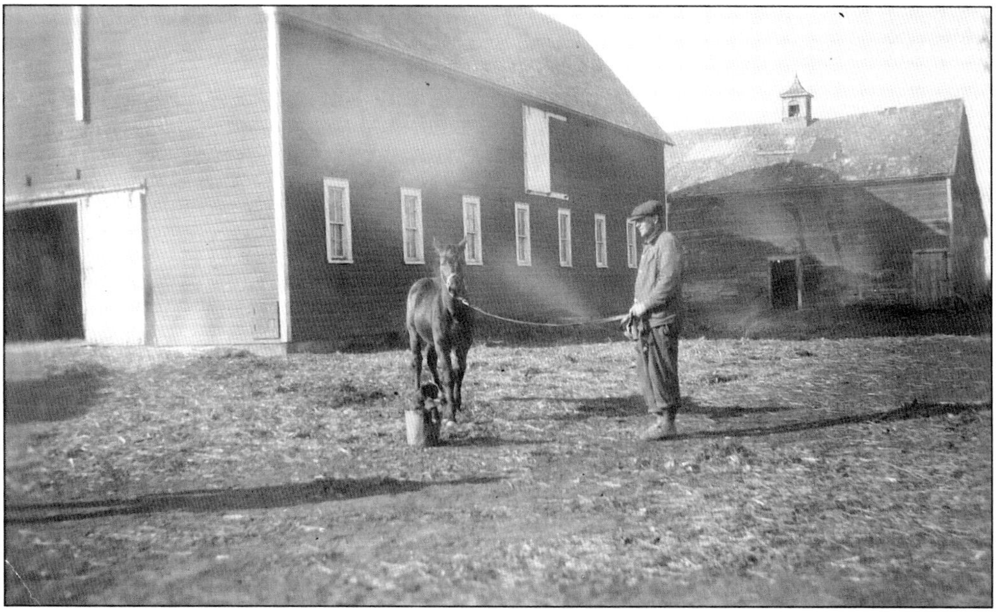

Big barns were needed to house the horses, the cows, and the calves. Kids played in the hay on the second floor of the barn when it was too cold to be outside in the wintertime. Today, these barns are gone, standing empty or leaning into the wind. Tractors replaced the horses, and many North Dakota farms no longer milk a large number of cows.

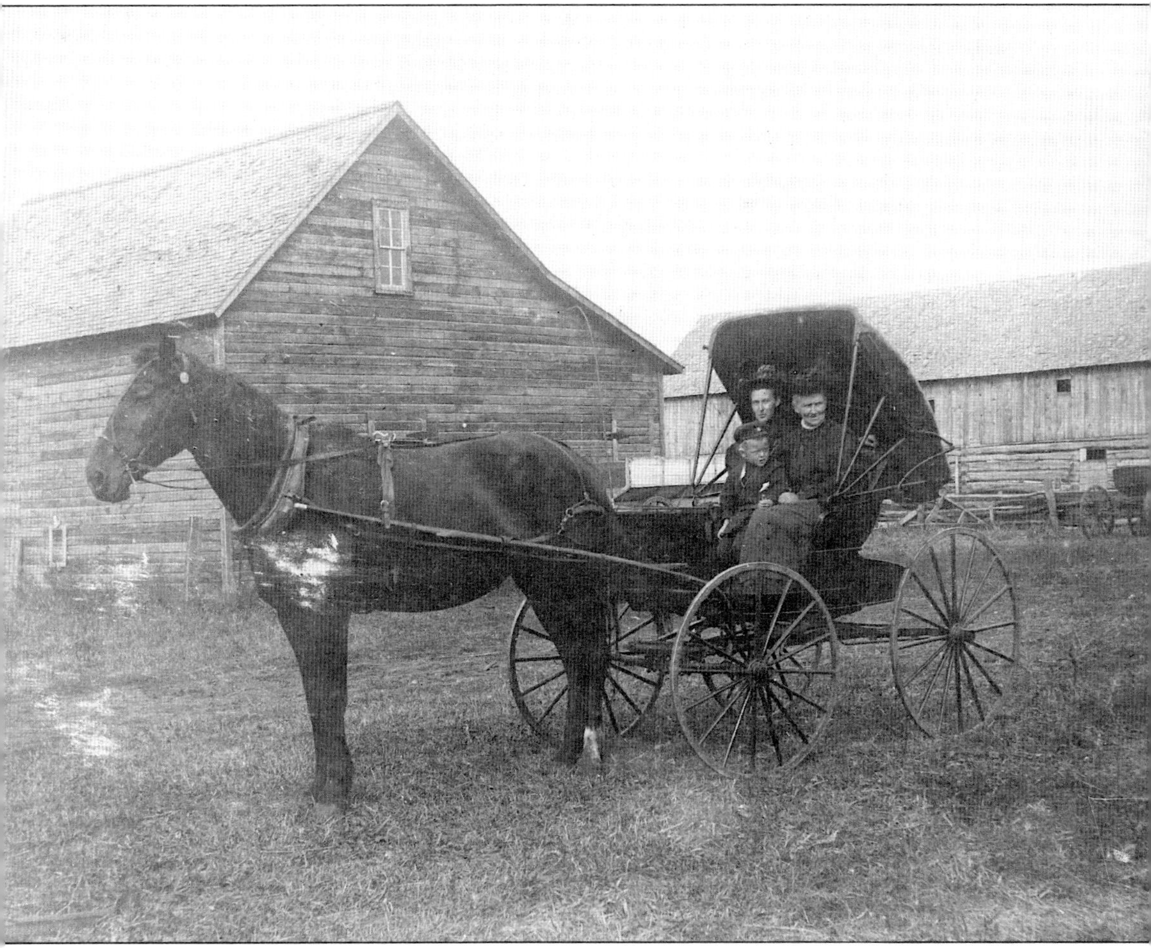

At the turn of the century, almost everybody, both farmers and people in town, owned a horse and a buggy for transportation and fun. Some of the buggies and harnesses were very elaborate. If this photograph had been taken in the summertime, the horse would probably be wearing a "nose basket" to protect the soft skin on its nose from horse flies and other insects.

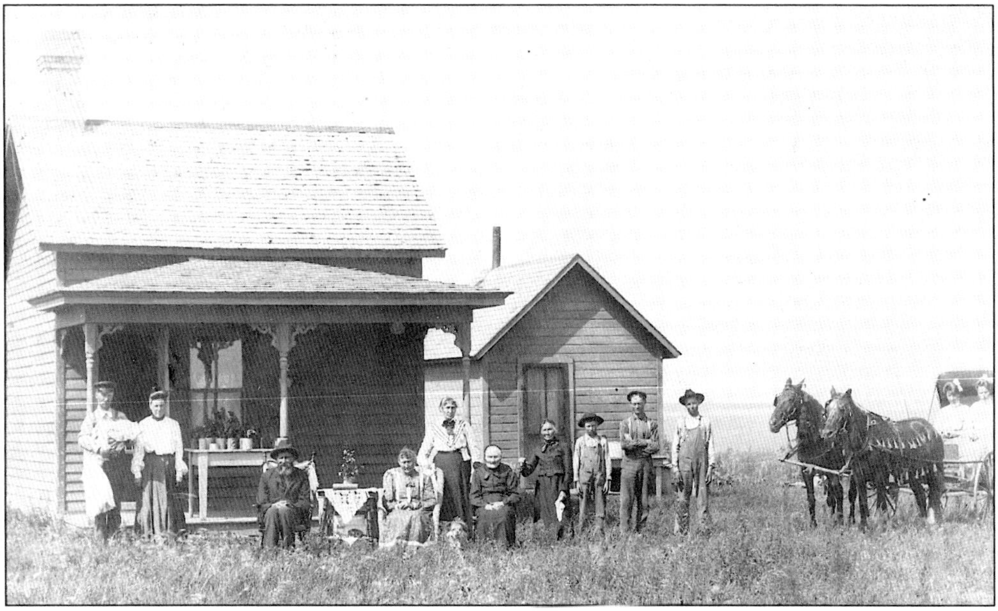

This photograph shows a typical farm from the turn of the century. The farmers had gone from sod huts to log houses, and here they were proud of their houses made from lumber. A surrey, which may have had a fringe on top, can be seen in this image. Note the older people in the photograph. In those days, each farmhouse had about three generations living in it. There were few "rest homes" for the aged.

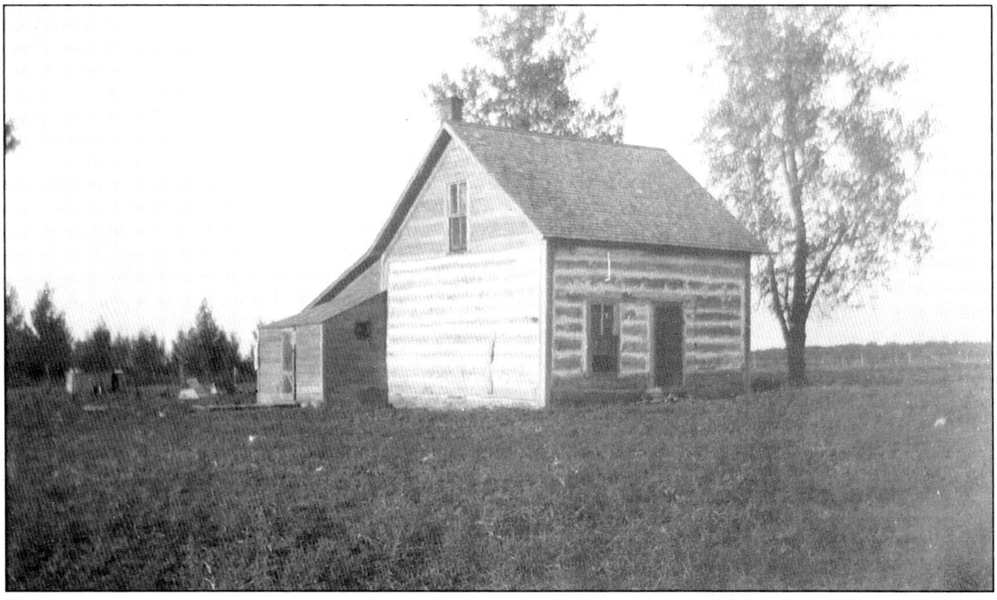

Many North Dakota farmers lived in log houses like this one, *c.* 1900; the houses were often made from logs cut nearby and lumber. They had no electricity or running water. Kerosene lamps provided the light and a cistern or well provided the water. The author and his two brothers were born in this log house.

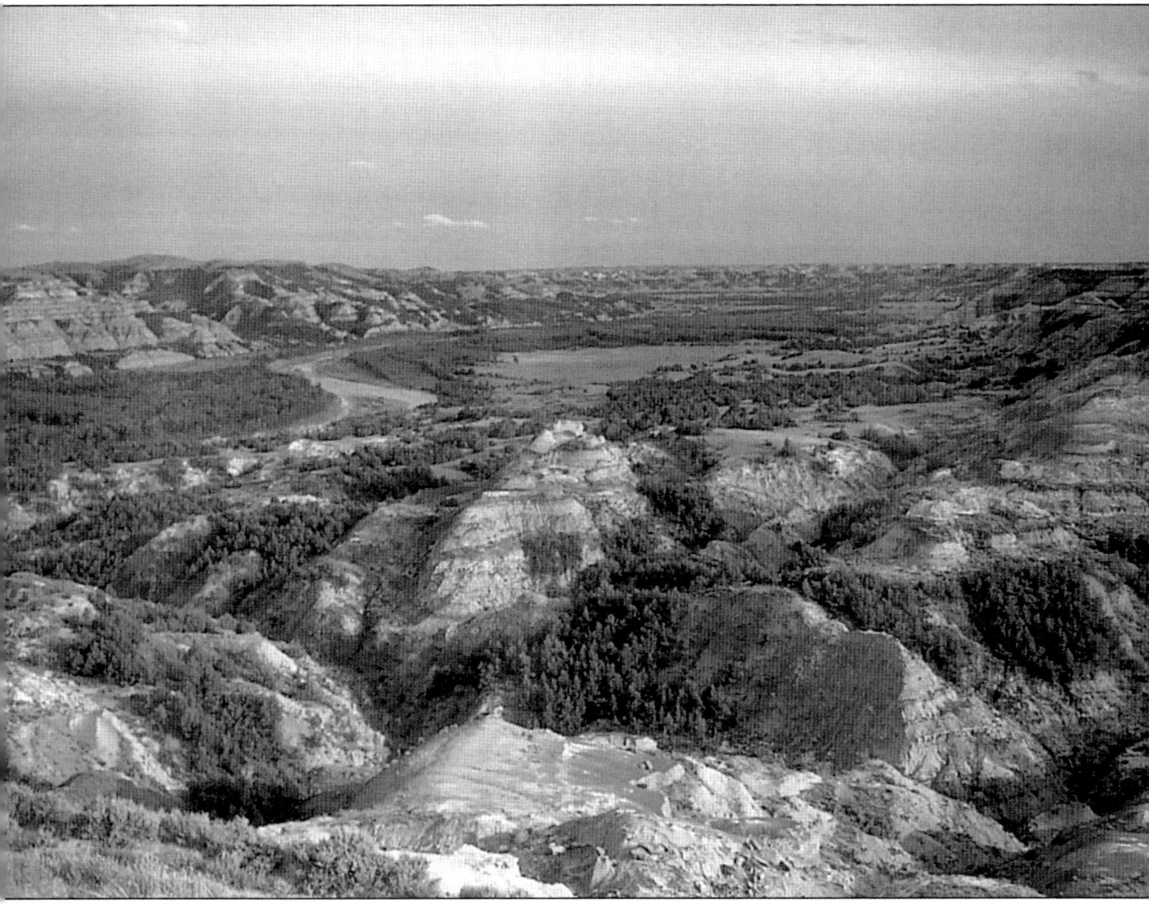

Teddy Roosevelt described the North Dakota Badland as "a land of vast silent spaces, of lonely rivers, and of plains where the wild game stared at the passing horseman." Marquis De Mores, early North Dakota entrepreneur, said "there is a strangely fascinating desolution to the badlands . . . I like this land because it gives me room to turn around without stepping on . . . others."

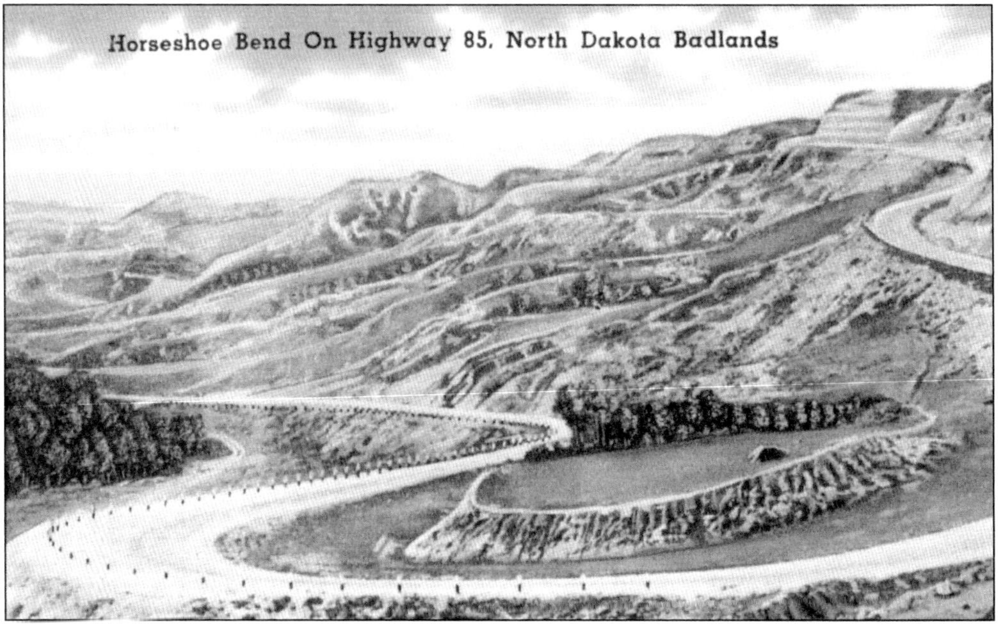

This old postcard shows a part of the North Dakota Badlands in the western part of the state. Theodore Roosevelt operated two ranches in the Badlands in 1883. In 1947, the U.S. Congress established the Theodore Roosevelt National Park, 70,000 acres of badlands and prairie.

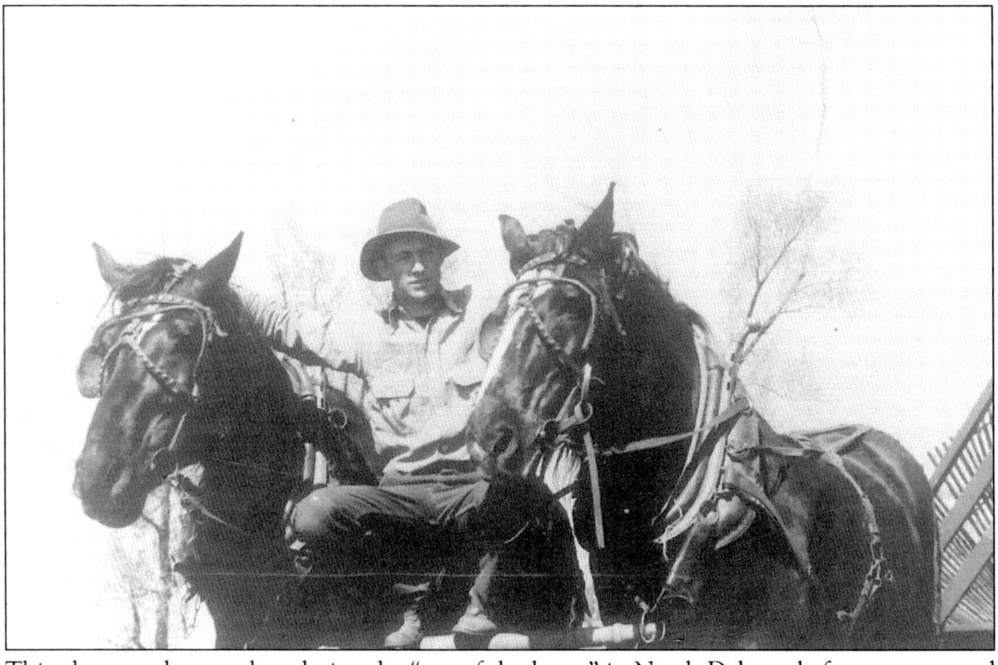

This photograph was taken during the "age of the horse" in North Dakota, before tractors and automobiles came into the state replacing the horses. However, many farmers, like Milton Aasen of Hillsboro, kept some of their horses for sentimental reasons. They didn't need them anymore but they hated to see them go. Milton loved the two horses shown here, for they had served him well for many years. He was not about to sell "Jig" and "Nig" to a manufacturer who would probably turn them into products we shall not name.

Many farms in North Dakota have been in the same family for more than 100 years. Here, the author holds his family plaque.

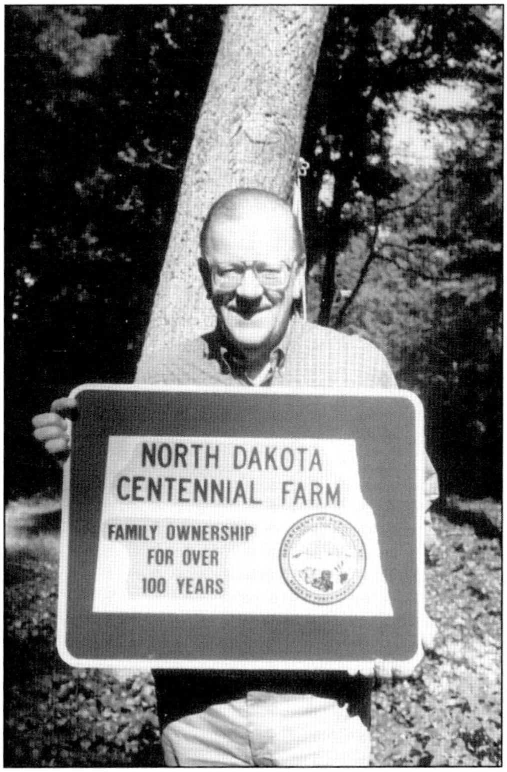

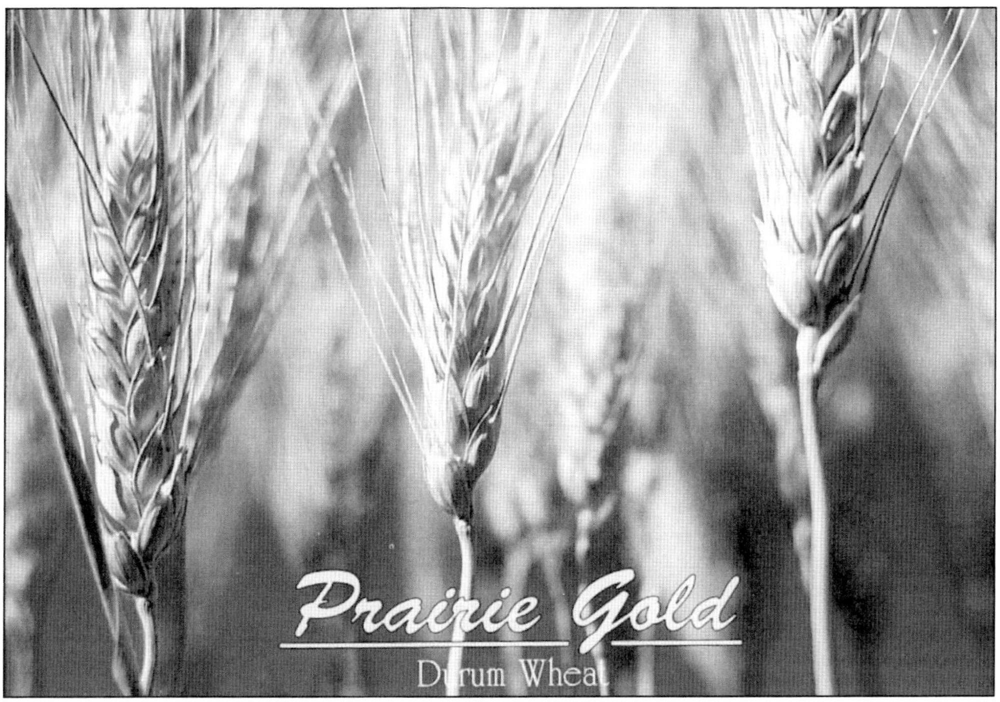

North Dakota has often led the nation in the production of durum wheat. Durum wheat is made into bread, macaroni, spaghetti, and other pastas.

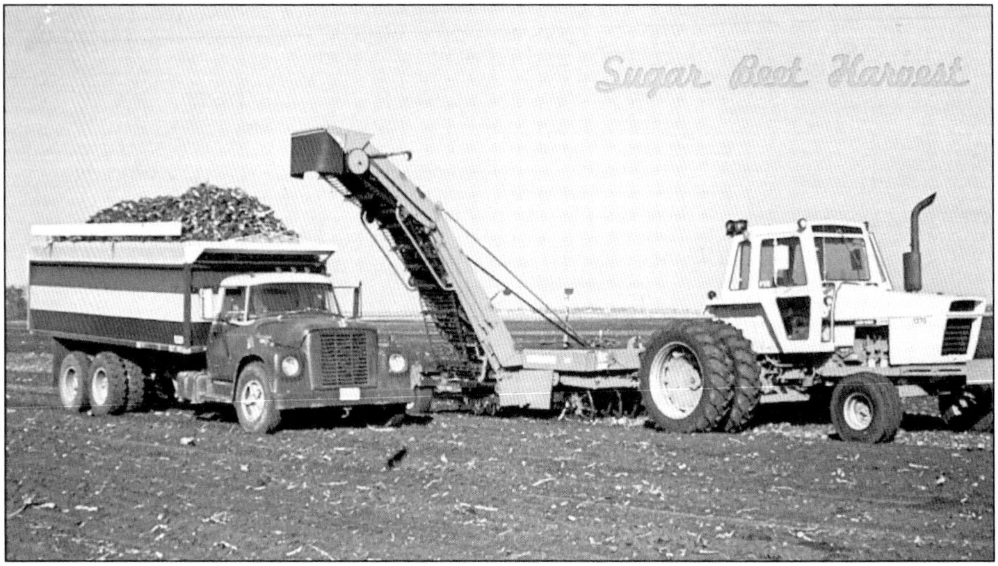

Between 1900 and 1930, North Dakota farms primarily grew grains like wheat, barley, oats, flax, and corn; some also planted potatoes. In the 1920s and 1930s, farmers started raising sugar beets, and sugar beet factories were built in East Grand Forks, North Dakota; Moorhead, Minnesota; and Hillsboro, North Dakota. Other new crops included soybeans, sunflowers, pinto beans, turtle beans, great northern beans, navy beans, and millet.

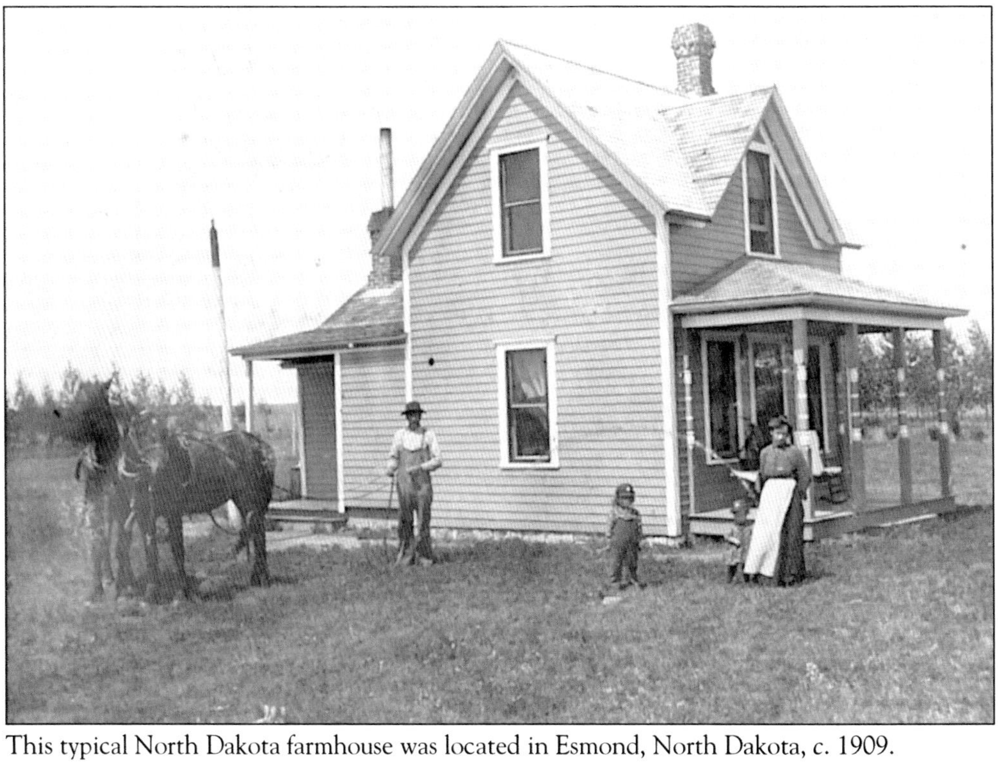

This typical North Dakota farmhouse was located in Esmond, North Dakota, c. 1909.

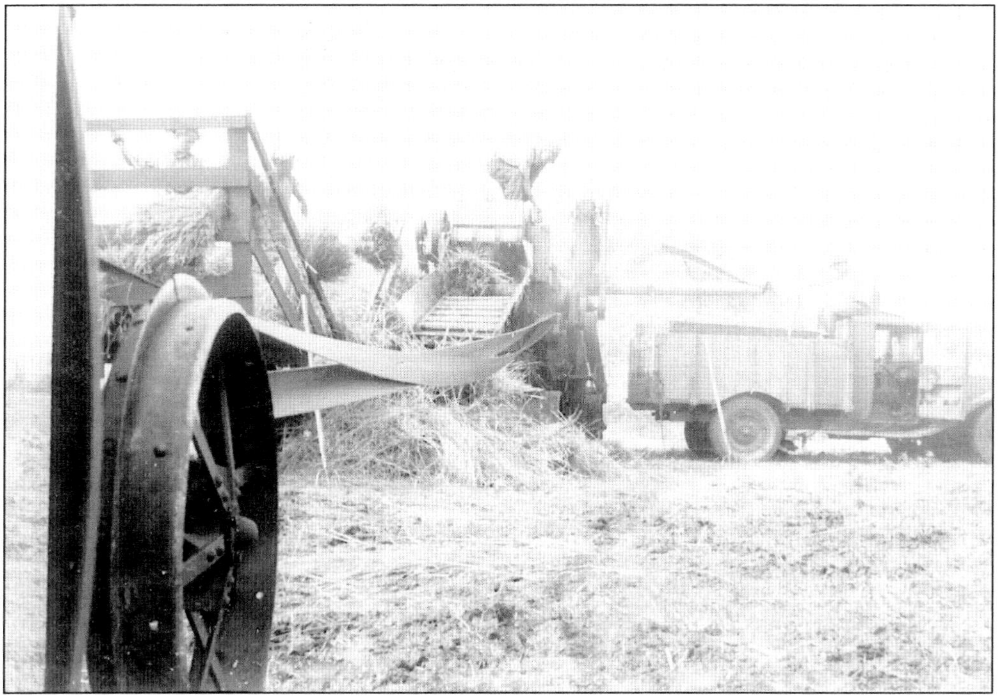

Farming in North Dakota has had many "booms" and "busts." This photograph was taken in the late 1930s, which were lean years. Today, news reports indicate the price of grain does not cover the cost of raising crops.

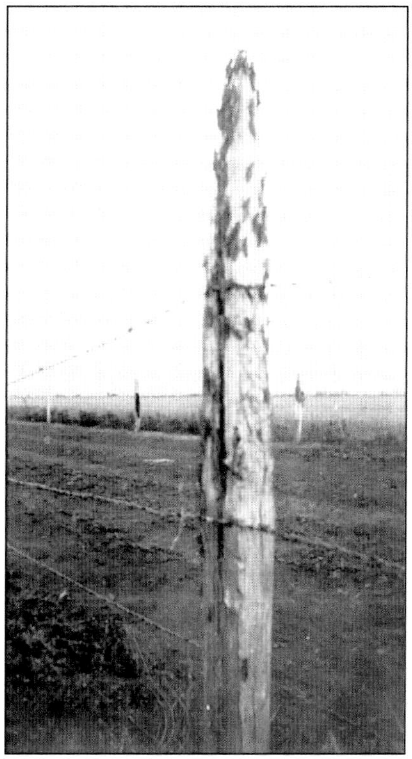

In 1932, North Dakota had a terrible infestation of grasshoppers that cost the state millions of dollars. Here, they rest on a fence post. (Photo by Tilford Aasen.)

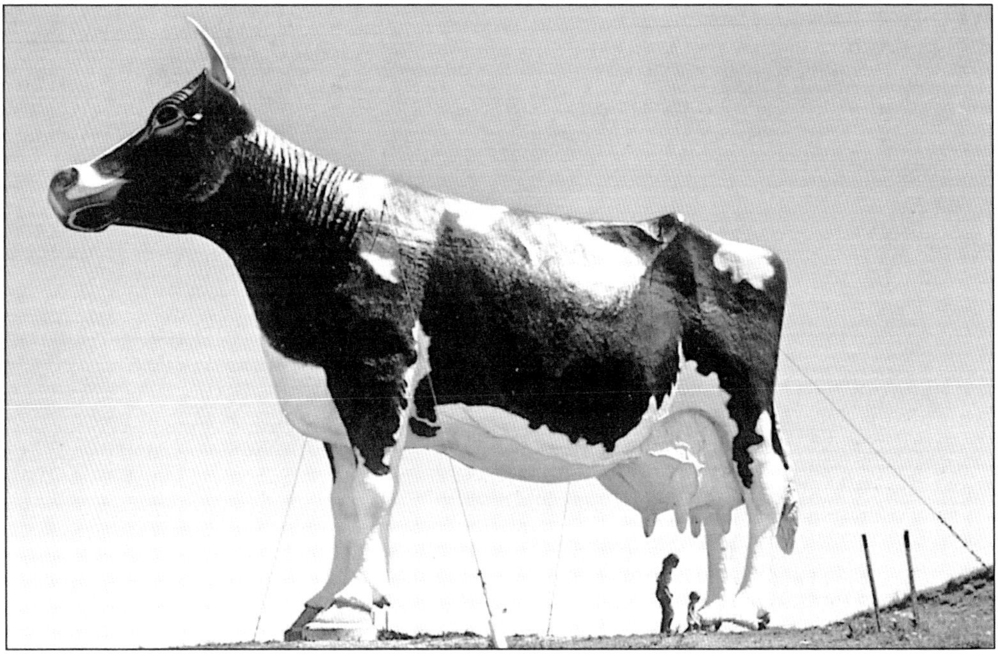

The world's largest Holstein cow—38 feet high, 50 feet long—stands on a hill near New Salem, North Dakota. Made of reinforced plastic fiberglass, it weighs 12,000 pounds. The Holstein cow is very popular in North Dakota because of its high milk production. In the early 20th century, every North Dakota farm had some milk cows for family needs and for extra income. Because dairies are a very hand intensive operation, few farms have milk cows today.

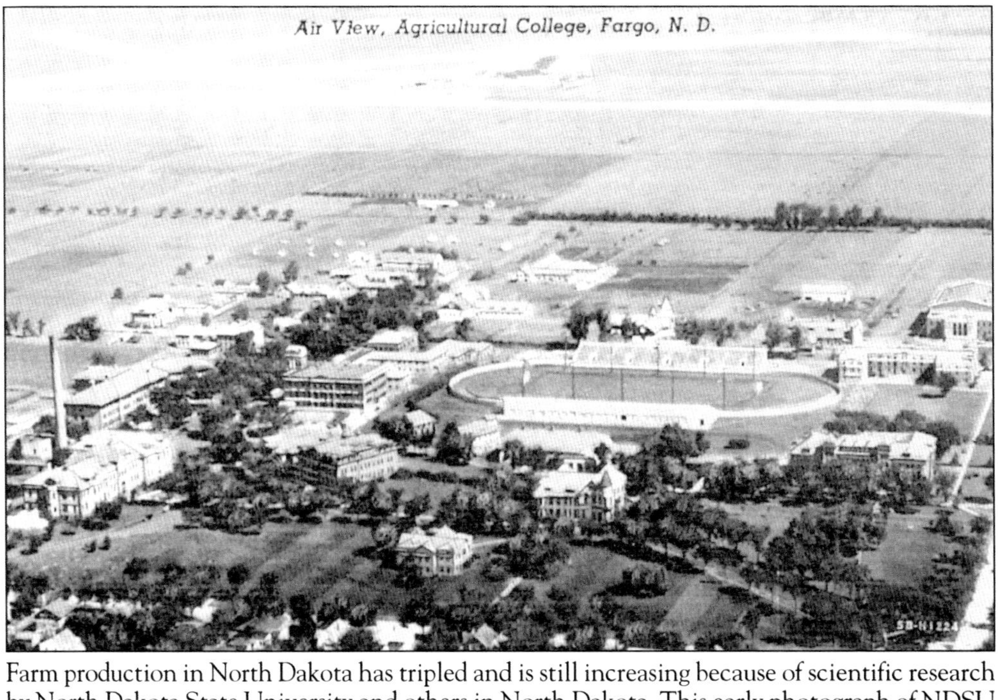

Farm production in North Dakota has tripled and is still increasing because of scientific research by North Dakota State University and others in North Dakota. This early photograph of NDSU was probably taken in the late 1930s.

Four

North Dakota People and Fashions

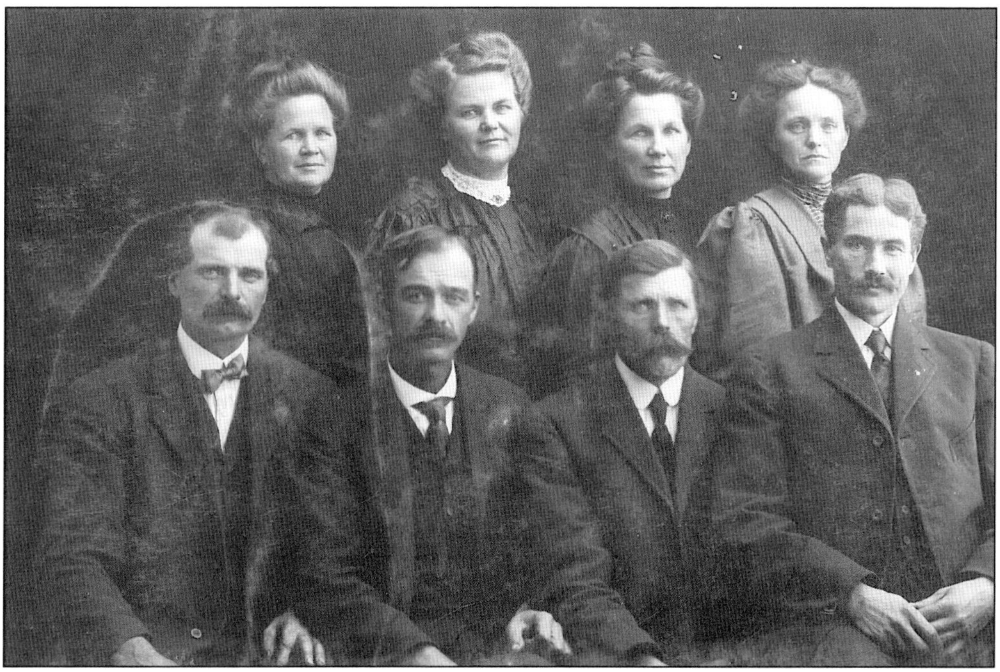

Most early North Dakota photographs show unsmiling people. That was the custom of the day, and it had nothing to do with North Dakota weather.

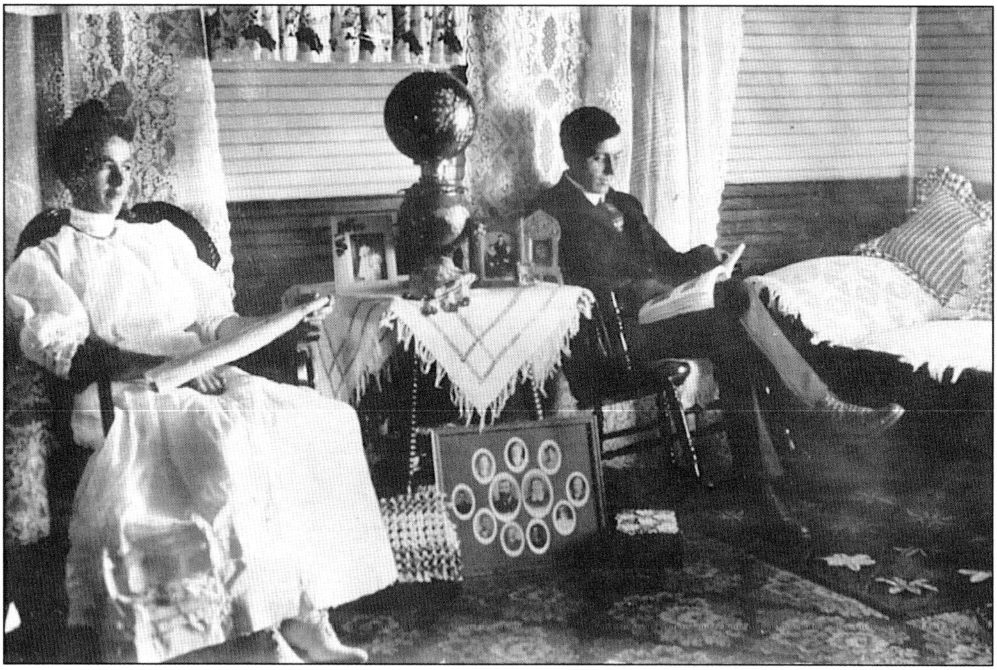

This couple managed to get a photograph taken inside their house before flash cameras were invented. Most pictures from this period are taken outside on sunny days. Note the couple's elegant clothing.

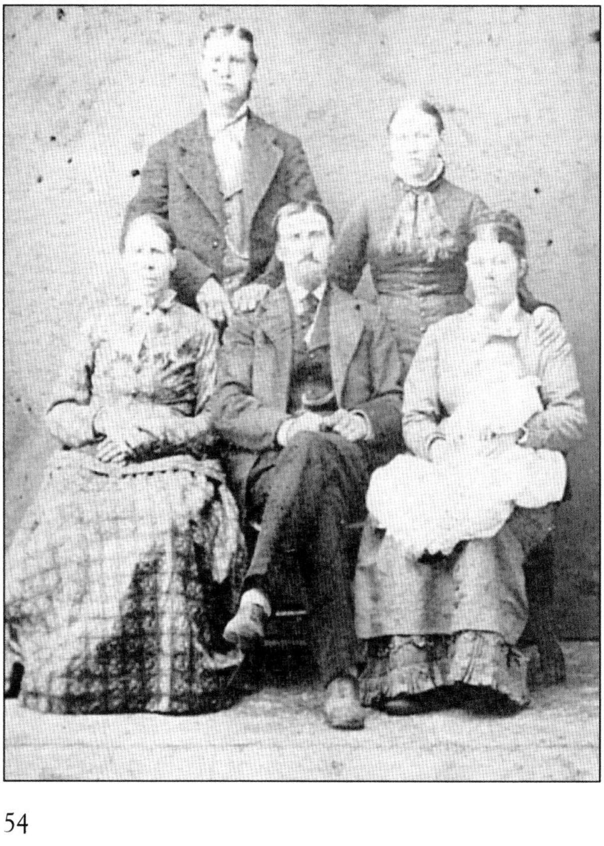

Many early photographs were staged similarly to this one. The author's grandmother, Bertha Brenden (upper right), and her family appear in this picture, c. 1877. The photographer told them to put their hands in their laps, stand up straight, and, for heaven's sake, DO NOT SMILE.

Large families were normal at this time. Many hands were needed for the farm work, which was not yet mechanized.

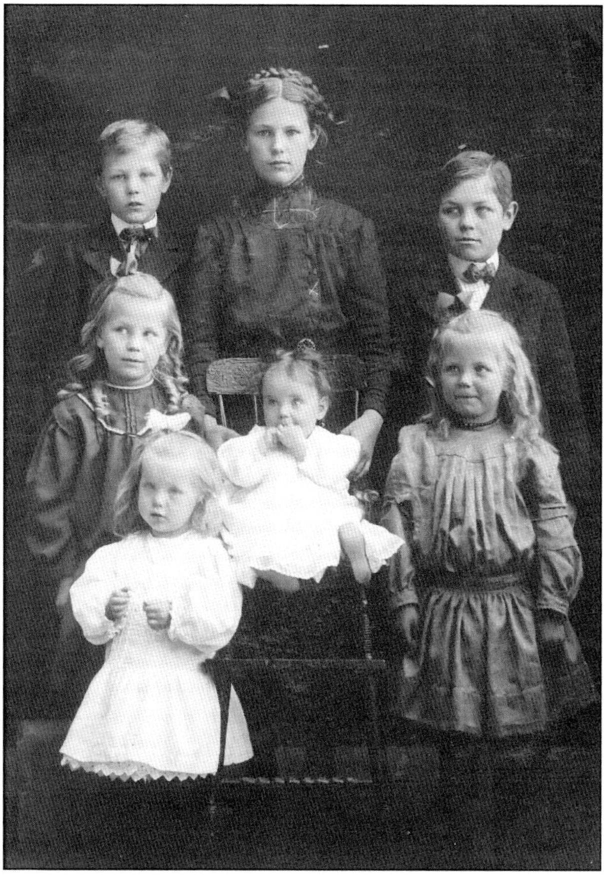

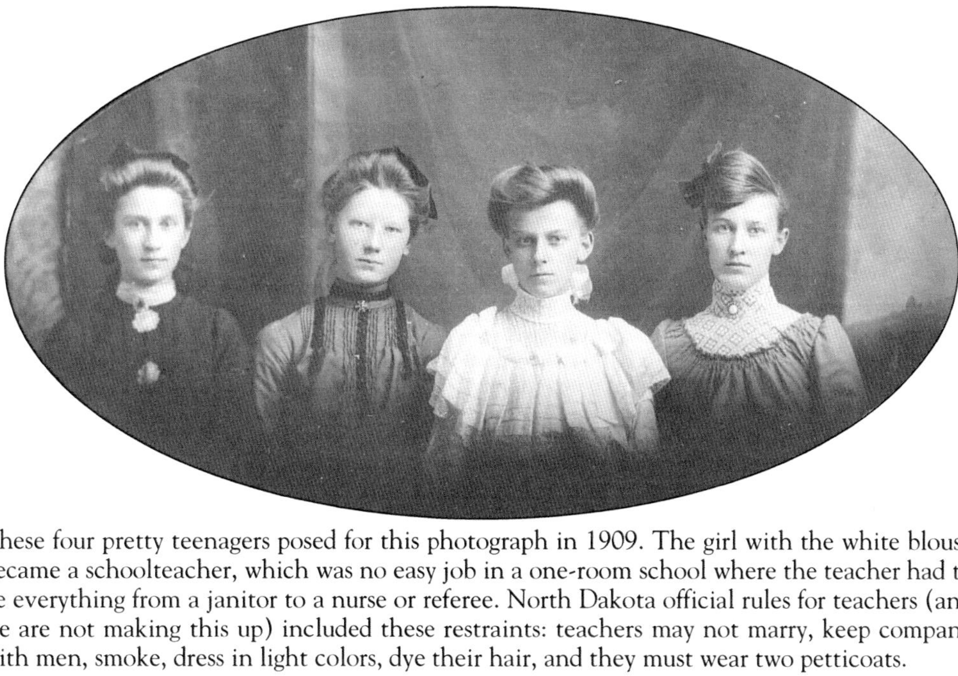

These four pretty teenagers posed for this photograph in 1909. The girl with the white blouse became a schoolteacher, which was no easy job in a one-room school where the teacher had to be everything from a janitor to a nurse or referee. North Dakota official rules for teachers (and we are not making this up) included these restraints: teachers may not marry, keep company with men, smoke, dress in light colors, dye their hair, and they must wear two petticoats.

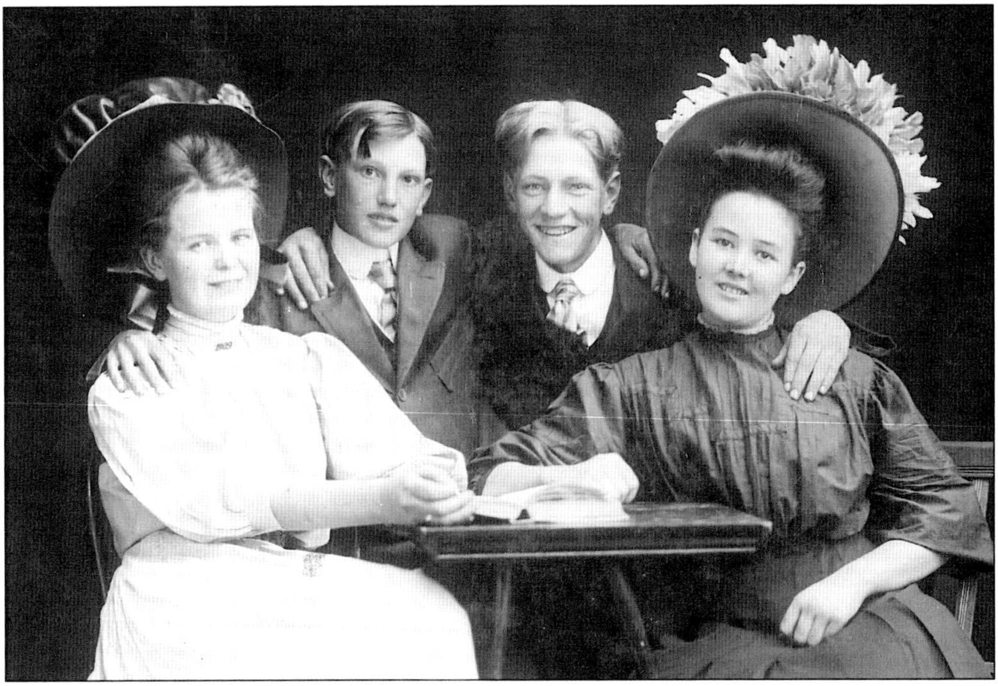

Women loved big hats at the turn of the century.

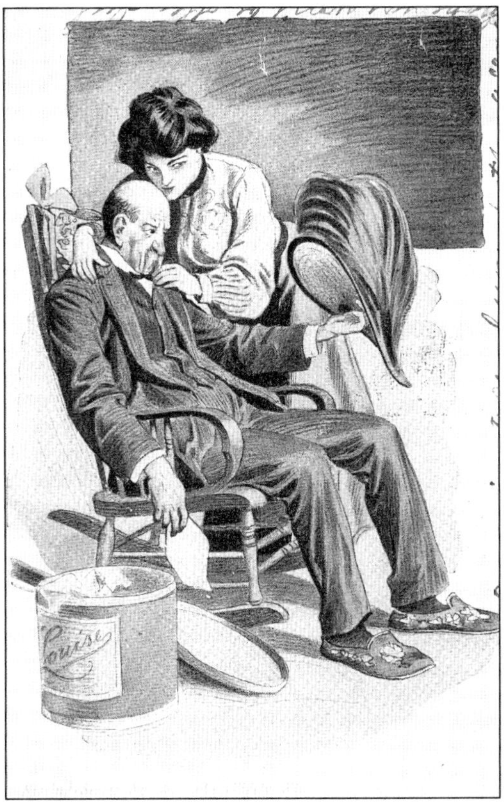

The wifely kiss apparently does not overcome the shock of the price tag in this postcard.

Note the wonderful hat the woman in this postcard wears.

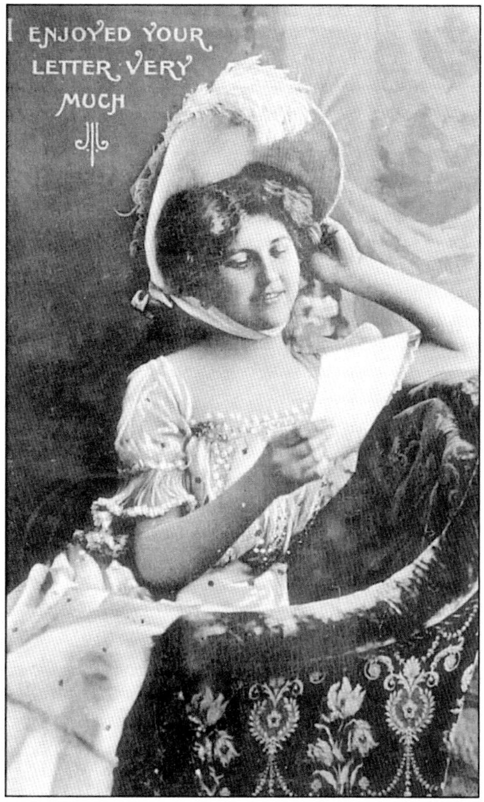

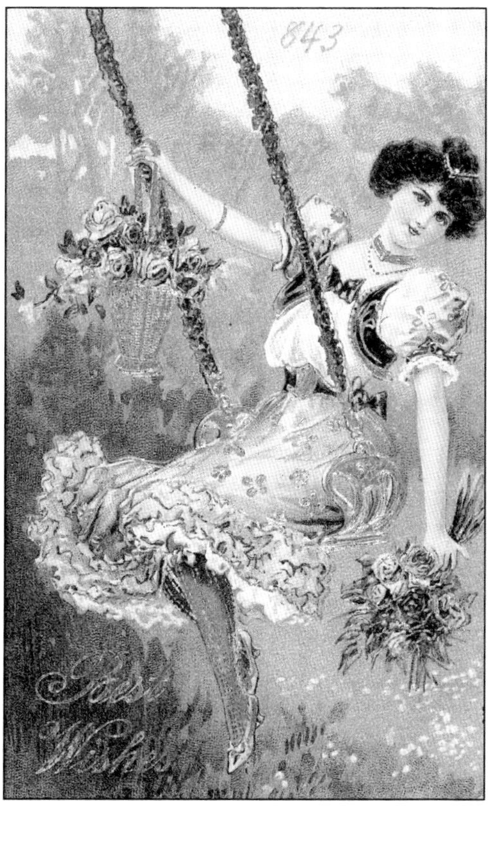

This beautiful card, which is embossed in four colors, was probably a top-of-the-line postcard in the early 20th century.

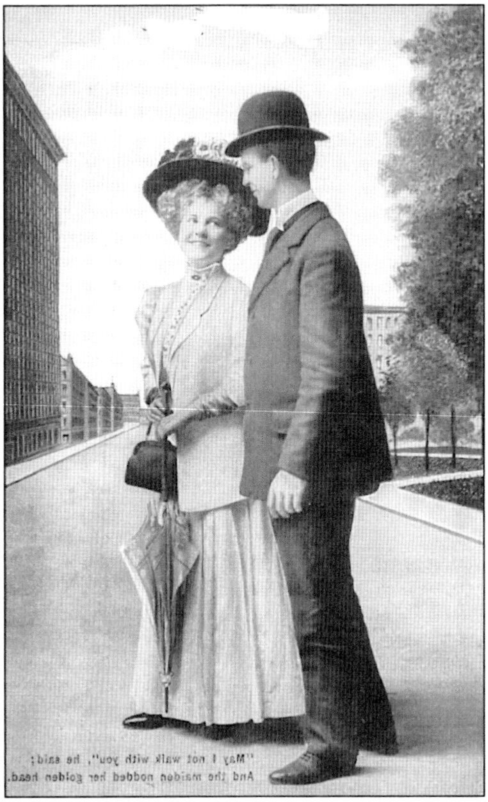

This couple mingles fashion with romance. The caption reads, "May I not walk with you," he said; And the maiden nodded her golden head."

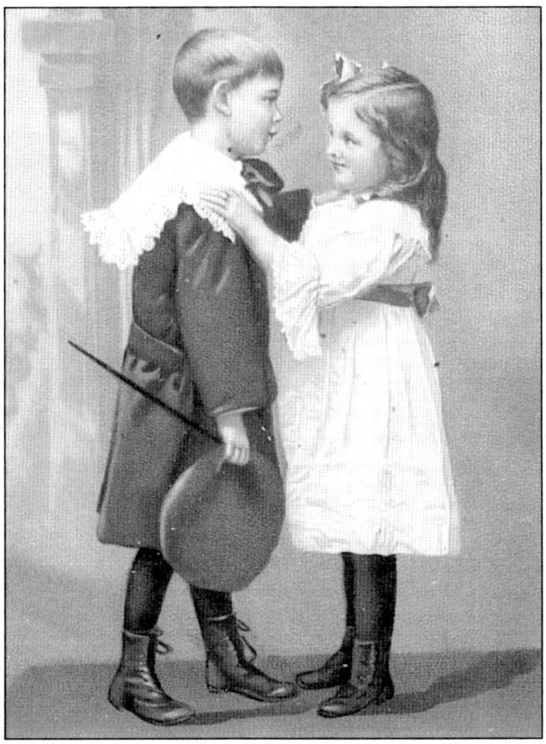

Even some of the children during this period wore fancy clothes. Jeans were not worn at this time.

Note the long, warm sweater and the high button shoes.

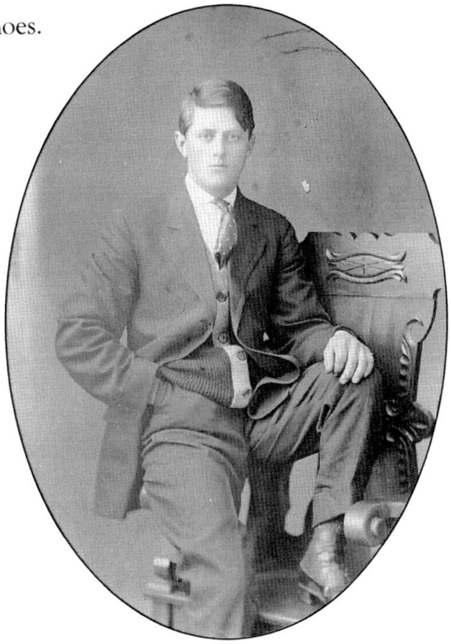

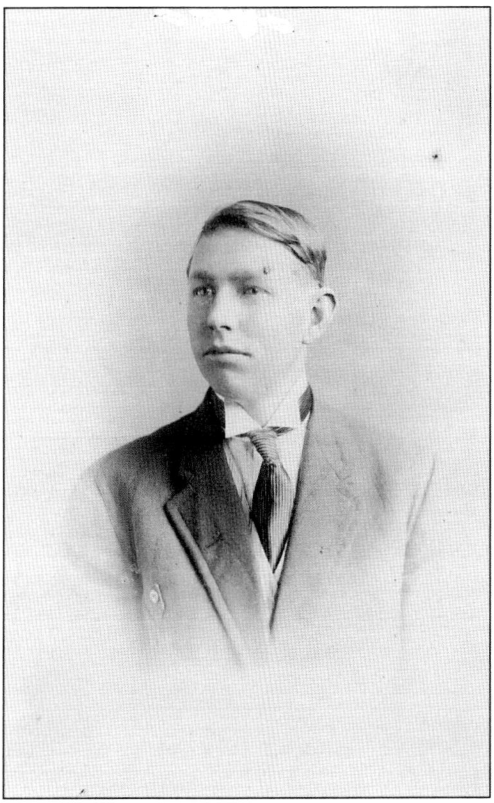

Check out the wing tip collar that Norwegian farmer Alfred Brenden wears in this image. Brenden was a bachelor who really dressed up on a Saturday night. He loved to go to "barn dances," which were held in barns far from town and not subject to local police ordinances.

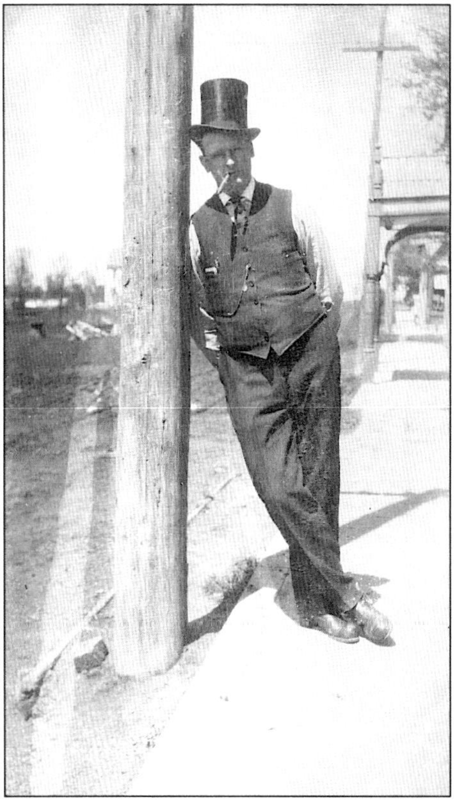

People liked to dress up crazy and have their photographs taken.

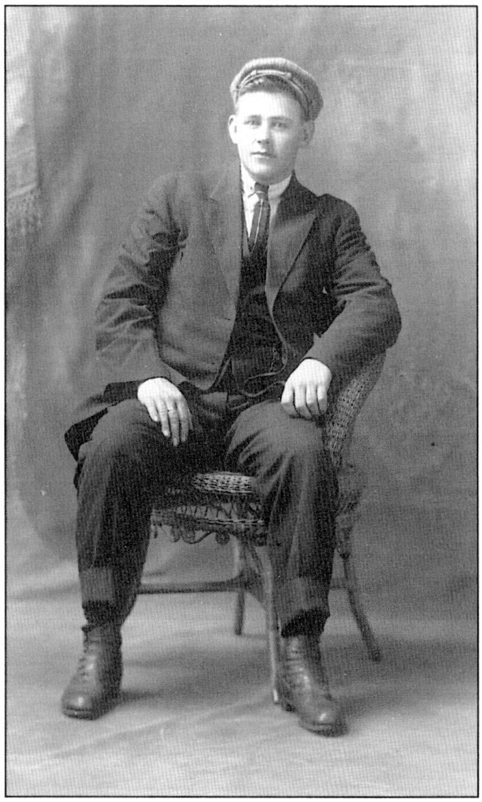

See the cap on this good-looking gentleman. He married young and, like many in Traill County, fathered eight children.

All three men are wearing the white, celluloid collar popular at this time.

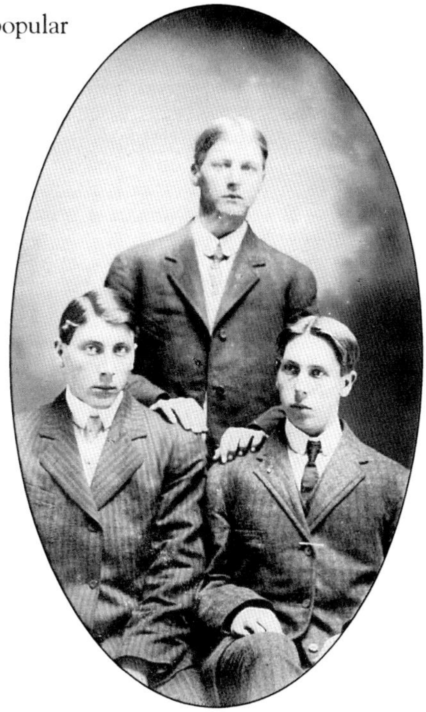

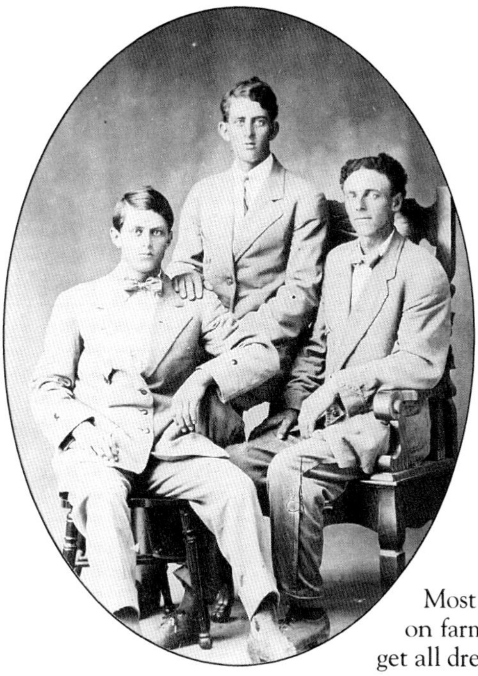

Most of the men during this period lived and worked on farms. They loved to take off their work clothes and get all dressed up.

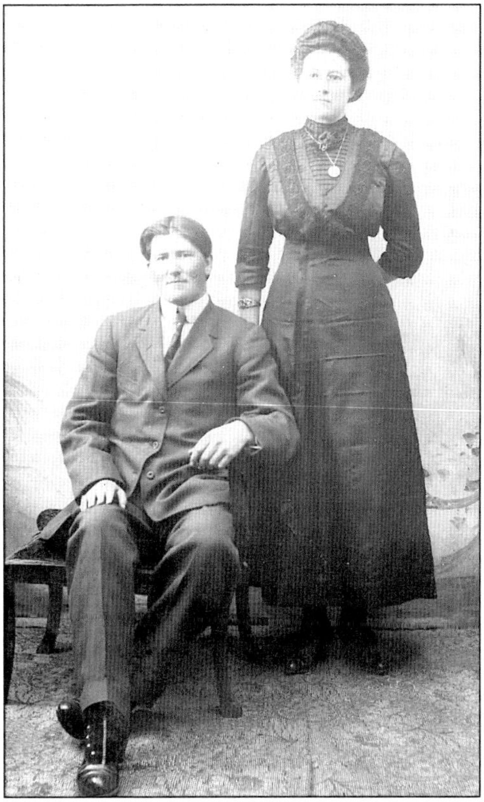

This wedding photograph shows the fashions of the day. The bride often stands in wedding photographs taken in the early 20th century.

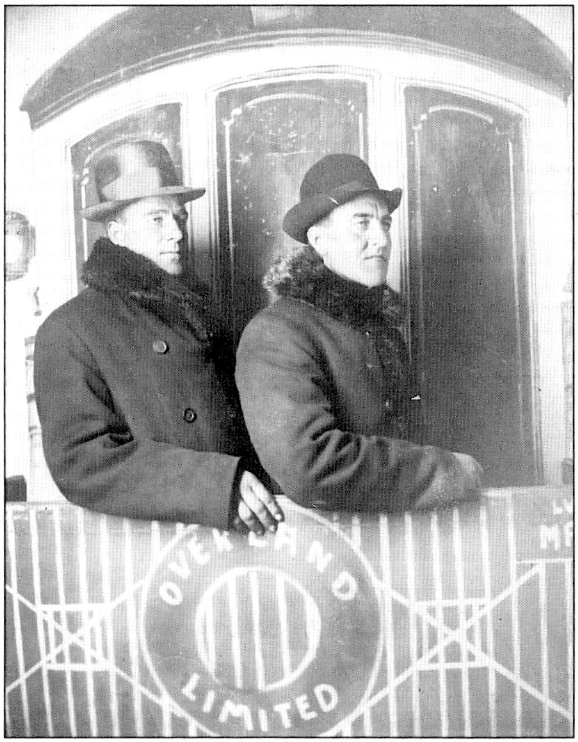

As the winters can be brisk in North Dakota, the men, like the author's father, on the left, wore bulky coats with fur collars.

Five

ROMANCE

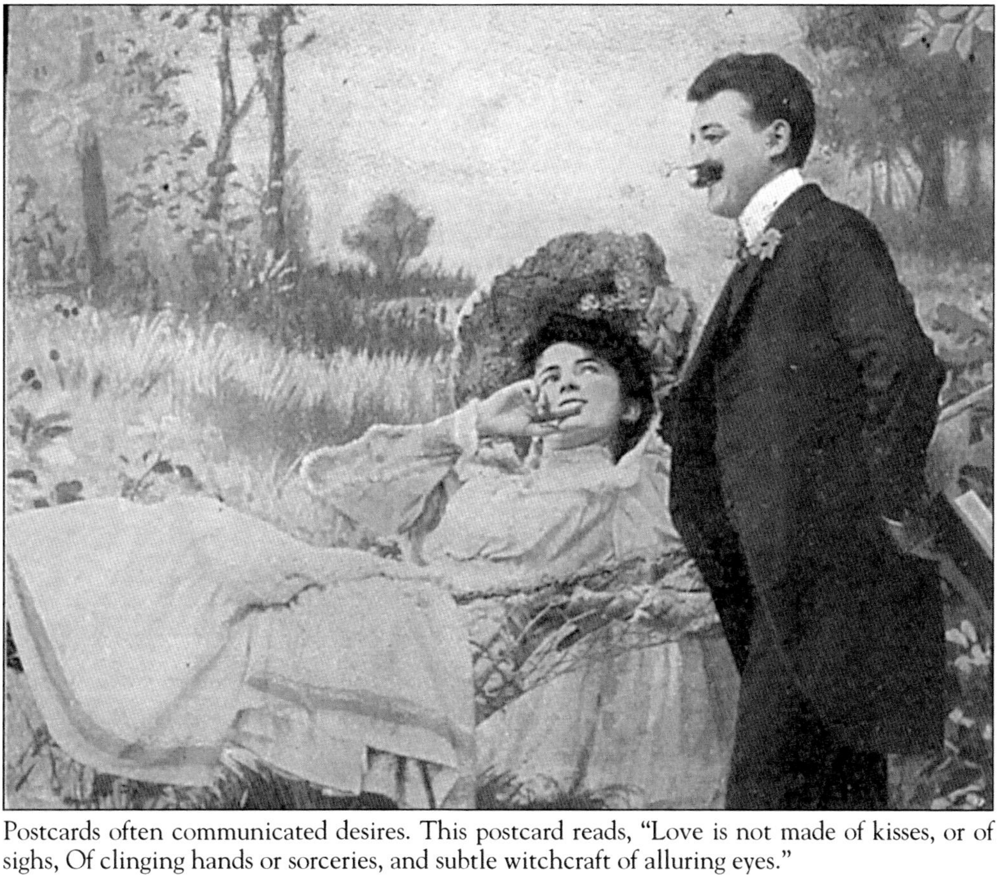

Postcards often communicated desires. This postcard reads, "Love is not made of kisses, or of sighs, Of clinging hands or sorceries, and subtle witchcraft of alluring eyes."

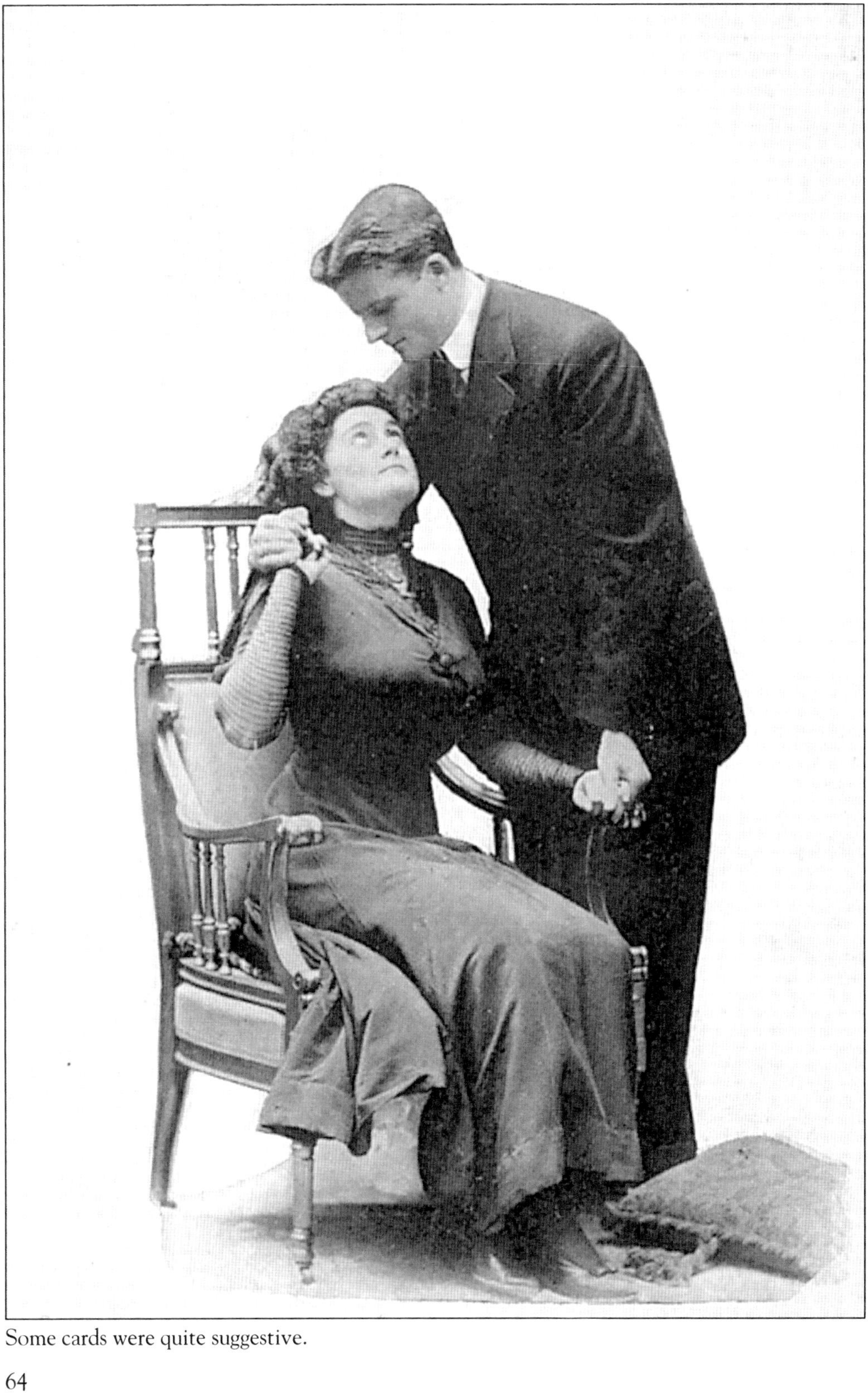

Some cards were quite suggestive.

Leap Year is mentioned on many postcards. Today, little is said about Leap Year.

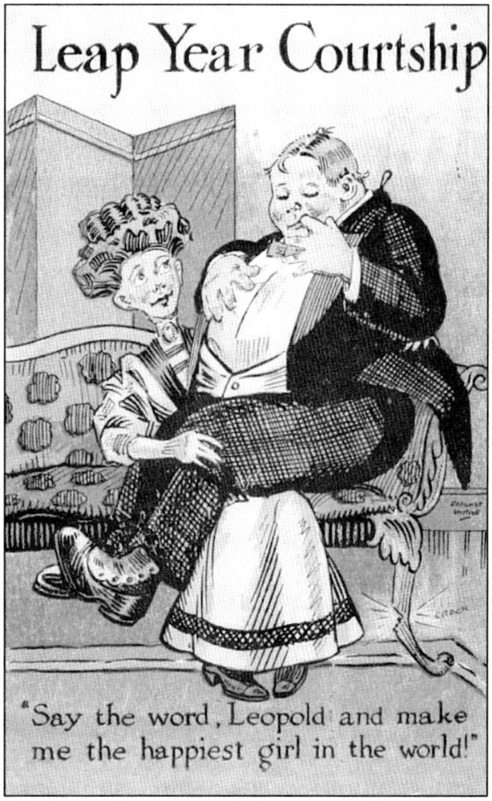

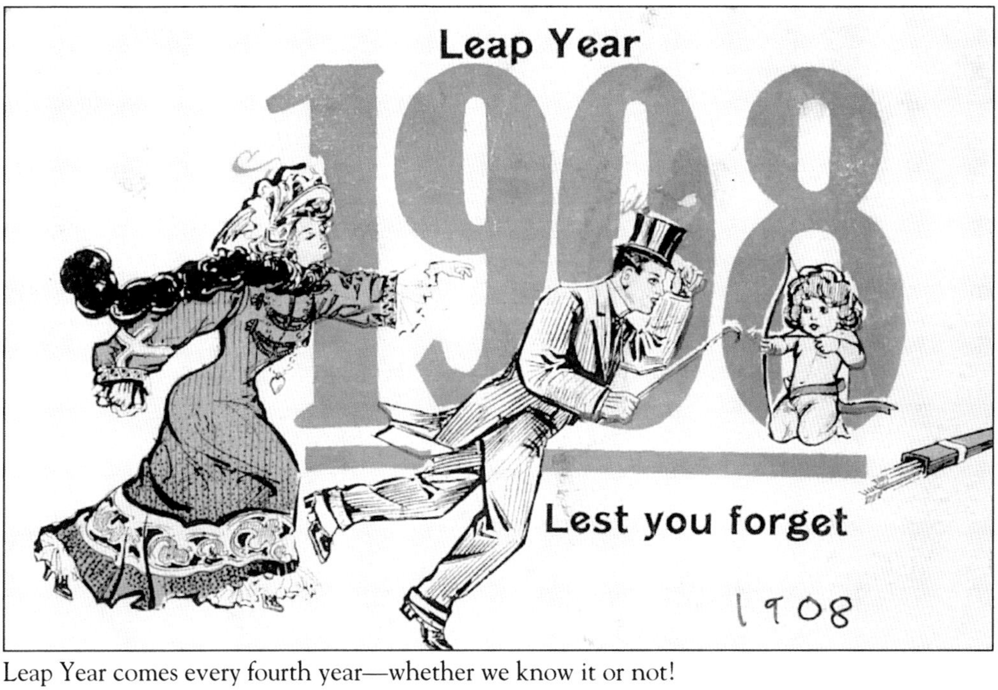

Leap Year comes every fourth year—whether we know it or not!

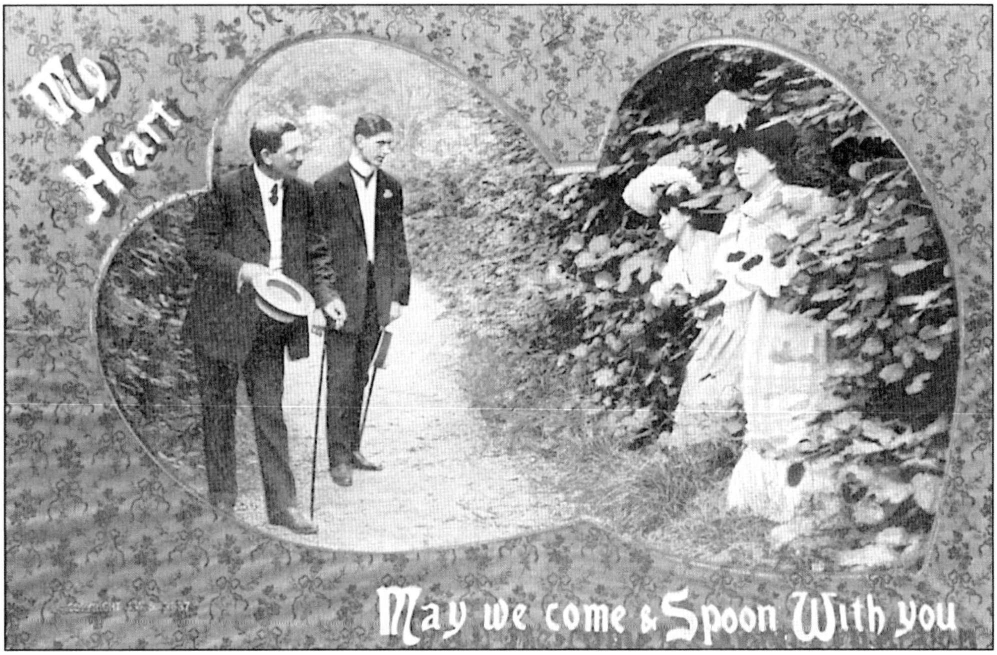

The word "spoon" was used on many of the "romance" postcards.

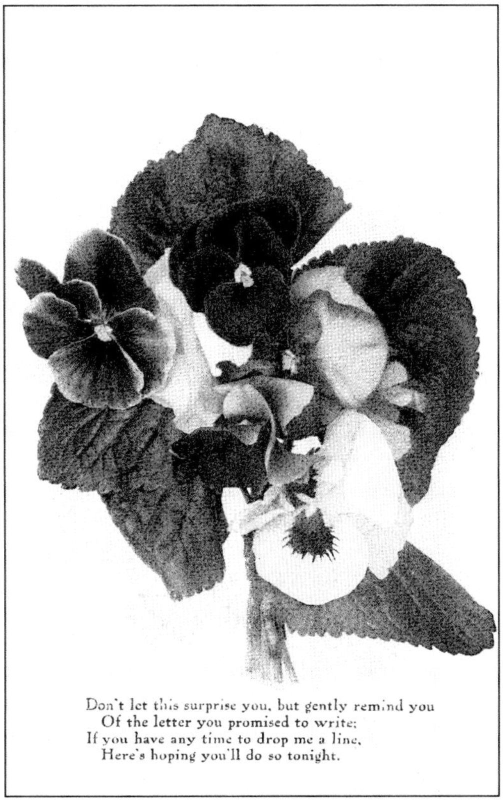

Postcards were also used to get a friend to write a letter. This postcard reads, "Don't let this surprise you, but gently remind you, Of the letter you promised to write; If you have any time to drop me a line, Here's hoping you'll do so tonight."

The author's mother, who was single in 1903, got this postcard from somebody who signed it, "FROM ME!"

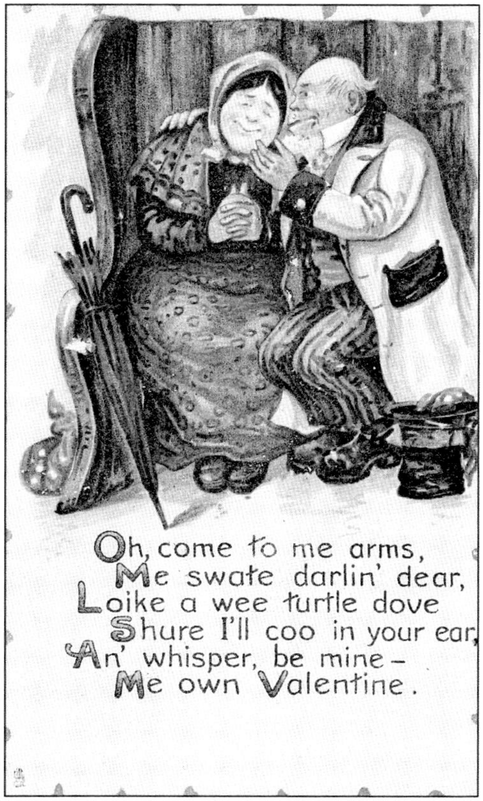

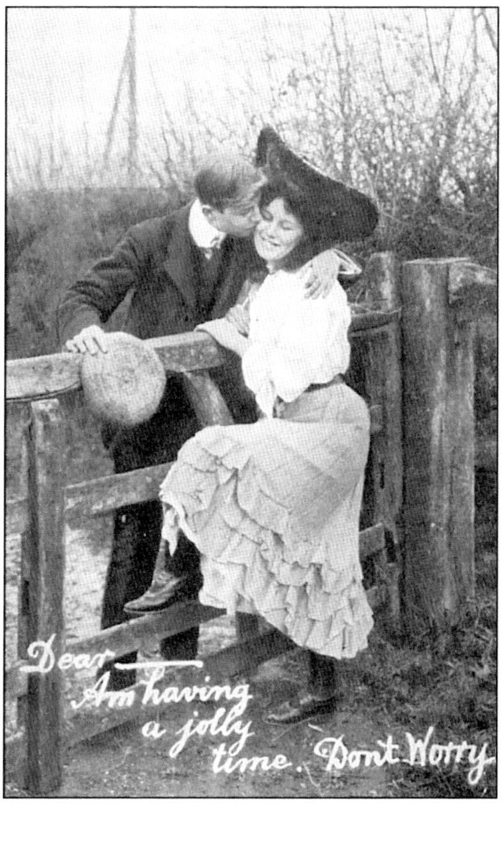

The author's mother sent this postcard to her boyfriend Ted Aasen to make him jealous. Postcards like this one began to be sold in North Dakota *c.* the 1890s. In North Dakota, between 1900 and 1930, most cards were mailed inside the state. Today, most postcards are mailed from out-of-state vacation places like California, Arizona, and Hawaii.

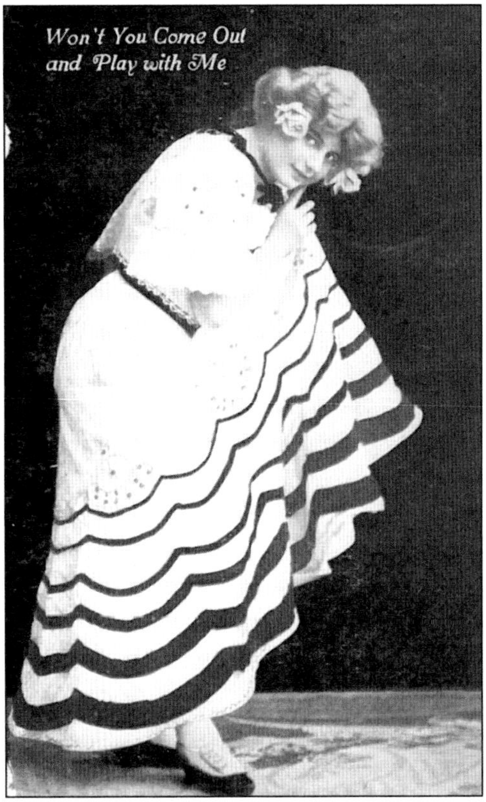

Some postcards were bolder than others were. This one reads, "Won't You Come Out and Play with Me."

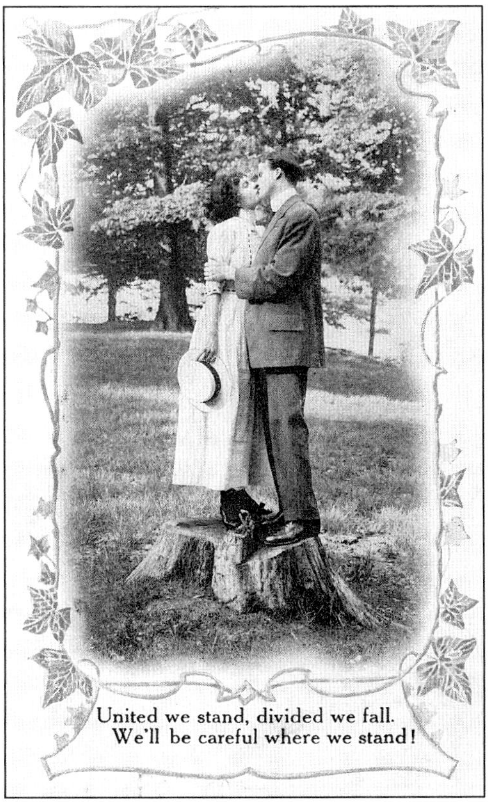

The caption on this postcard reads, "United we stand, divided we fall. We'll be careful where we stand!"

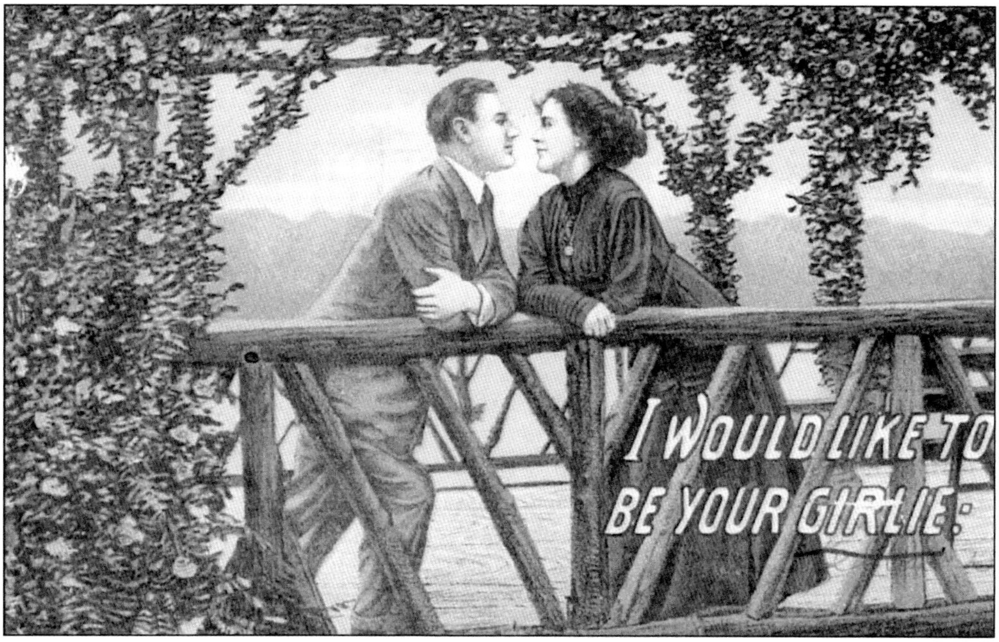

In 1911, "Girlie" was a popular word.

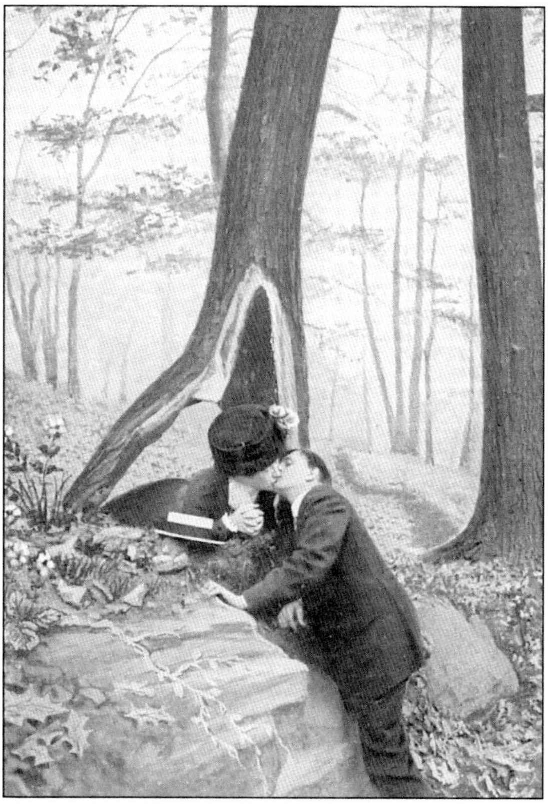

The author's mother got this card from an obvious cad in Minnesota.

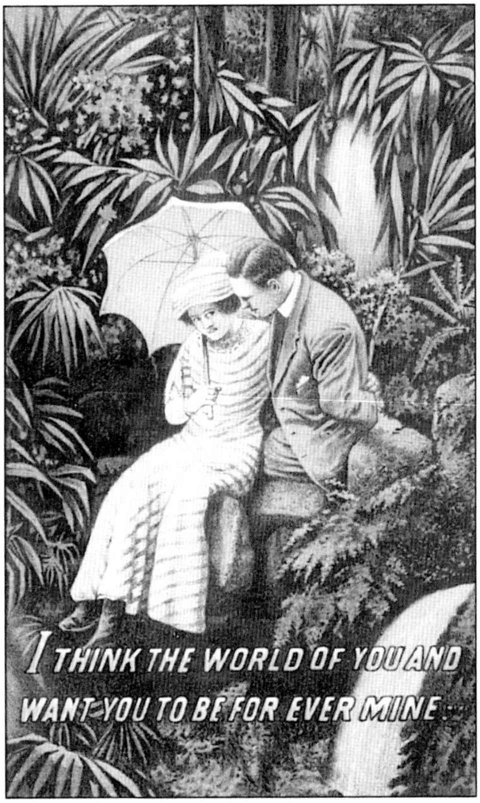

The postcard is an interesting way to pop the question.

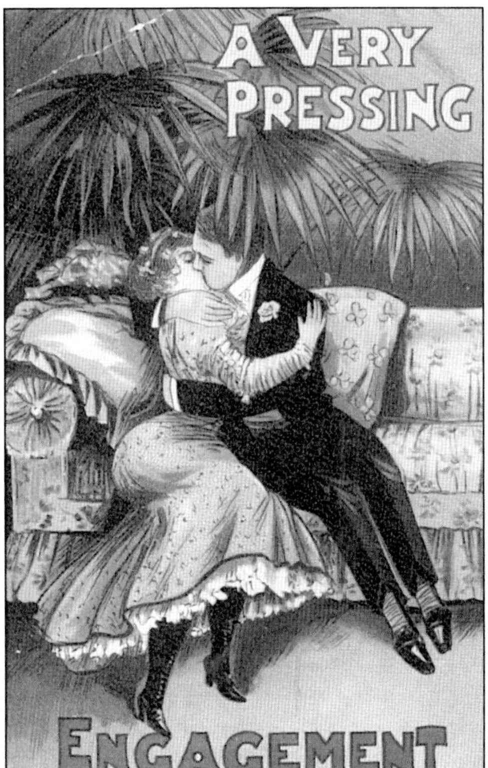

In 1911, this postcard probably shocked some people.

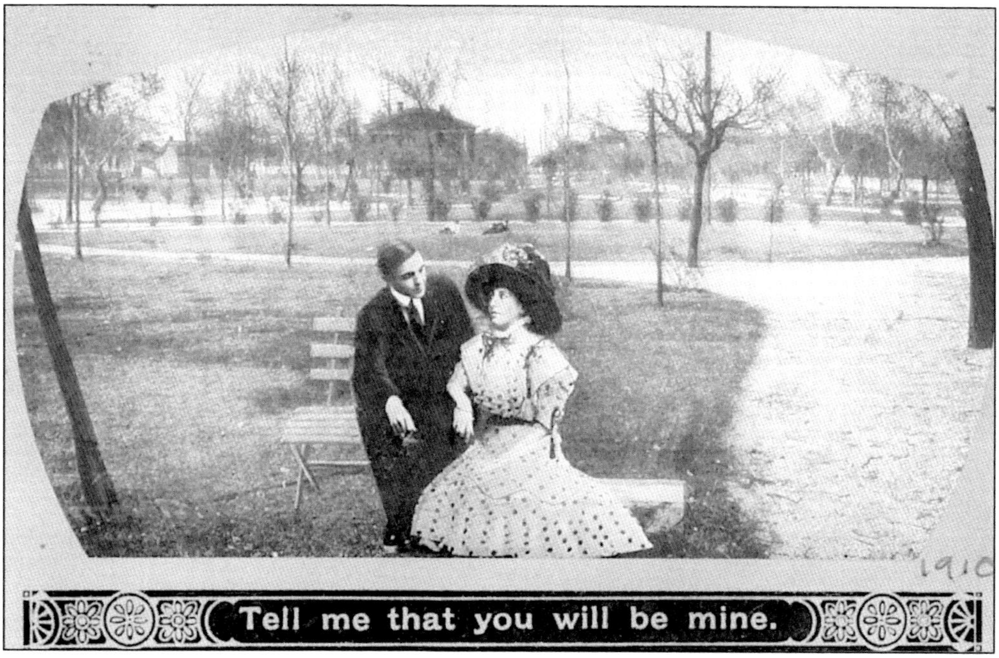

Here is another proposal by mail.

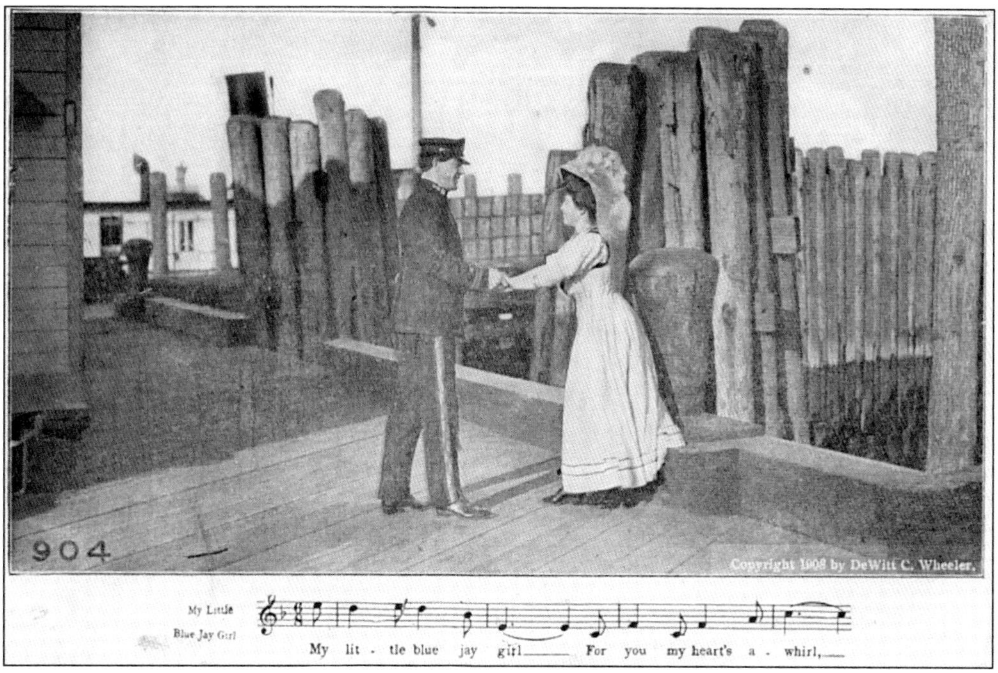

Music adds to the message here.

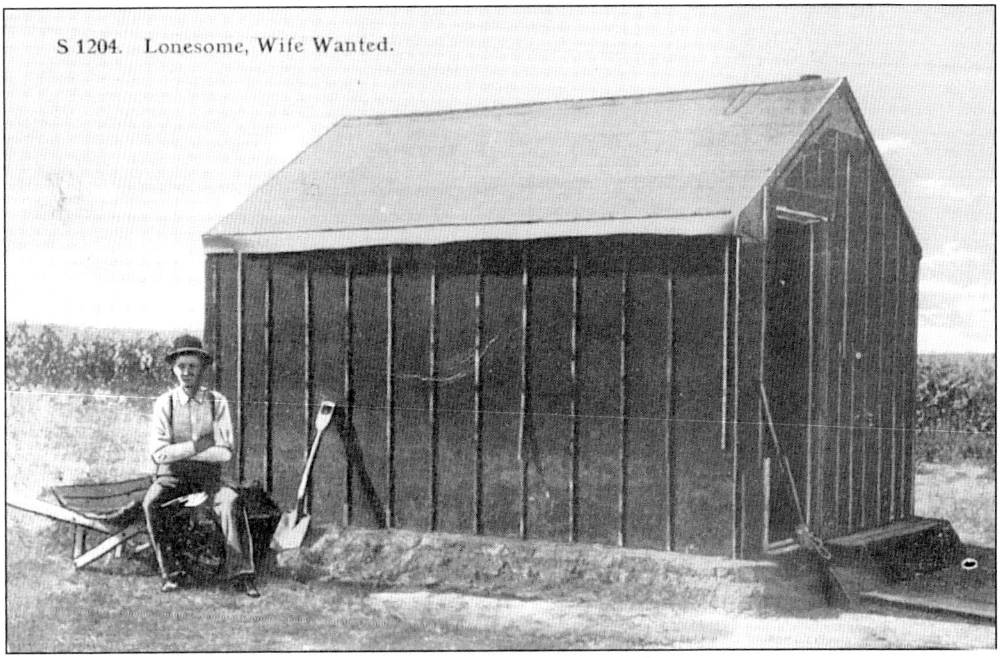

This bachelor says in this postcard, "Lonesome, Wife Wanted."

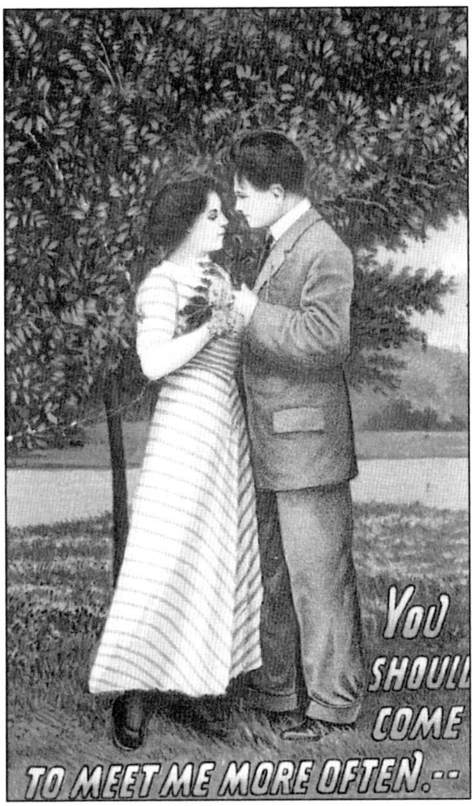

Postcards were often sending a blunt message.

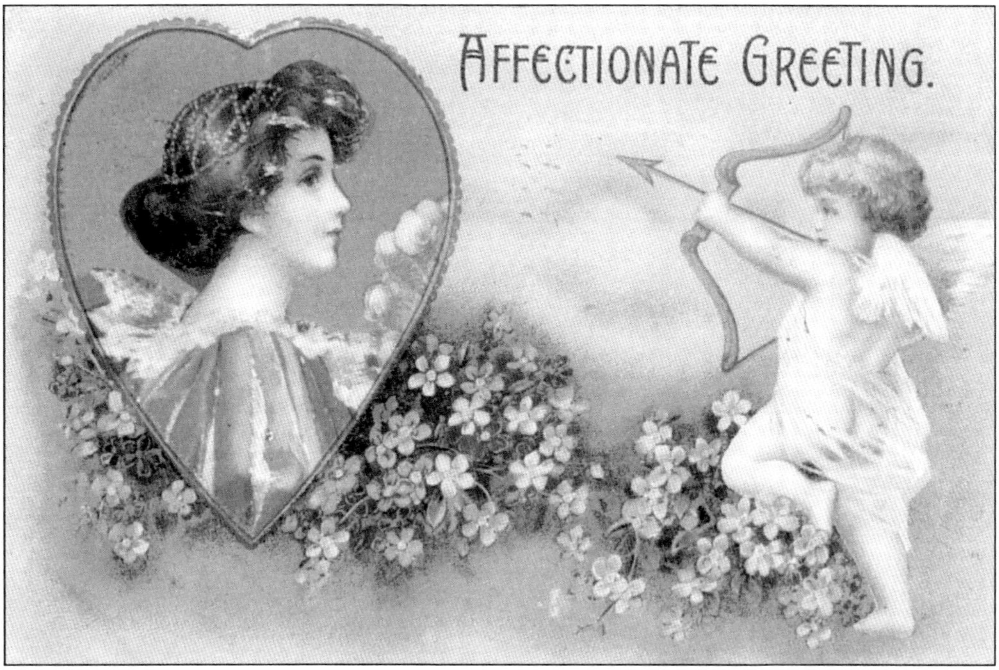

A large number of postcards in this collection dealt with romance—in some form.

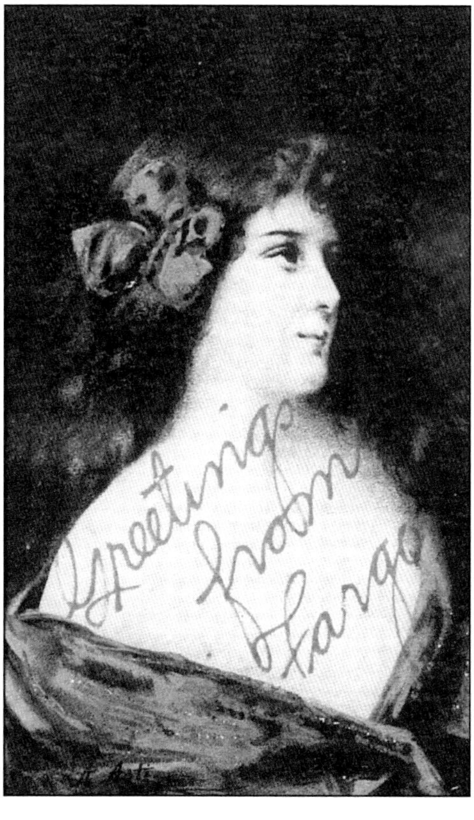

The purpose of this postcard was to sell the idea that there were a lot of pretty girls in Fargo, North Dakota. There were! (Editorial comment.)

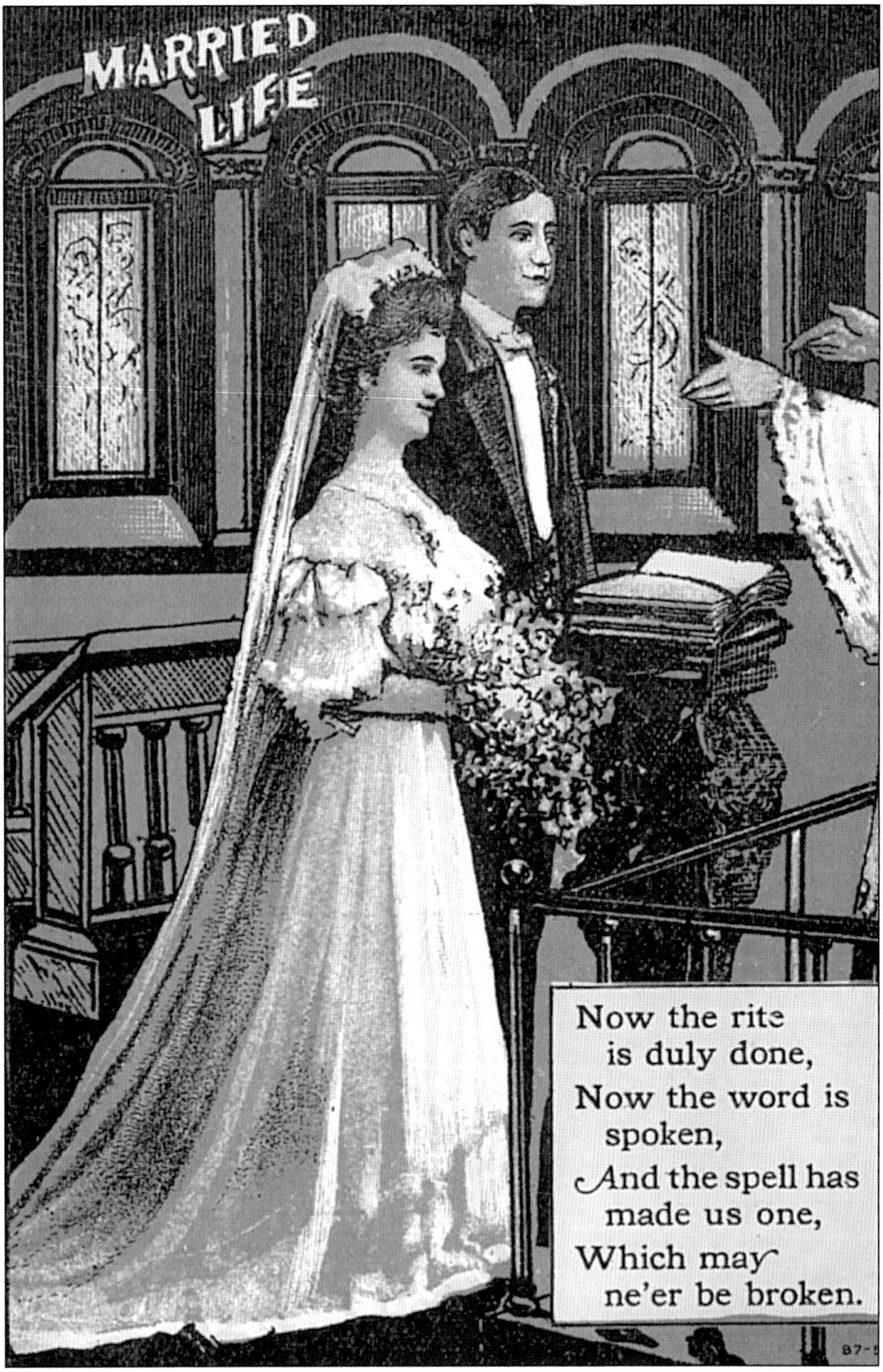

This postcard shows what a bridal couple might look like in the 1900s. The divorce rate in North Dakota was once one of the lowest in the nation. However, the percentage of divorced North Dakotans over 15 years old nearly quadrupled between 1970 and 1990 to six percent. According to the *History of North Dakota*, married women are the fastest growing of the work force in both rural and urban North Dakota.

Six

Humor

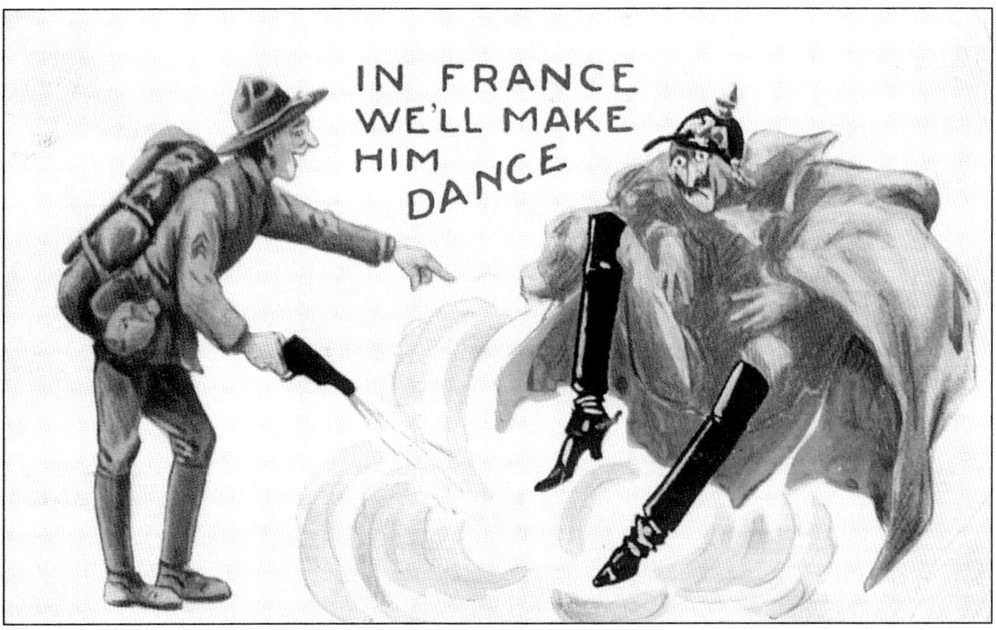

This 1918 postcard suggests what the U.S. troops in France would do to Germany's Kaiser.

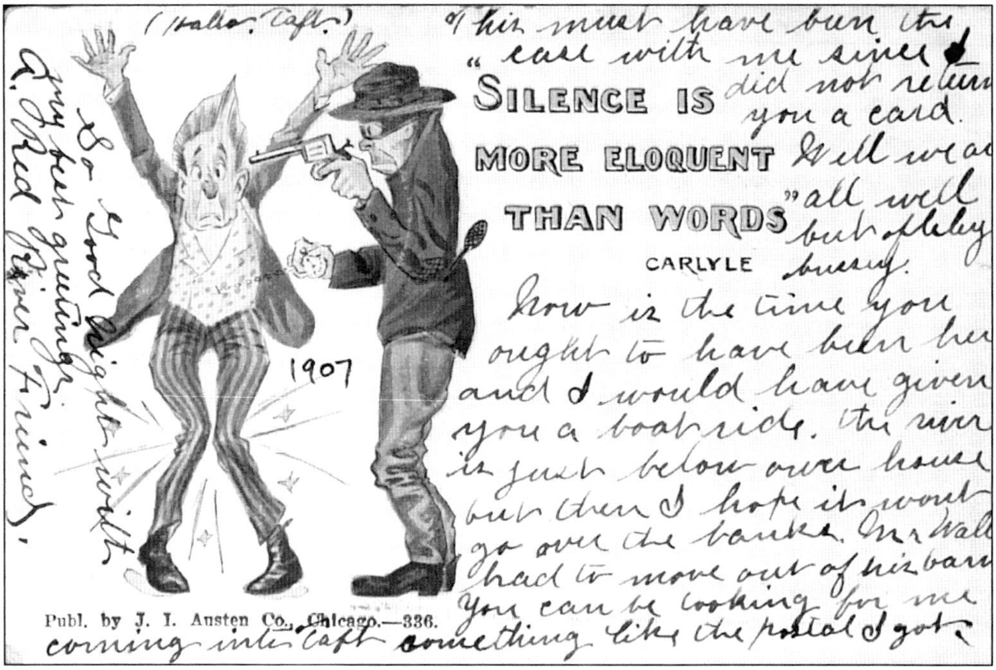

Although crime was a subject for humor on postcards, North Dakota has always had one of the lowest crime rates in the United States.

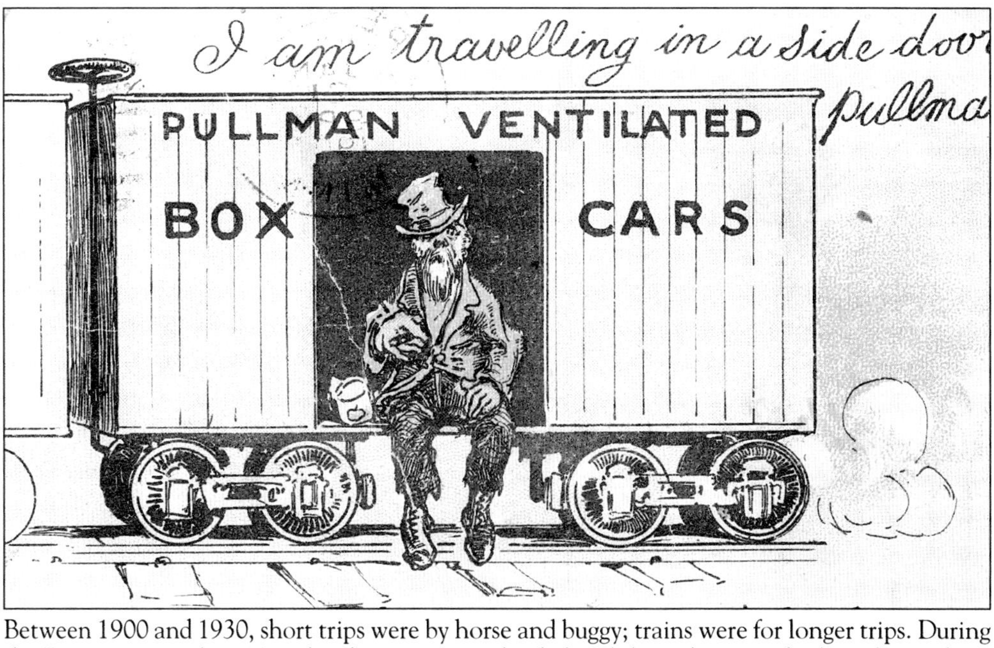

Between 1900 and 1930, short trips were by horse and buggy; trains were for longer trips. During the Depression in the 1930s, freight trains were loaded with homeless men looking for work.

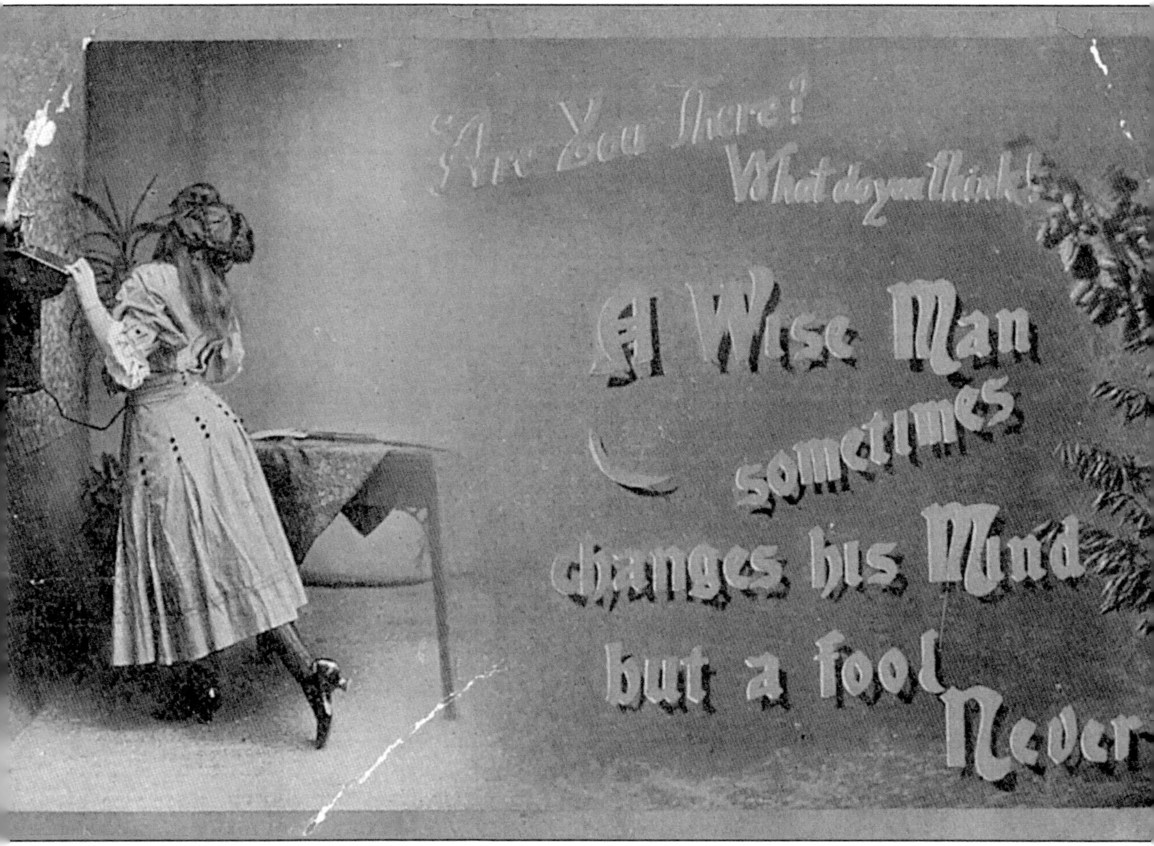

The caption on this postcard reads, "Are you there? What do you think? A Wise Man sometimes changes his Mind but a fool Never!" Postcards sometimes sent subtle messages.

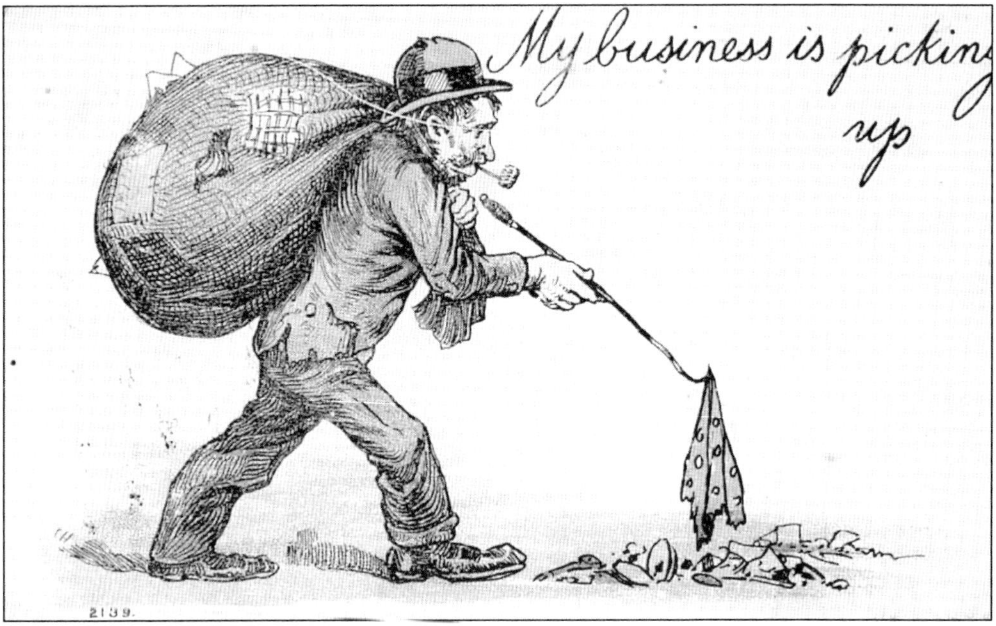

Many postcards like this were sent.

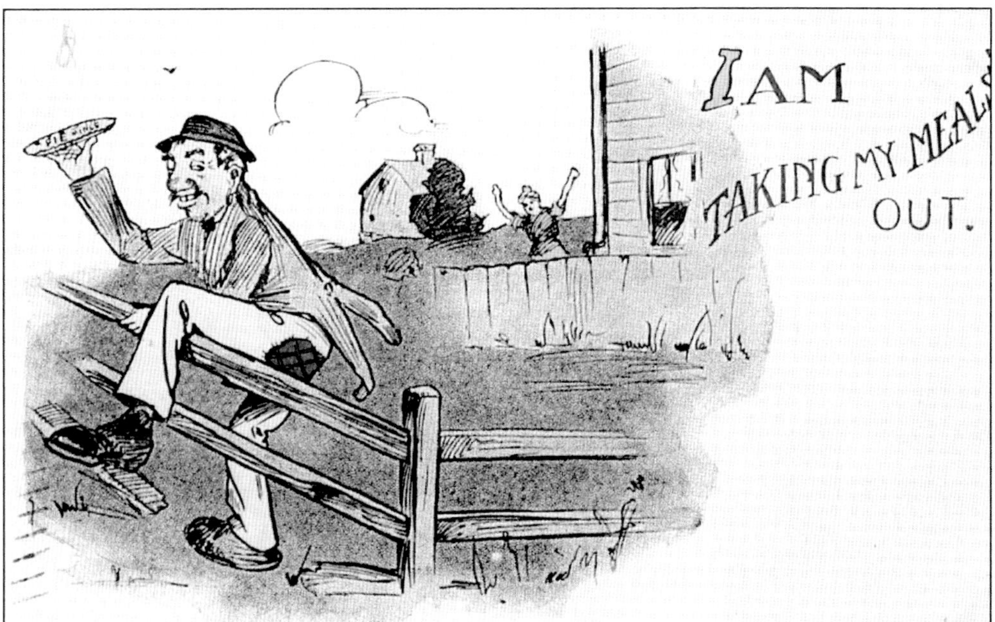

In depression days, some postcards were sent just to give a good chuckle. Many chuckles were needed during the Depression of the 1930s.

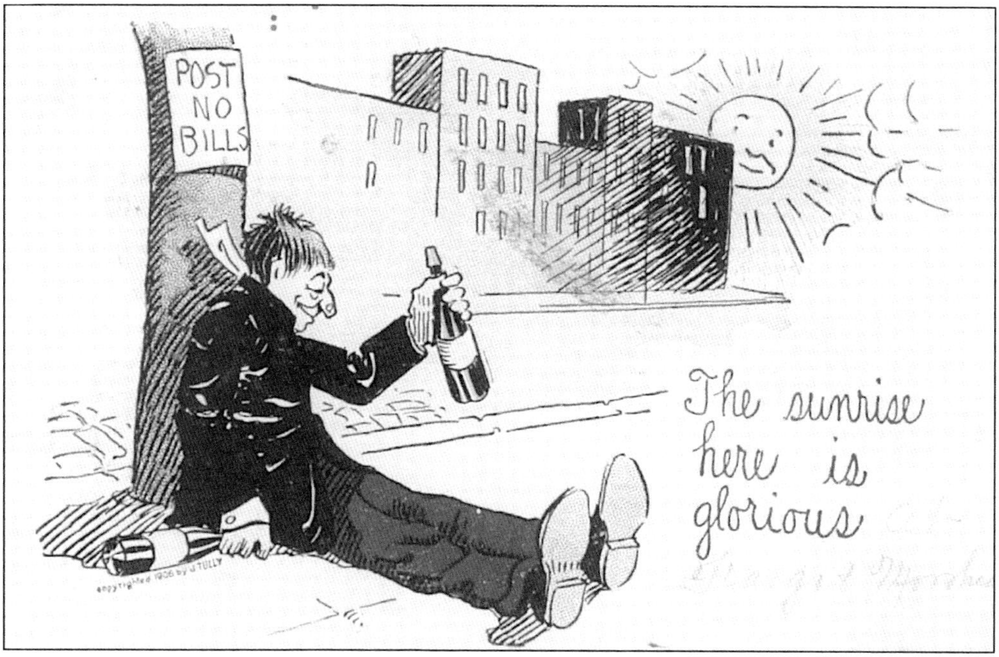

North Dakota women were very active in the Prohibition movement in the state. Some women in Hatton, North Dakota, once attacked a bar with axes!

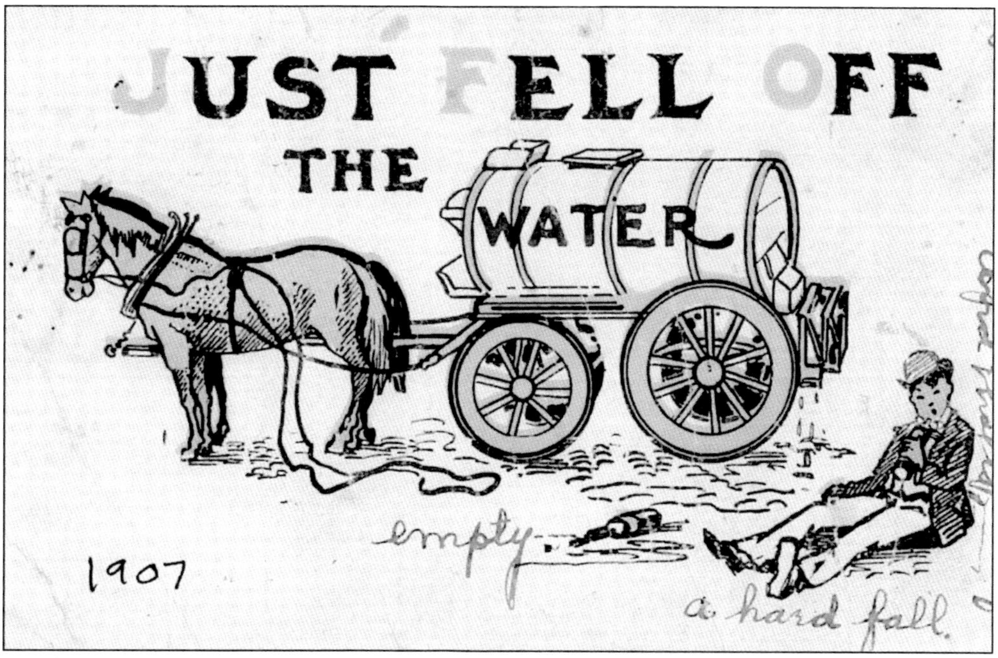

Bootleggers were common during the early 20th century. Some people drank alcohol with warm water and sugar. The alcohol came in a big tin can. A lot of bottled, illegal liquor was snuck into North Dakota from Canada; it was expensive.

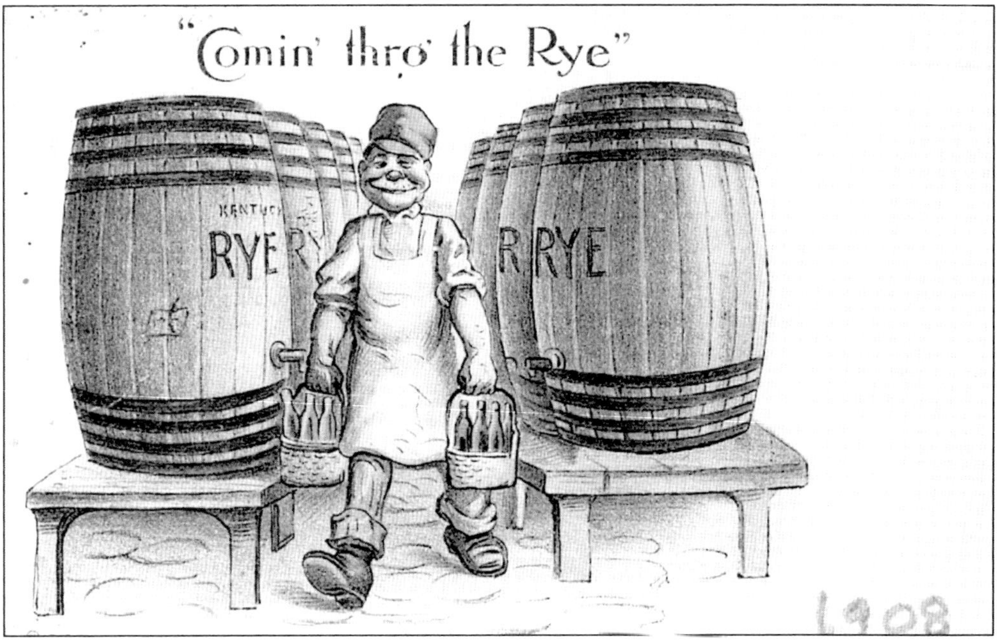

Liquor was featured on some of the cards.

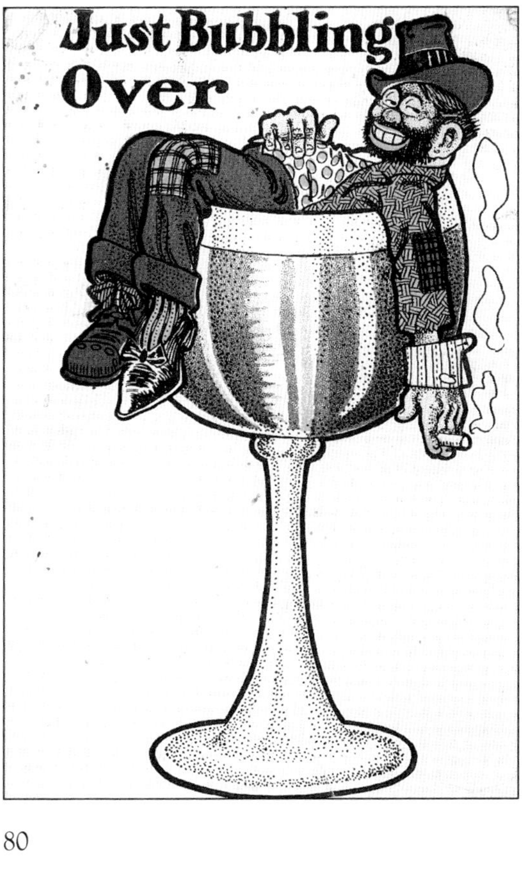

Some North Dakotans brewed their own beer in the 1900s.

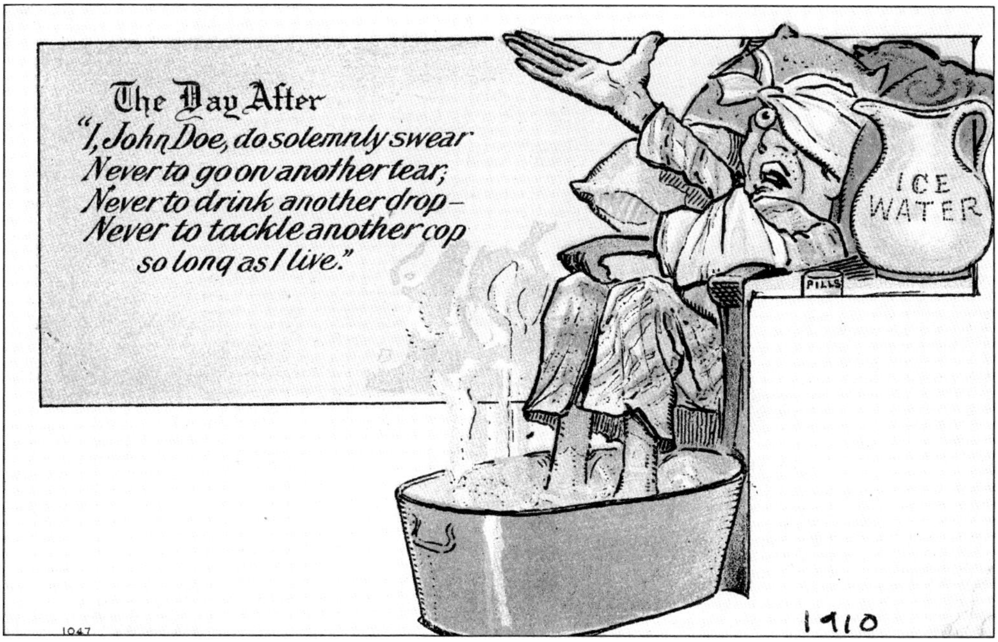

When faced with this condition, some drunks liked to joke, "I want some hair from the dog that bit me!"

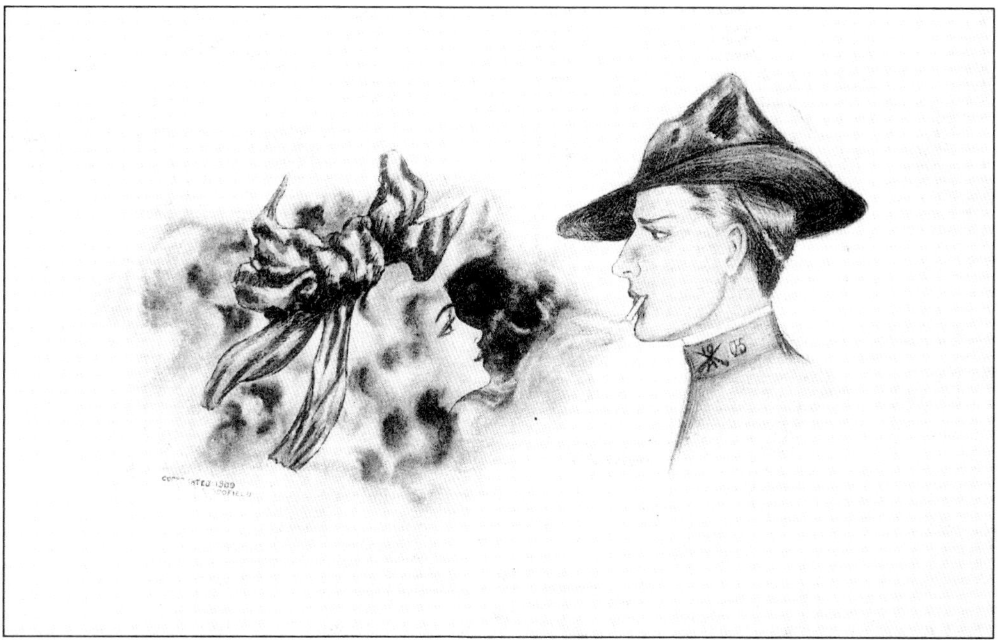
Although many of the early postcards showed the evils of drinking; smoking tended to be a glamorous thing, as shown above.

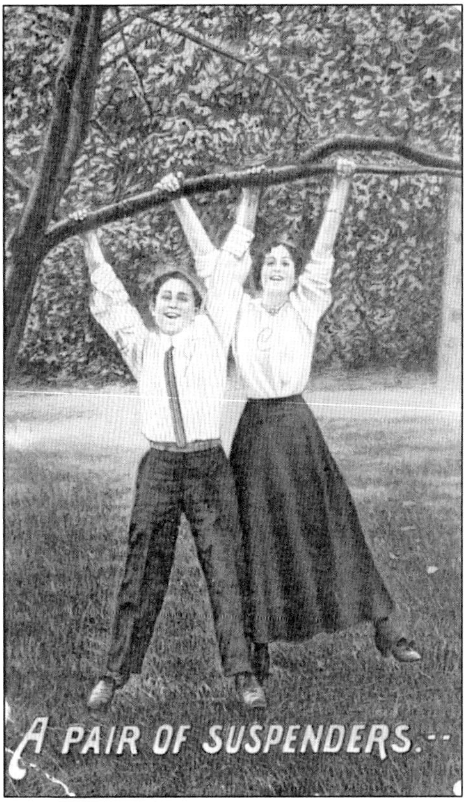

Early postcards liked to show funny stunts.

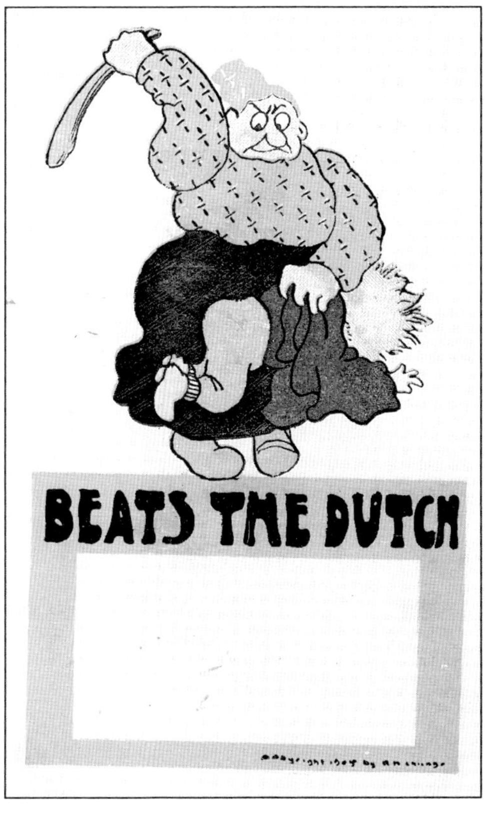

In 1908, I am sure this card sent a definite message.

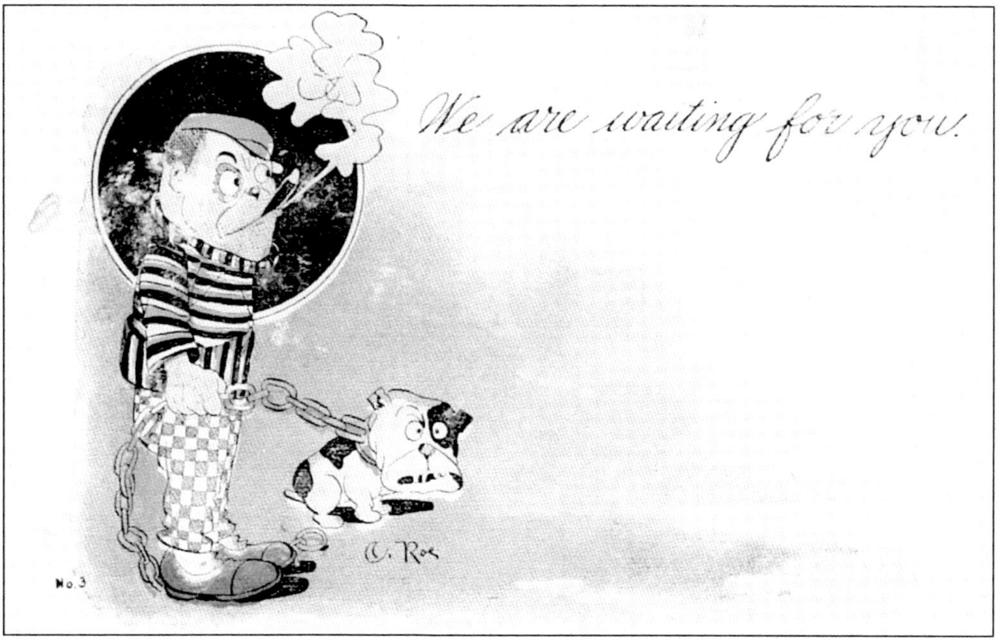

The humor portrayed on this postcard seems grim.

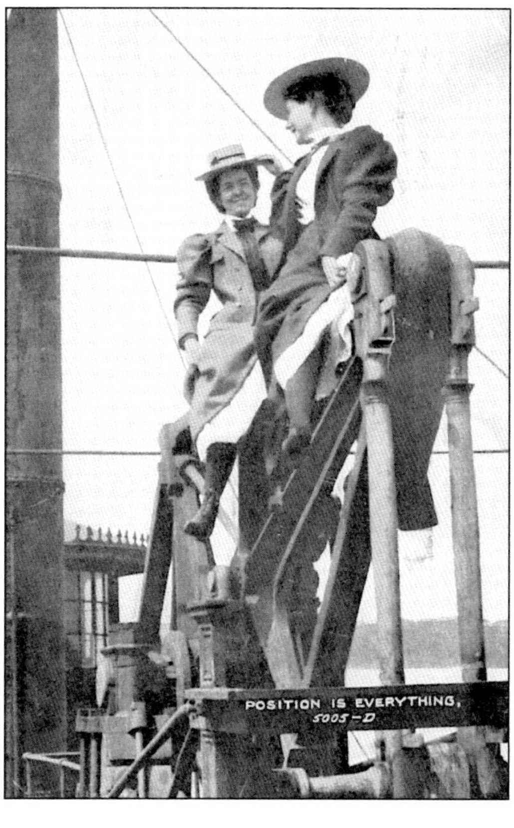

This 1908 photograph shows two North Dakota ladies riding a wooden Ferris wheel at a state fair.

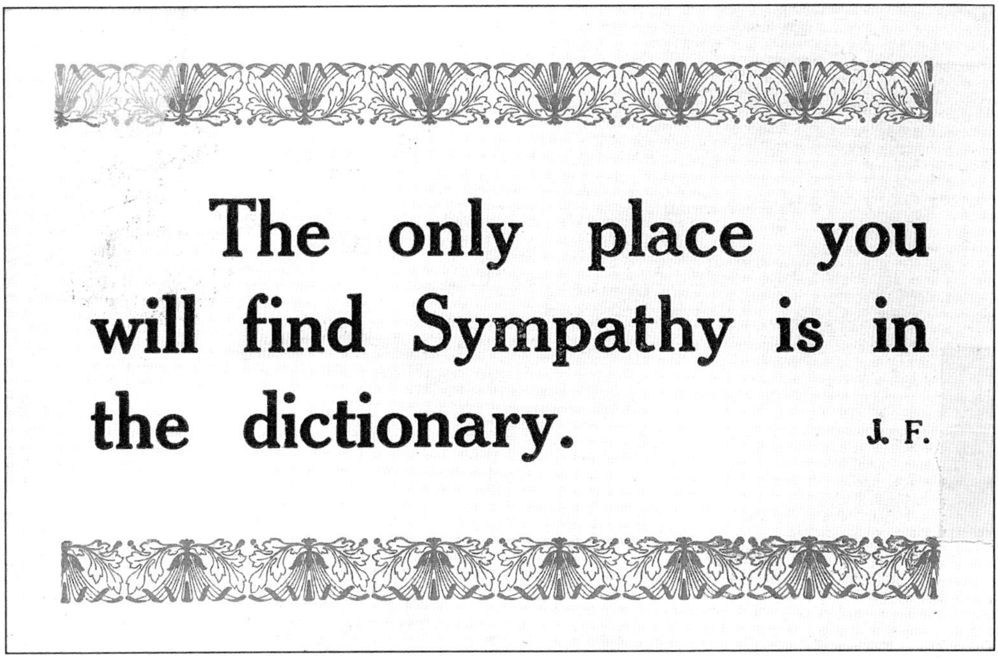
The only place you will find Sympathy is in the dictionary. J. F.

This funny, but harsh message was mailed in 1918 for 2¢. Postage went up from 1¢ to 2¢ during World War I. Today you might find this kind of statement on a bumper sticker.

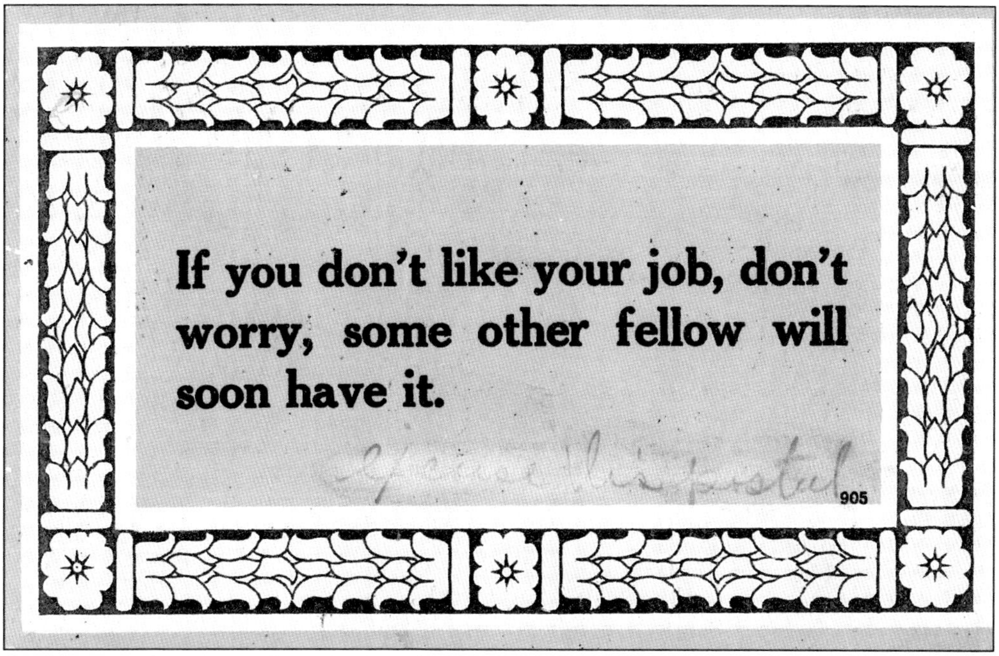

Some postcards contained words of wisdom.

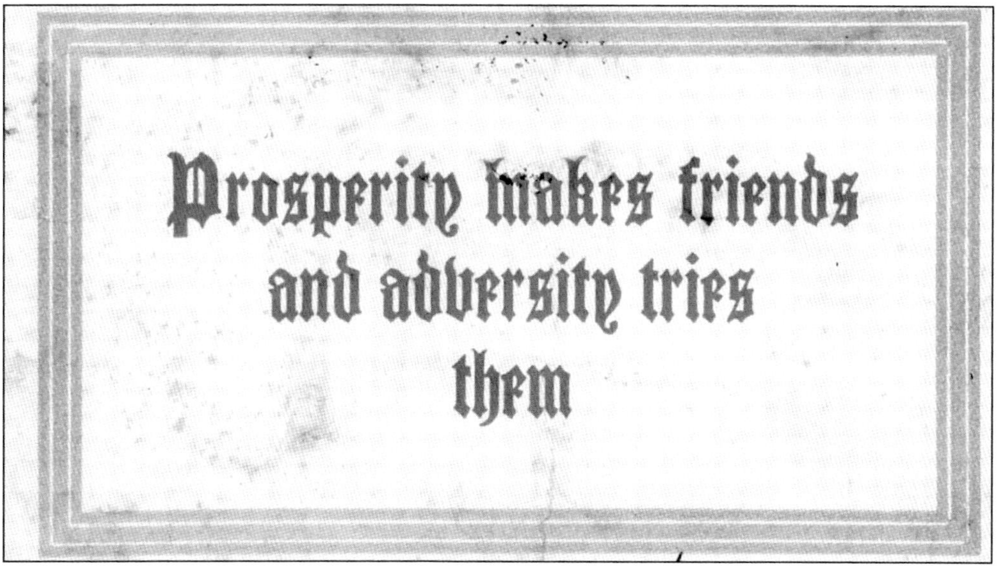

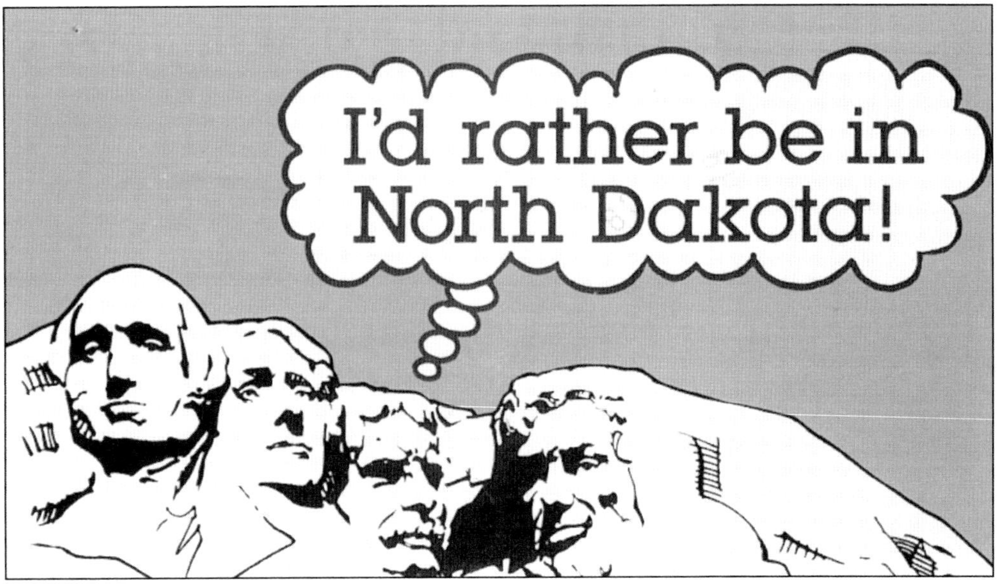

This has been a popular North Dakota postcard for many years. Teddy Roosevelt said he would rather be in North Dakota; he was in the state from 1883 to 1887. On September 5, 1910, in Fargo, Roosevelt said, "If it had not been for what I learned during those years I spent here in North Dakota, I never would have been President of the United States."

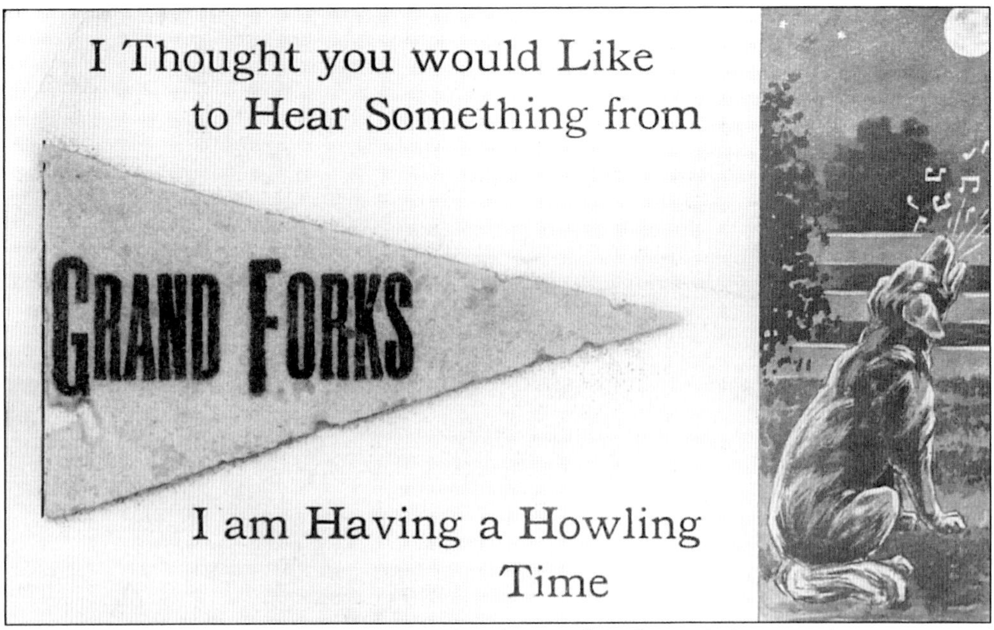

A pun was used to add humor to this Grand Forks, North Dakota 1912 postcard.

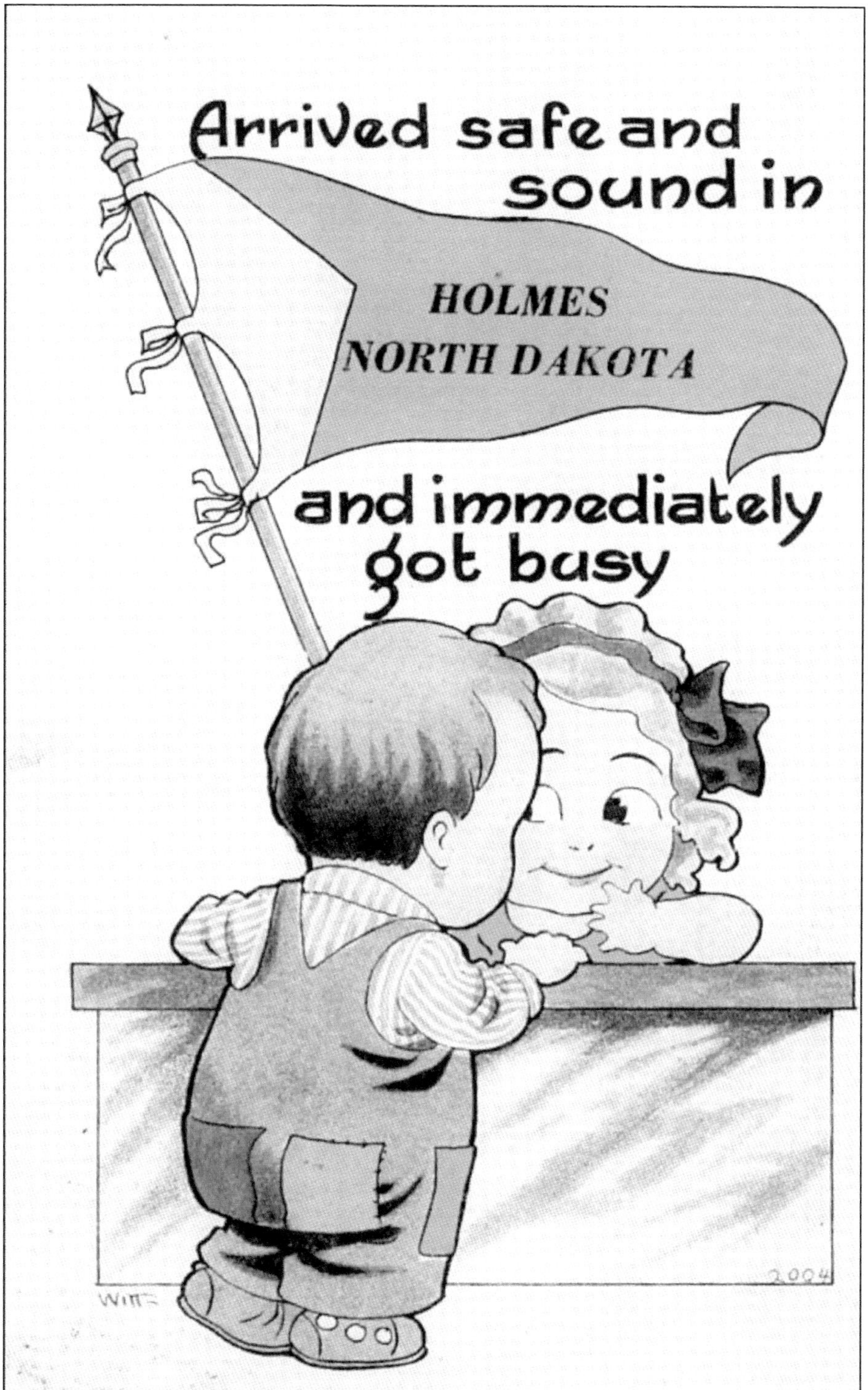

Miss Manna Lerfald of Hatton received this funny card in 1919. The little boy wears a clean, but patched, pair of pants.

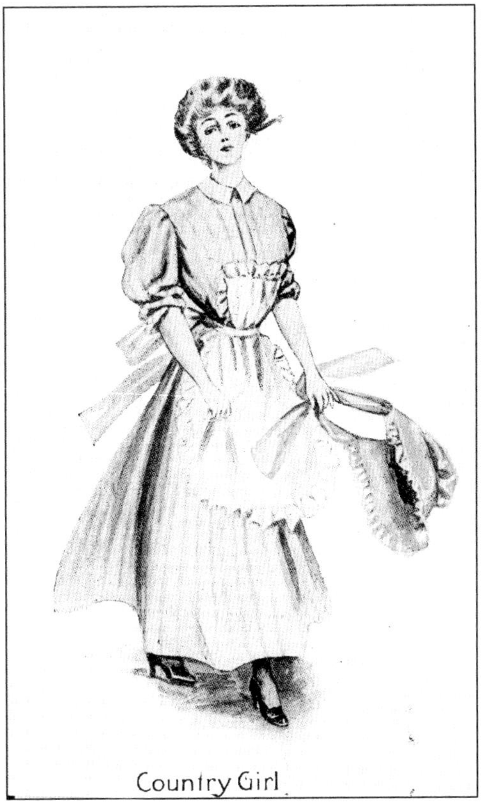

This "Country Girl" could go anywhere.

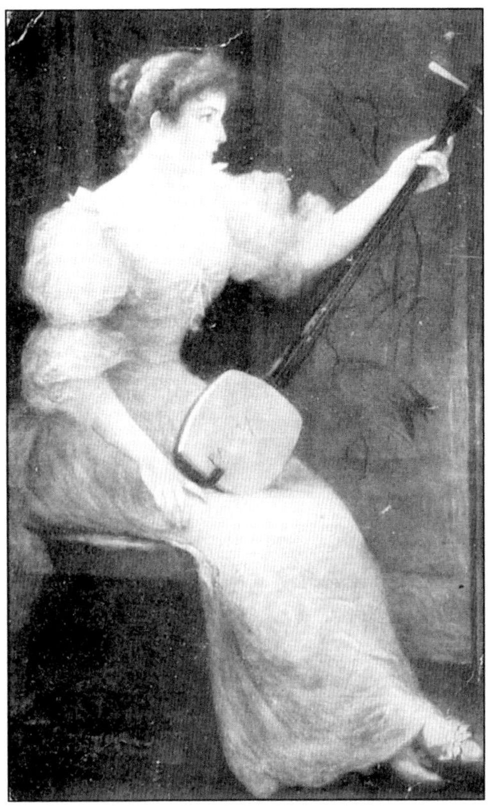

This beautiful card from 1907 was captioned "INSPIRATION."

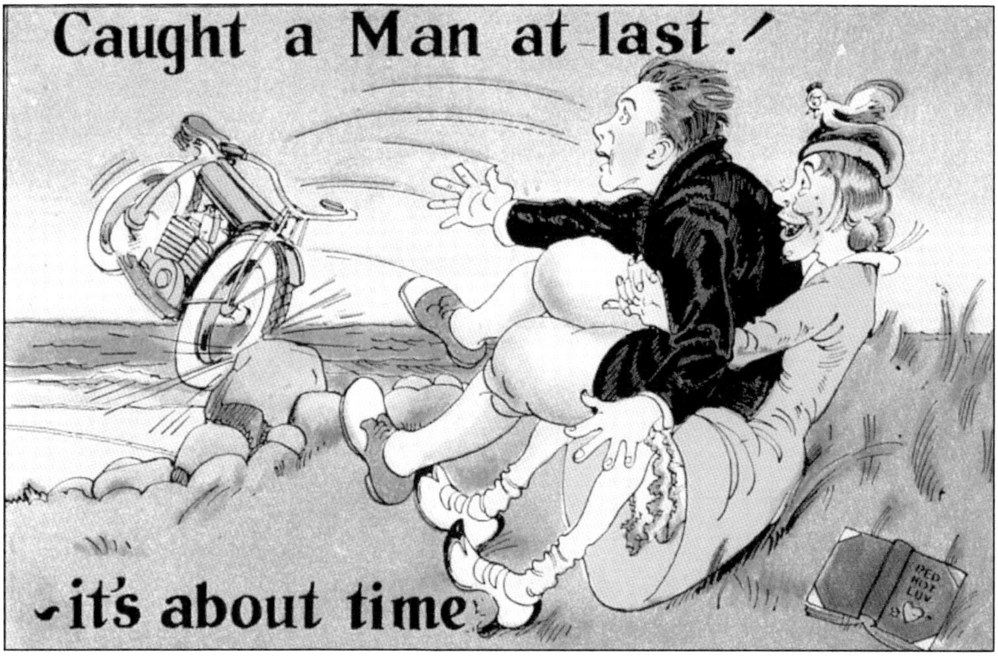

This postcard was probably only sent to carefully selected brides.

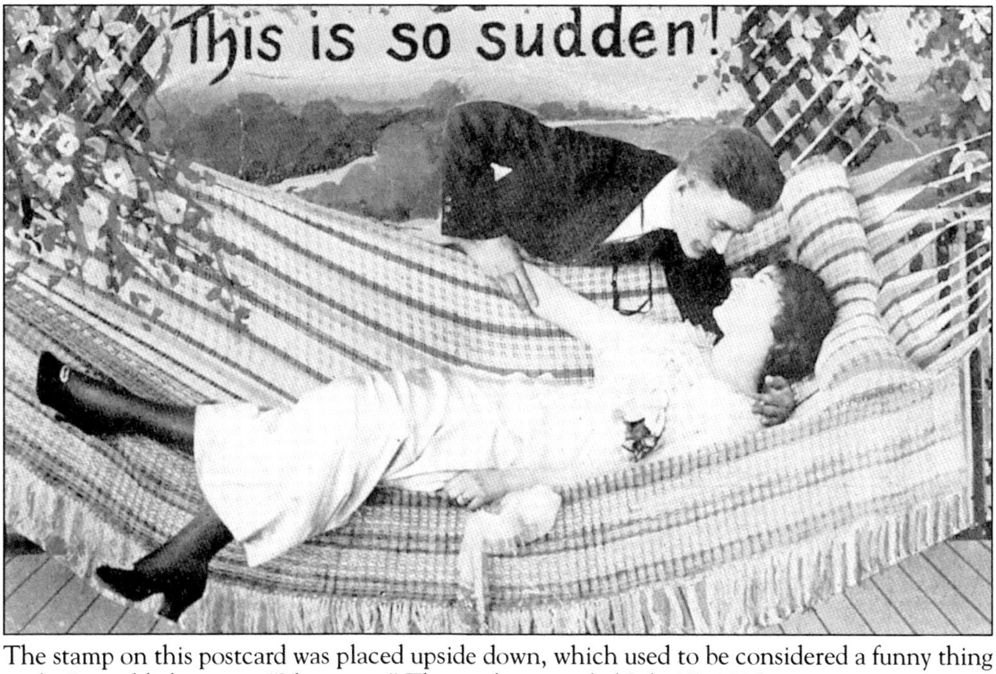

The stamp on this postcard was placed upside down, which used to be considered a funny thing to do. It could also mean "I love you." The card was mailed July 15, 1915.

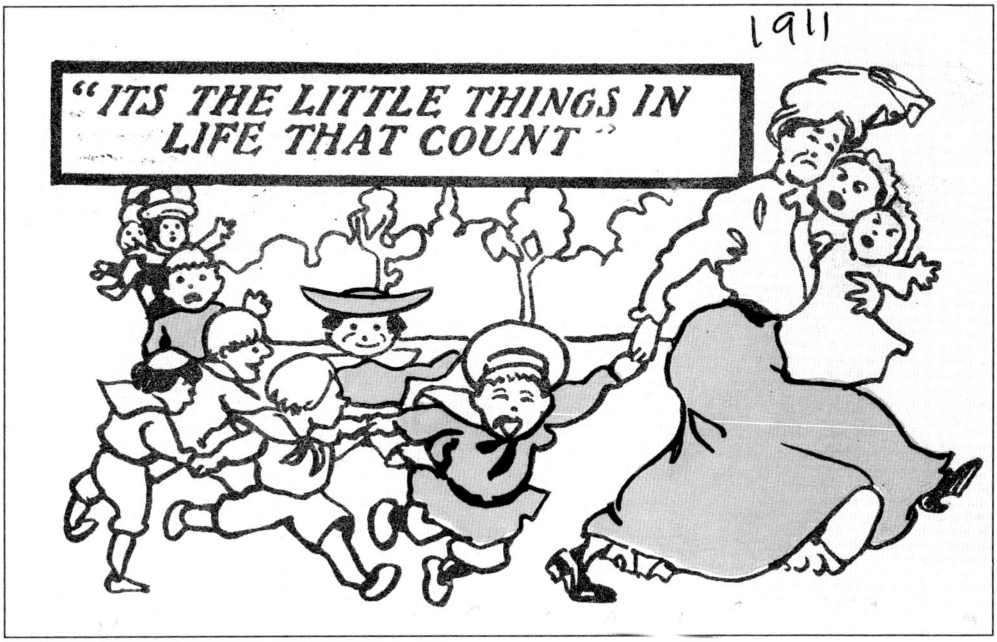

This postcard pokes gentle fun at the fact that in 1911, when this card was mailed, most families had many children.

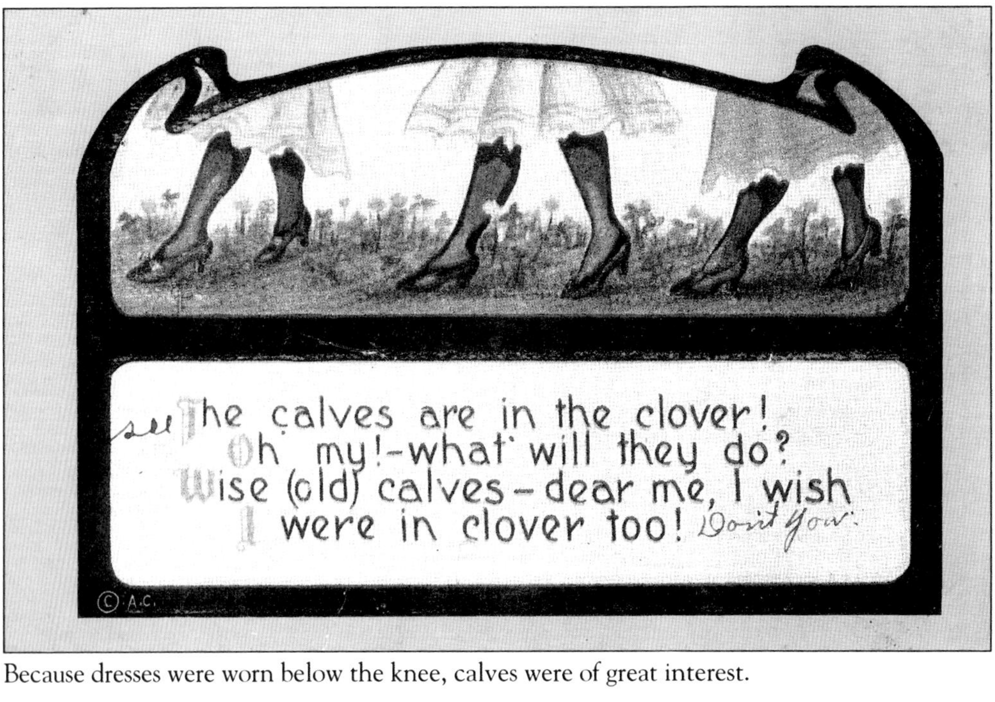

Because dresses were worn below the knee, calves were of great interest.

The postcard, like many others, was printed in England.

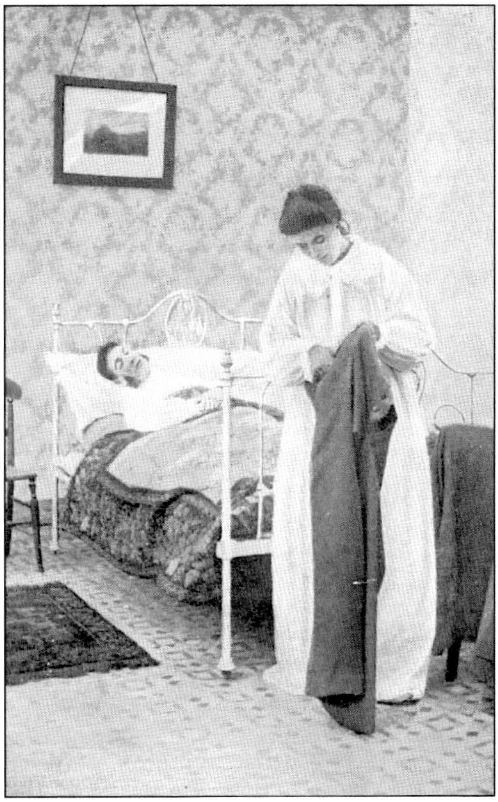

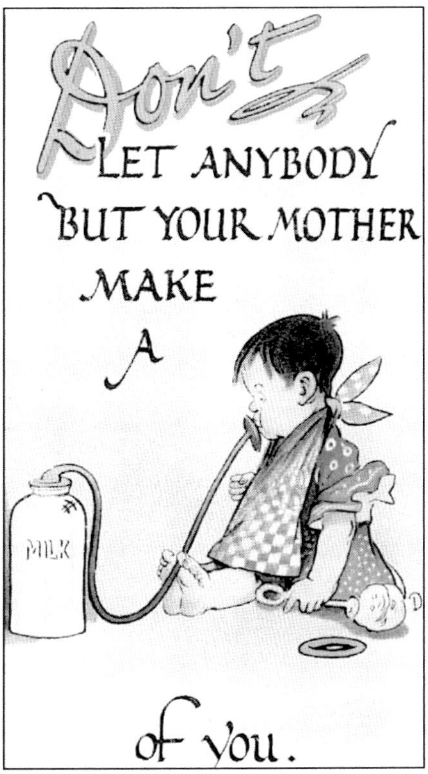

The personal messages on these cards seldom referred to the illustration or photograph on the other side. However, we are sure that the illustration was often selected to sent a "hint" or suggestion.

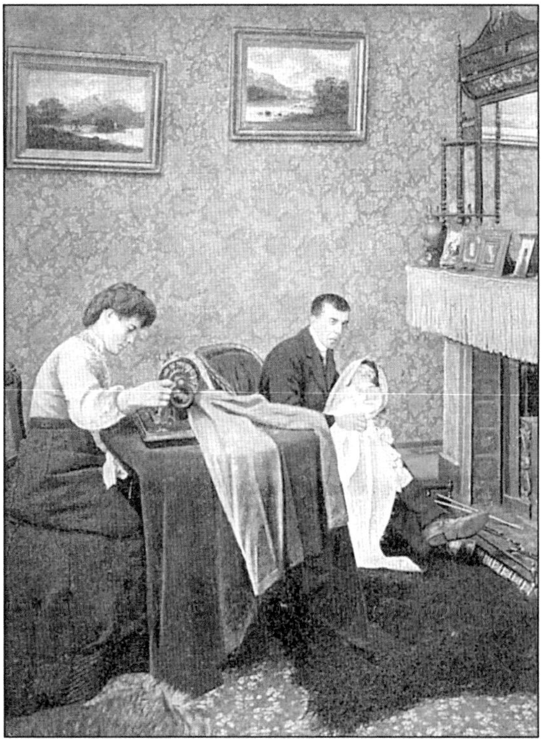

The caption for this postcard reads, "Matrimonial Bliss."

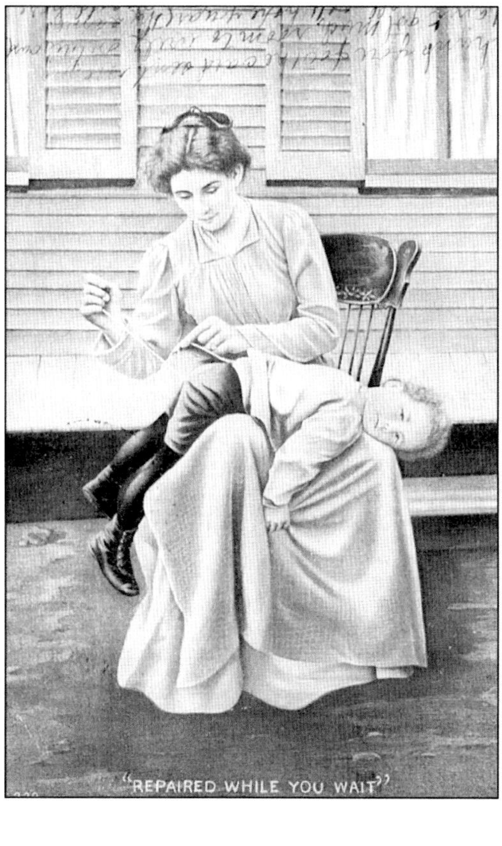

Little boys had to do what mother ordered.

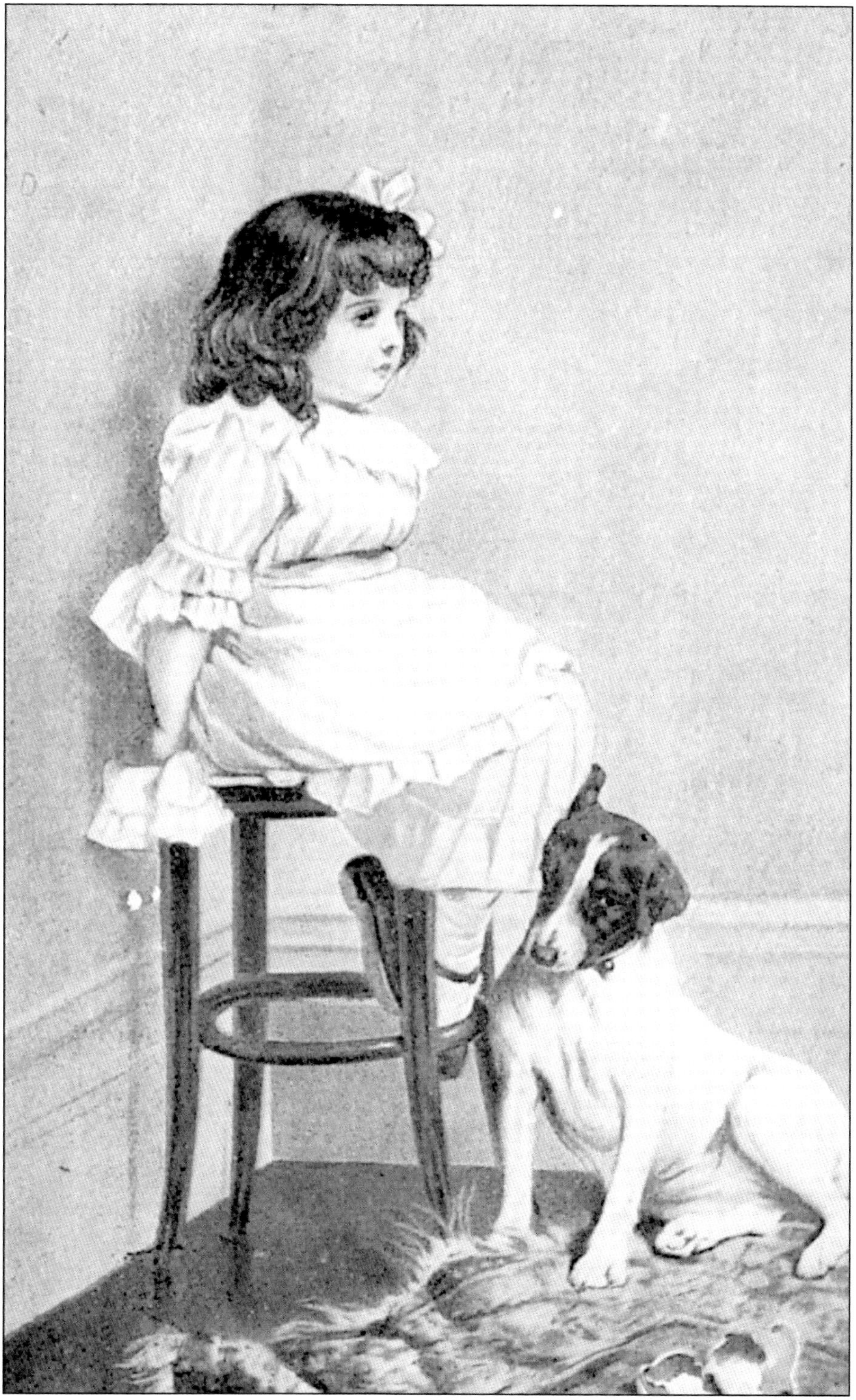

The little girl is "in disgrace" for breaking a flower vase, but her dog is still loyal.

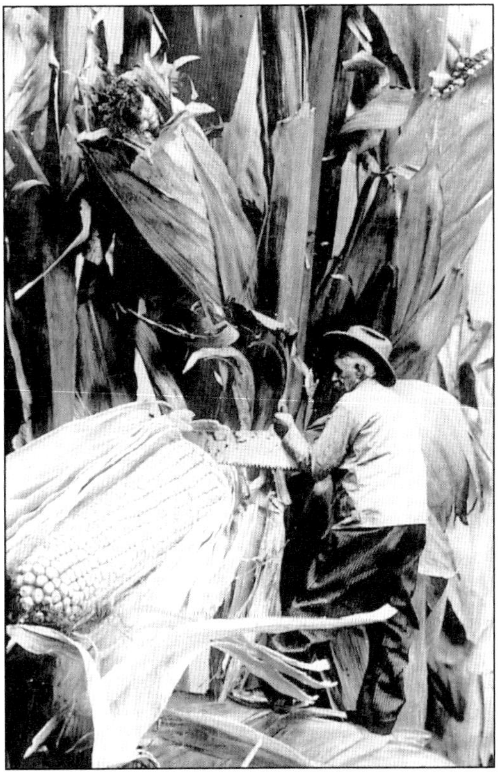

North Dakotans like to brag (a little) about their farm products. Okay?

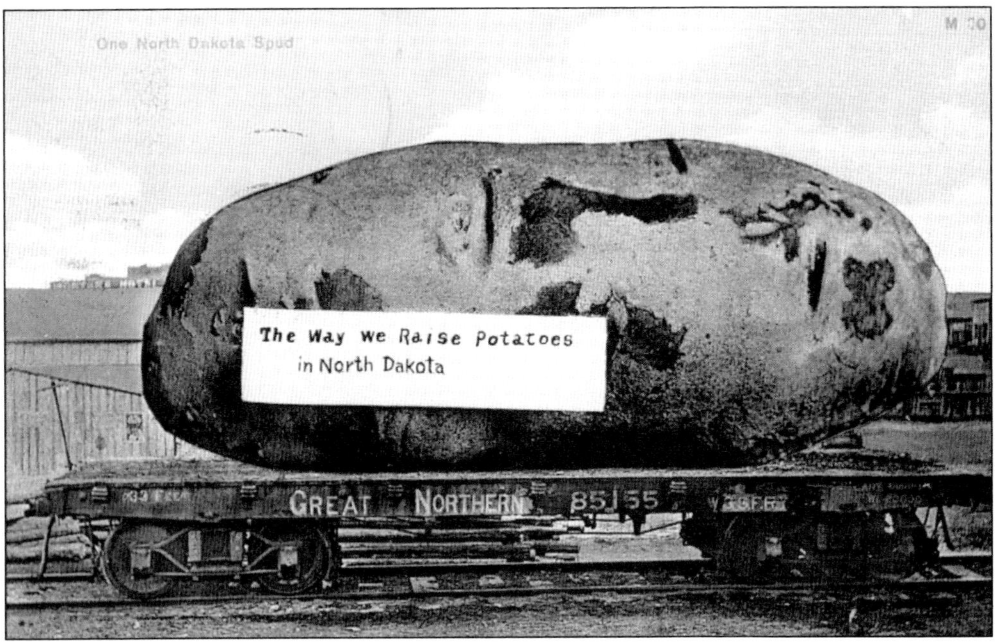

This may not be an actual photograph.

Seven

GREETINGS AND REPORTS

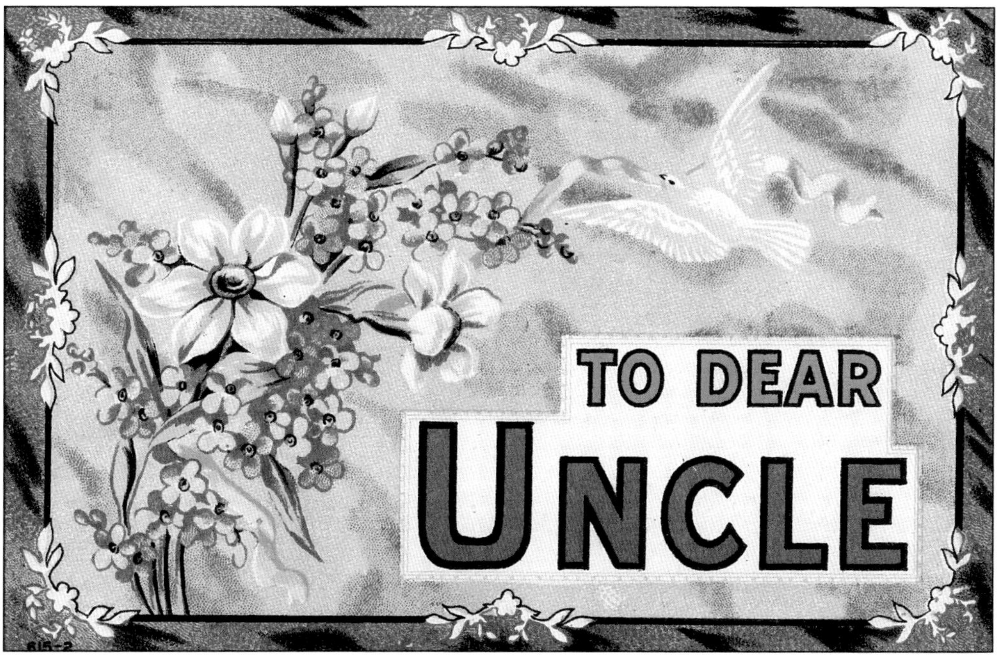

Postcards were also used to communicate greetings or news. This card expresses love for a relative. It is a very nice idea!

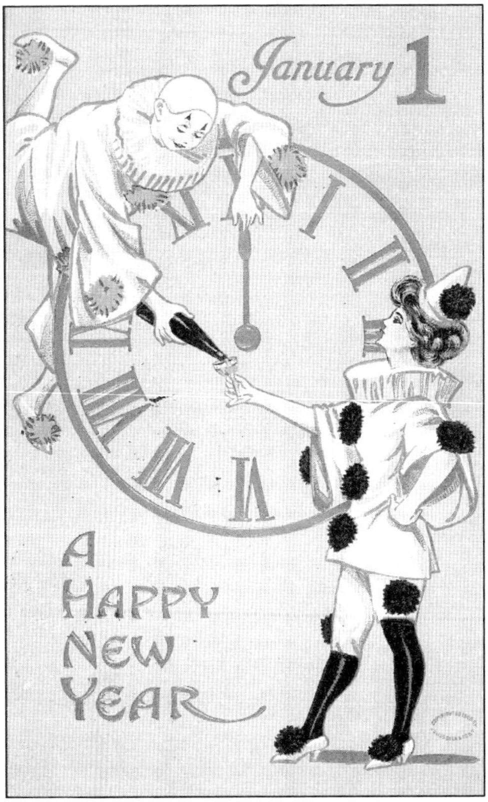

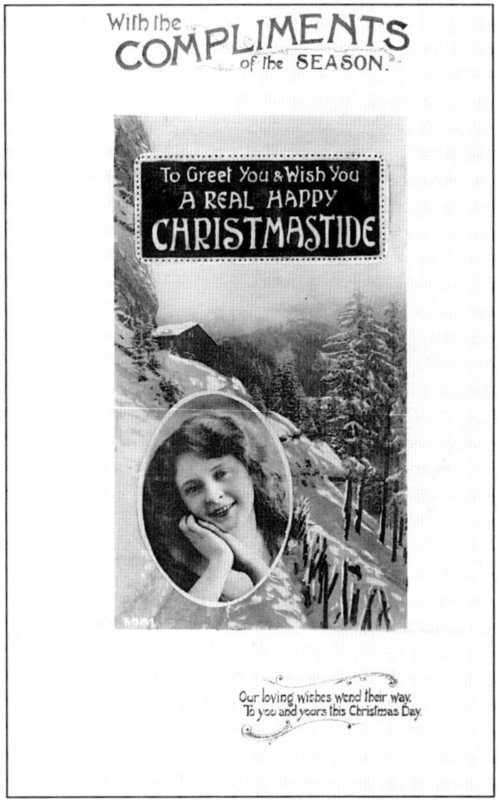

Postcards were used as Christmas cards; many also greeted other holidays as well. As the copier machine had not been invented. Few families sent out long family Christmas letters—reporting all the wonderful achievements of each child.

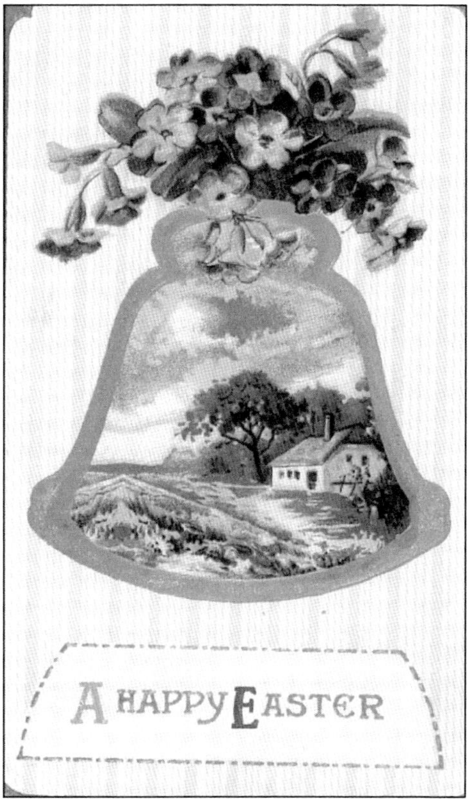

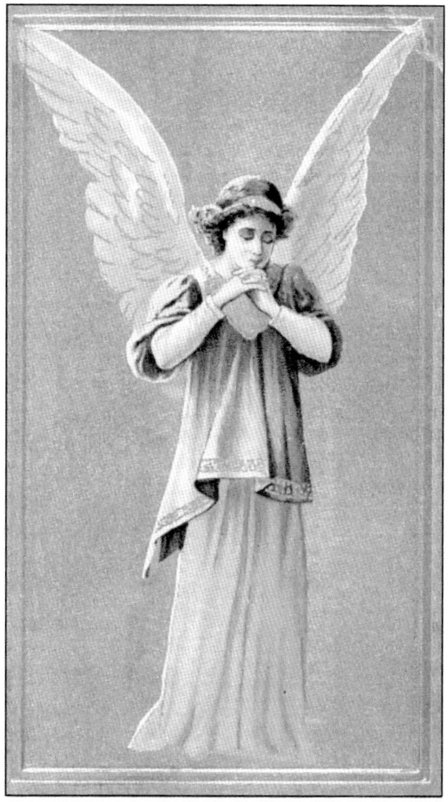

Easter is a very special day, marked by church services and maybe some new clothes.

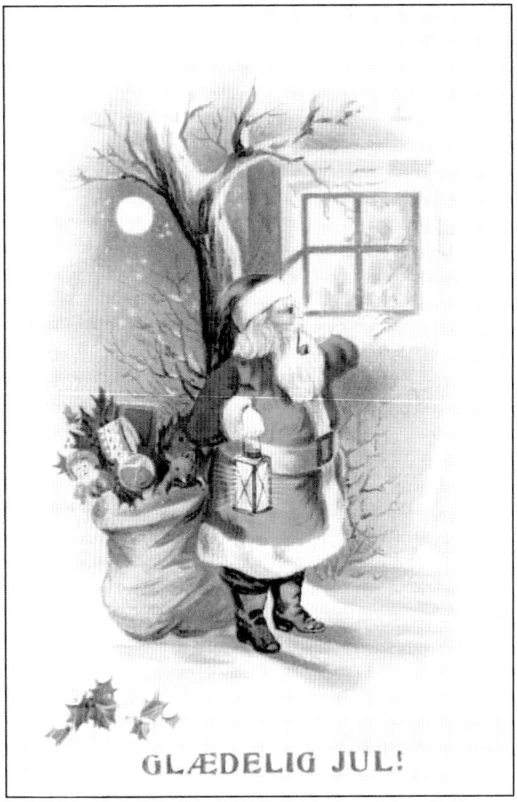

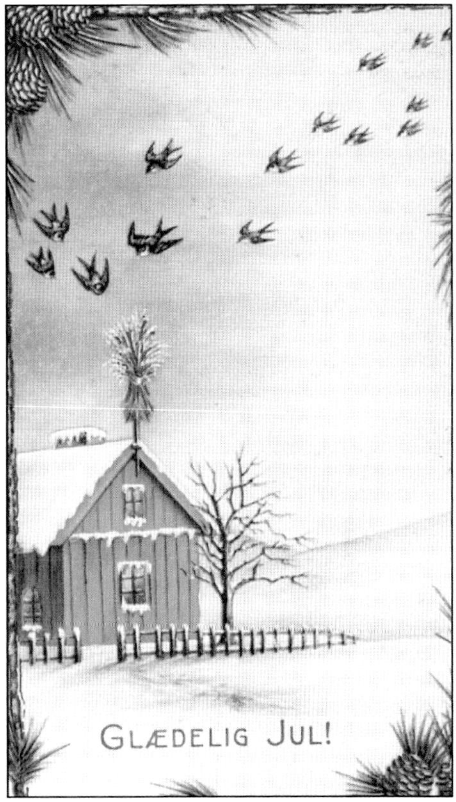

As Norwegians, Germans, and Russians comprised the major ethnic groups in North Dakota at the turn of the century, many greeting cards were in their languages. The postcards on this page are in Norwegian. Even Santa Claus smoked in these days.

Dressmakers have almost disappeared today, but there were many from 1900 to 1930. If you wanted a dress, you went to their house (or they came to yours). Dressmakers disappeared when people started to buy their clothes "off the rack."

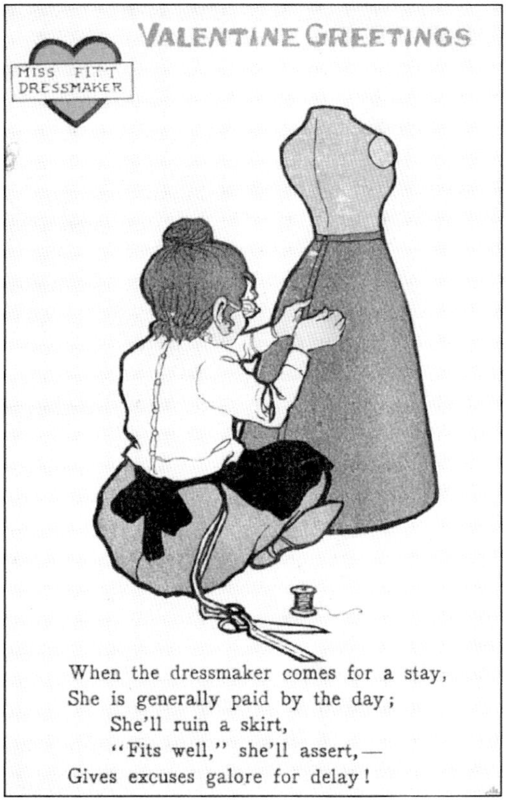

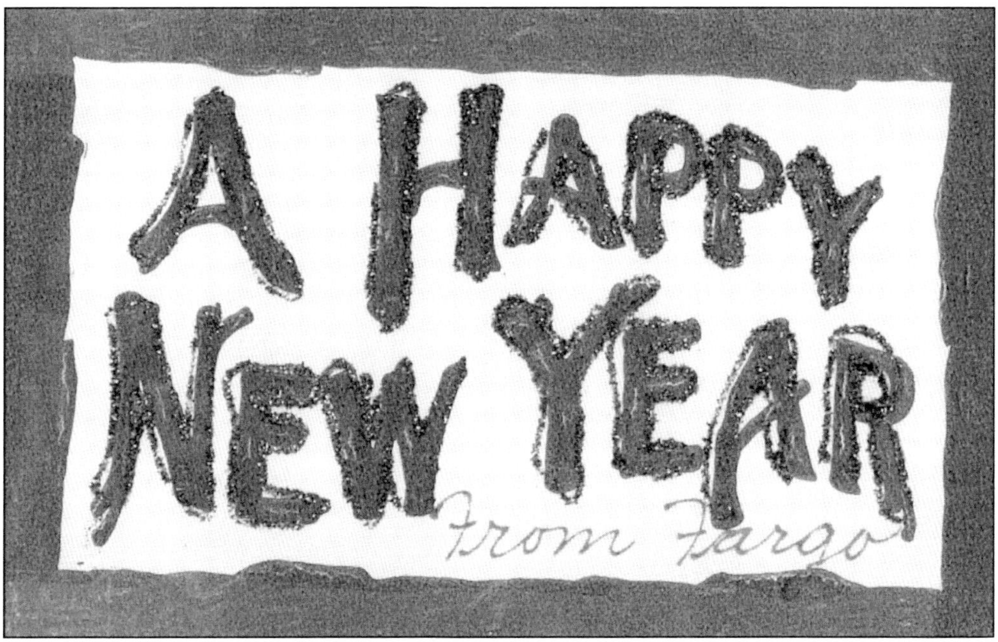

Many cards were not only embossed, they were sprinkled with shiny, sparkling glitter, like this one.

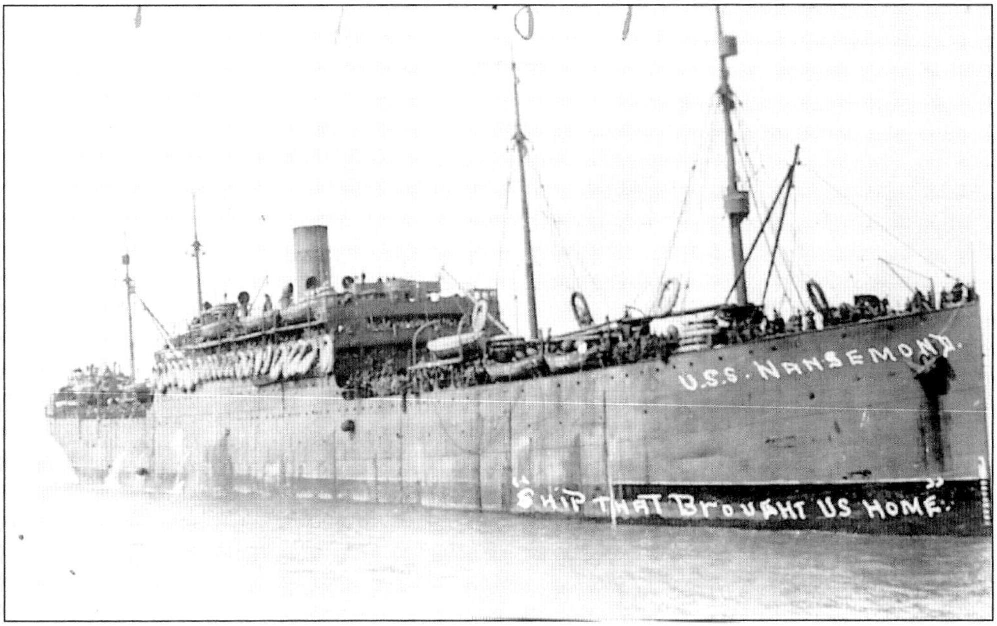

Postcards also recorded important news events. This image shows the U.S.S. *Nansemond* bringing back World War I veterans from France. The author's uncle, Oliver Brenden, came home on the U.S.S. *Nansemond*; he died a few years later because he had been gassed by the Germans.

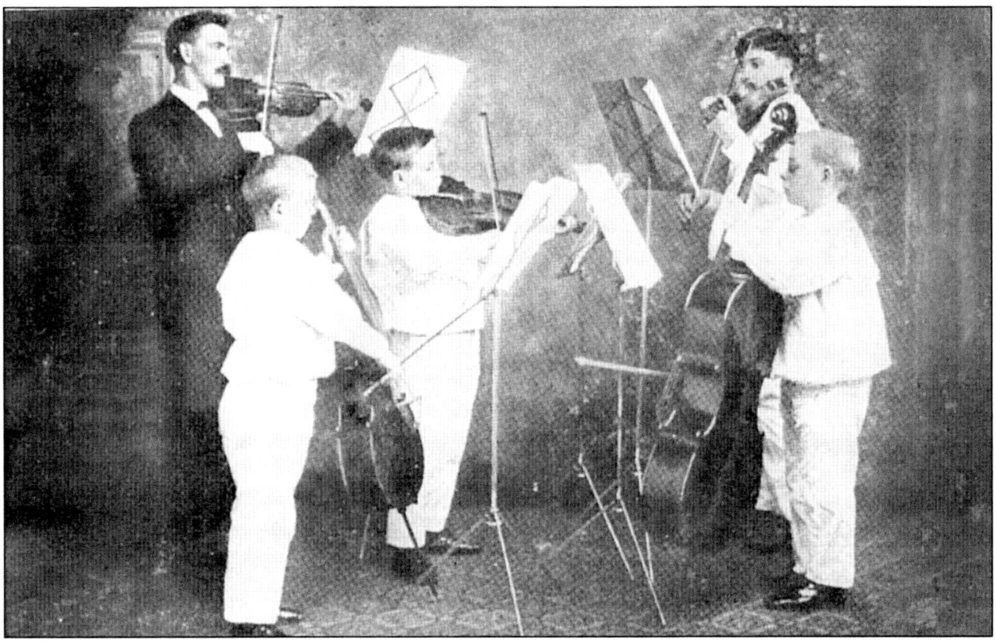

Postcards were also used to advertise. This card pictures a popular music group, the Christiansen family, who played at events all around the Fargo area. Leif Christiansen was the music director at Concordia College in Moorhead, Minnesota, for many years.

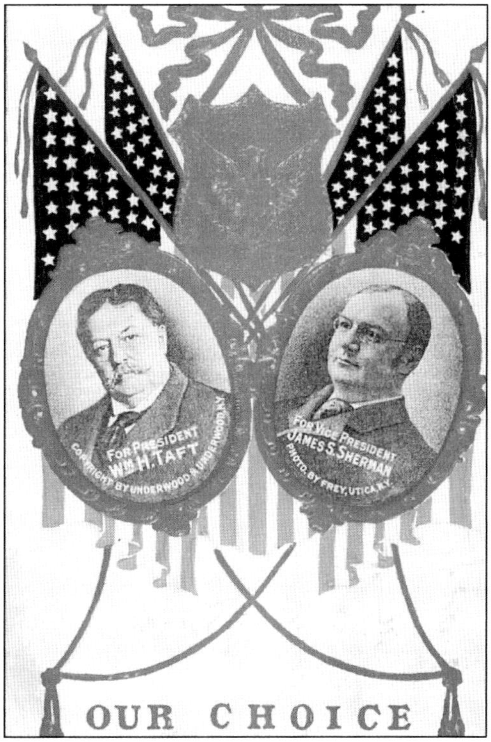

Postcards were also used to win elections. Candidates at this period had very few ways to reach the voter; postcards were not only read, they were cheap and easy to mail.

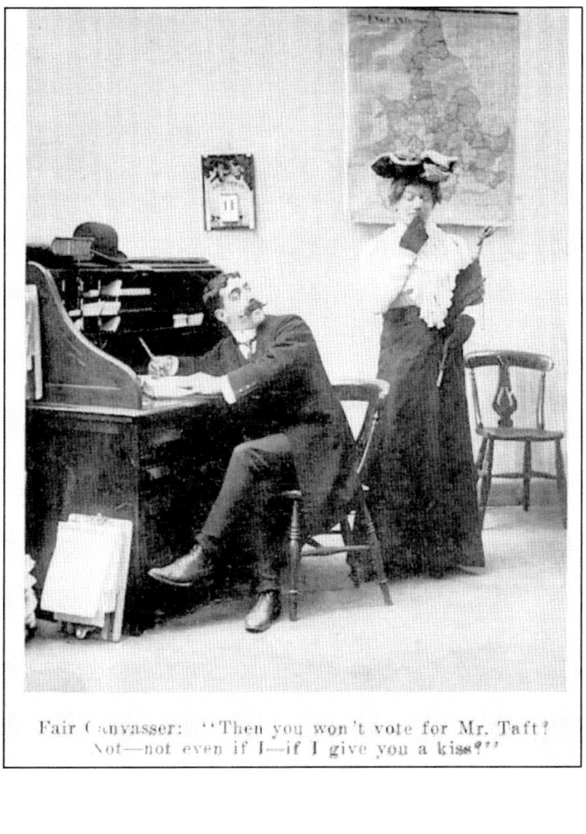

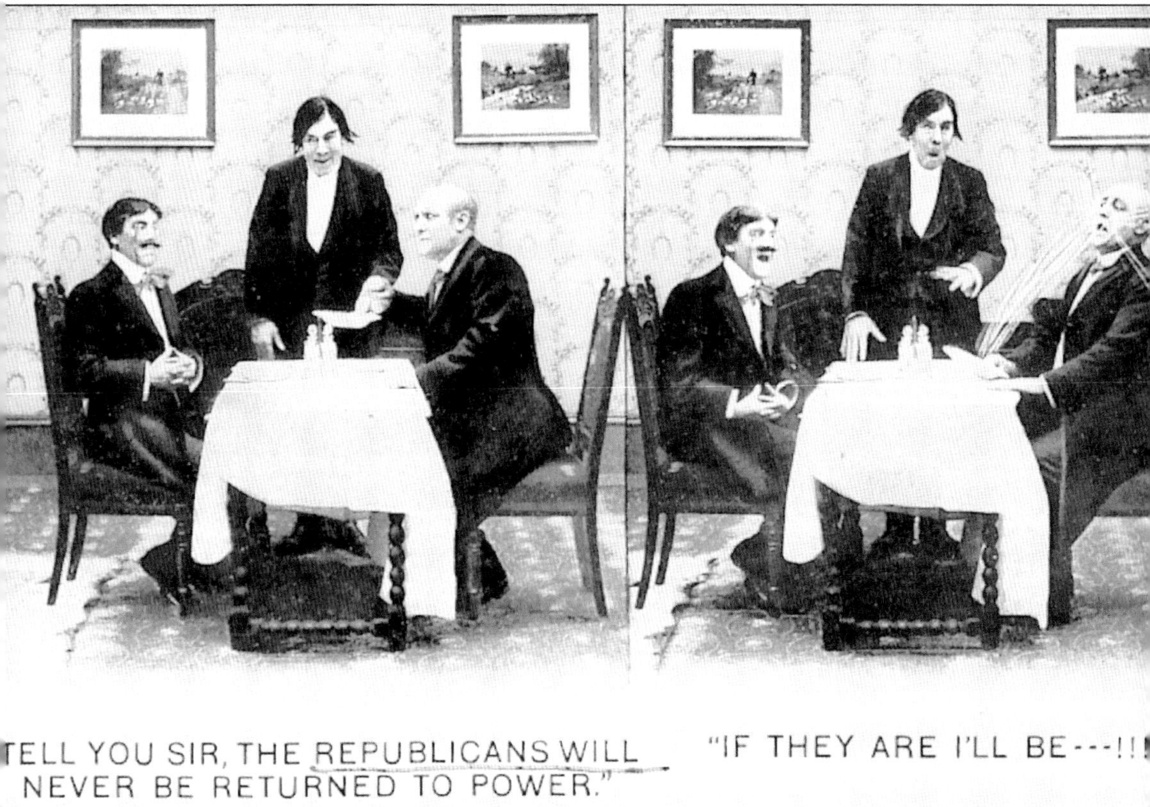

North Dakota is famous for its turbulent politics. For many years, the Republican Party held the majority, and the Democrats were very weak. However, the Republican Party had two wings; one wing, the Republican Organizing Committee (ROC), was conservative, while the other, the Non-Partisan League, was liberal. The Non-Partisan League joined the Democratic Party, in 1956, and the two parties are now about even.

Eight

Fun and Games in North Dakota

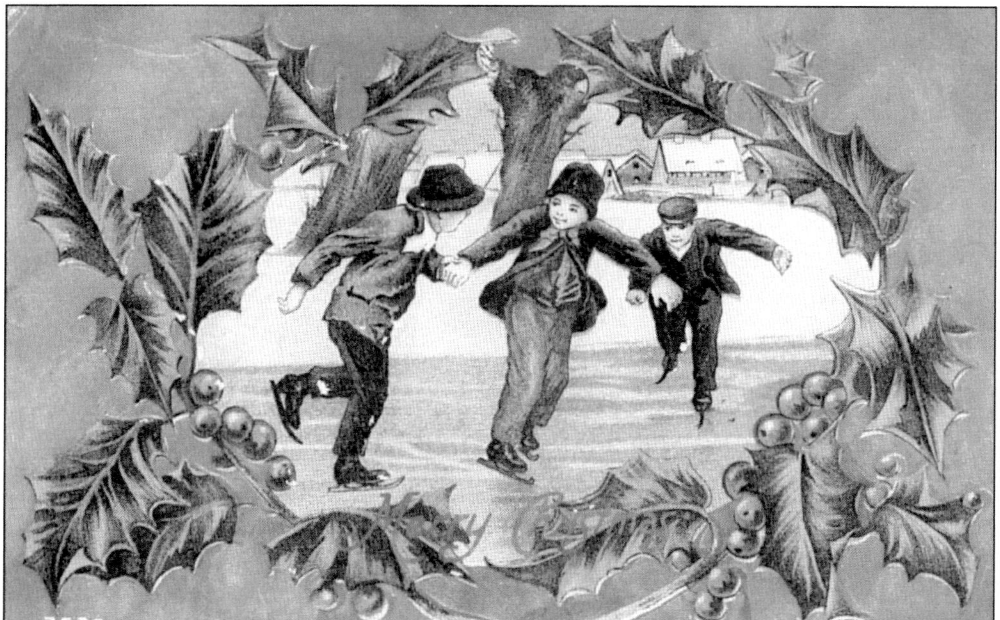

This postcard from 1900 shows that you can have fun during the winter in North Dakota, despite the fact that winters can be "chilly." Weather is always a popular subject in North Dakota. The coldest day recorded in the state was at Parshall in 1936 when the thermometer showed 60 degrees Fahrenheit. The warmest day was 121 degrees Fahrenheit at Steele that same year. North Dakota is one of the two or three states that has the highest average wind speed. Average wind speeds in the Red River Valley are 10 to 20 percent higher than the rest of the state.

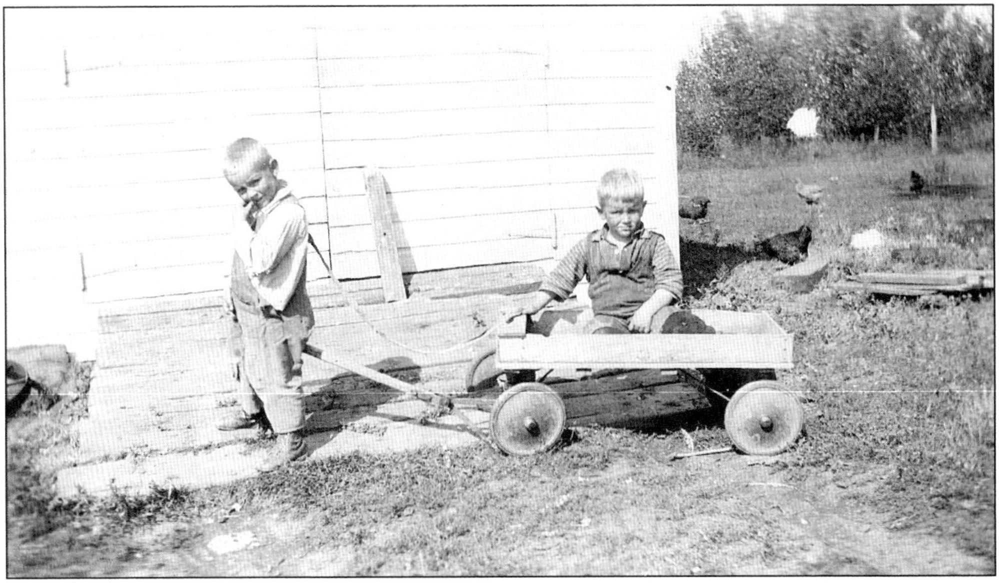

This picture shows a grim period in North Dakota history; life was not easy. Most people were poor, but their kids didn't know it. All these two boys needed was a wagon and a brother with whom to play.

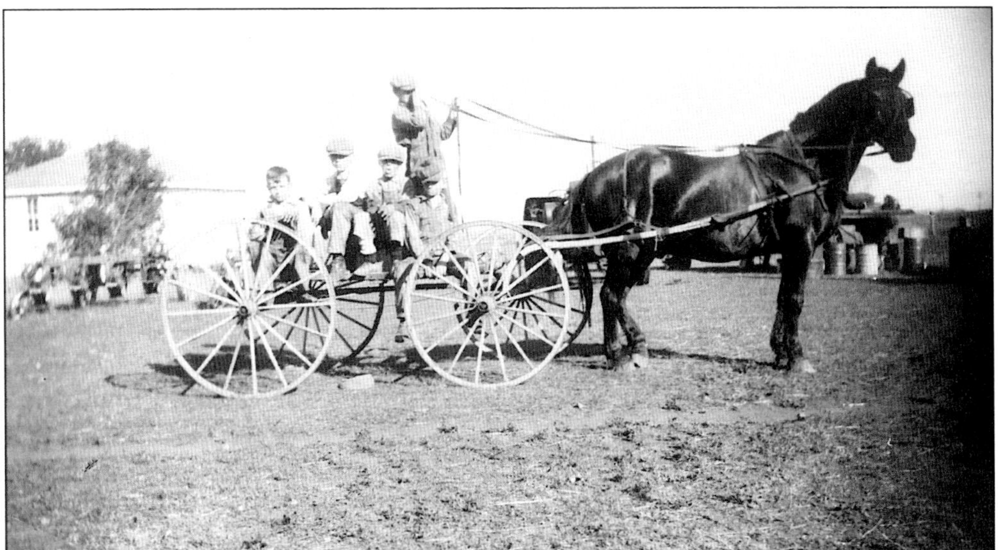

When the boys got older, they had a pick of eight work horses to hook up to buggies, wagons, or snow sleds. Growing up in North Dakota, Eric Sevareid said, "I wouldn't trade my boyhood for that of any other man." Mr. Sevareid grew up in Velva, North Dakota.

It was not fun for the little kids who would be dragged into a bathtub, rubbed, scrubbed, and later dressed in their best clothes. Note the ribbon the oldest boy, Tilford Aasen, is wearing. Even small towns had studio photographers in these days. Now only the big cities have them.

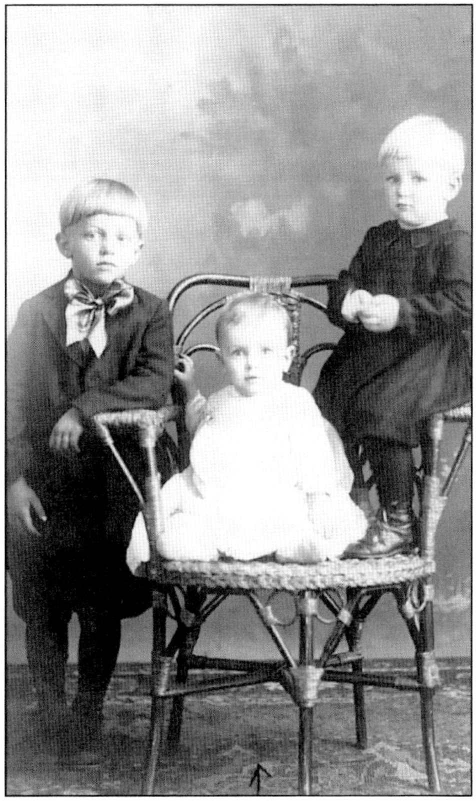

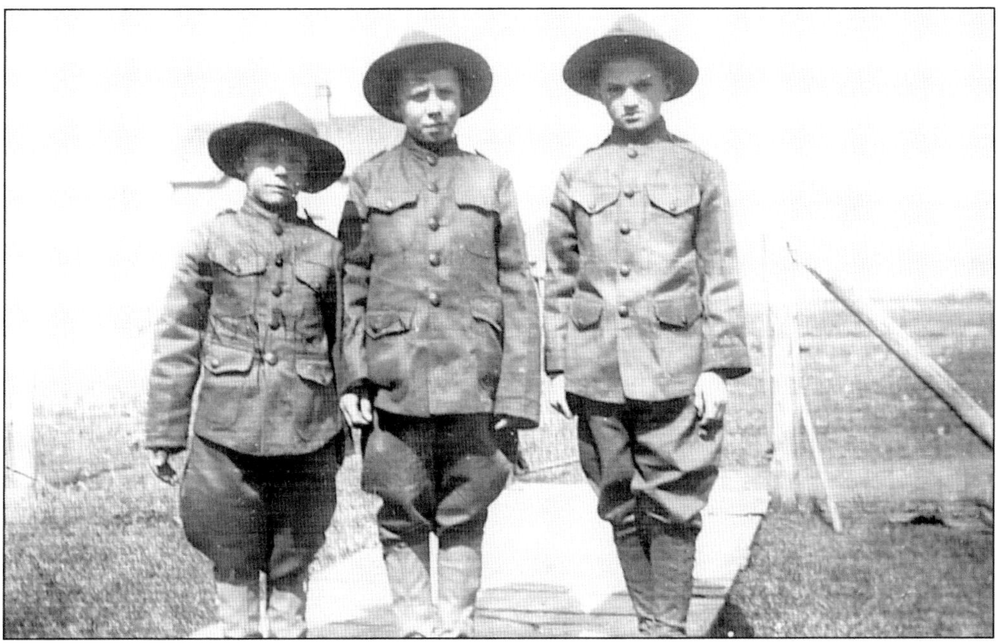

These children were too young to enlist in World War I, but they could play soldier.

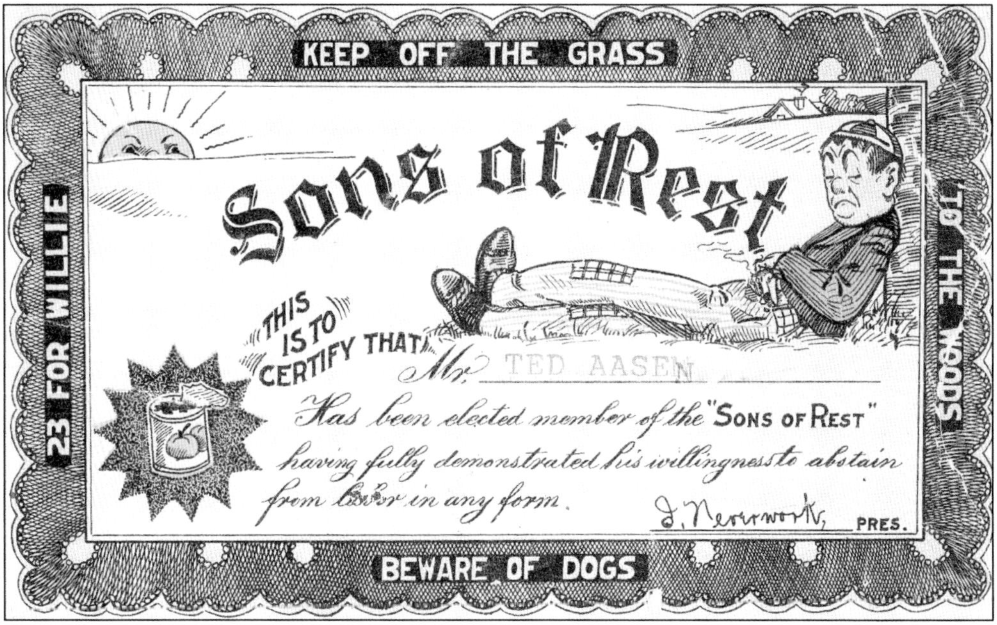

This joke postcard promised you a day of rest—and suggested you were lazy as hell!

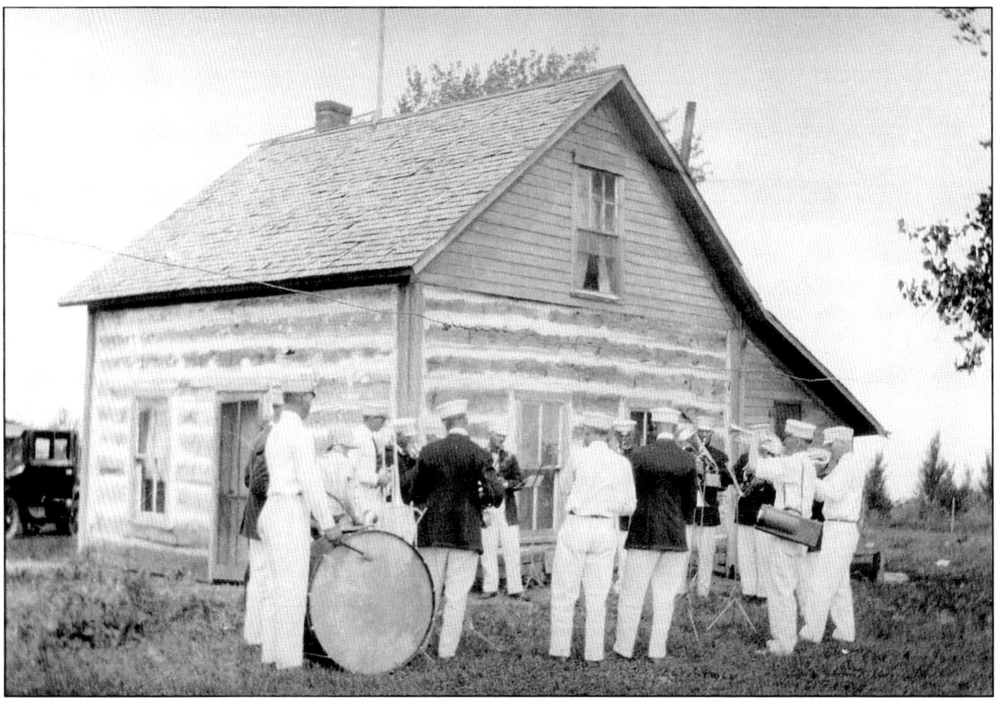
In the early 1900s, it was not all long days and hard work. The local community band might show up (on a Sunday) to give you a serenade!

Some would-be comedians of this period liked to send gag postcards to their friends. This image was taken in Perley, Minnesota, which is right across the Red River from North Dakota.

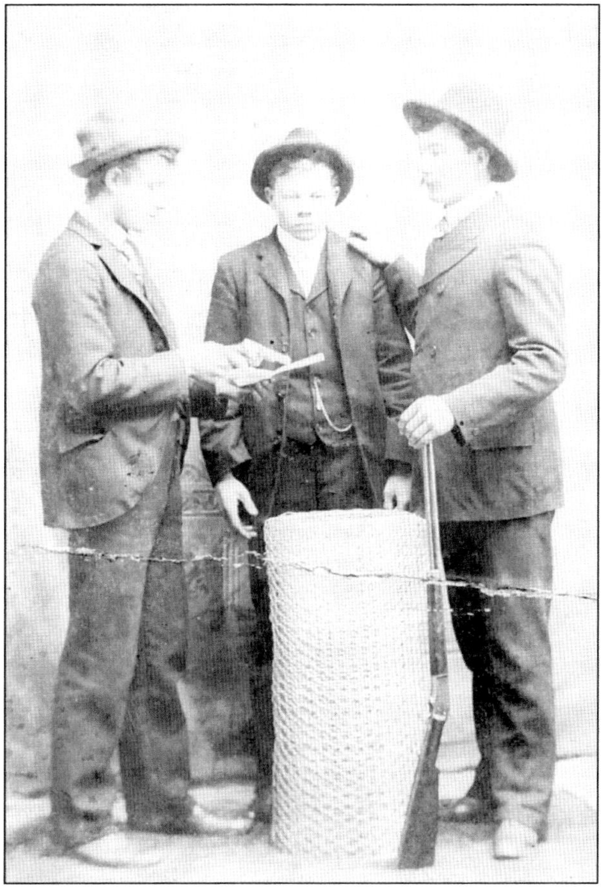

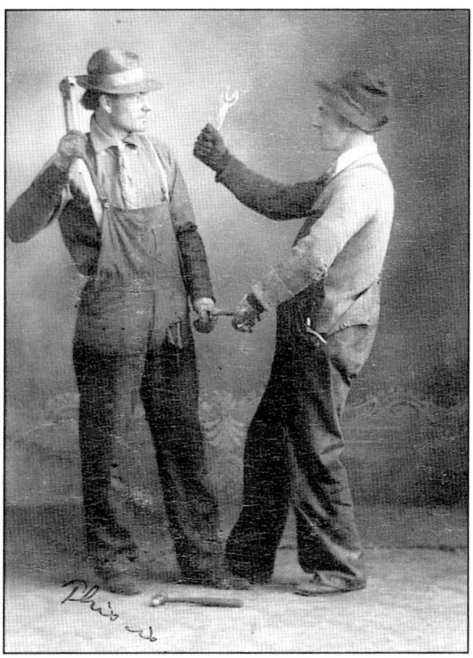

These two men were very good friends, and they loved to set up silly photograph opportunities like this one.

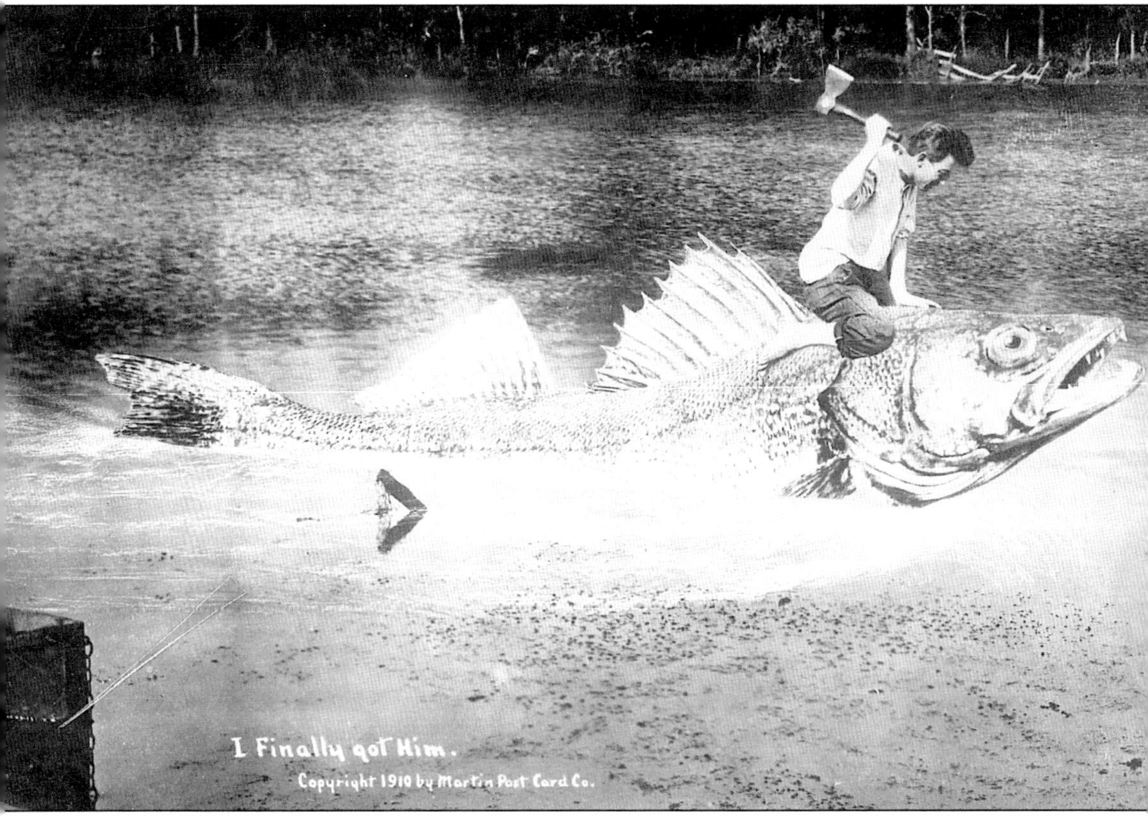

This may not be an actual photograph.

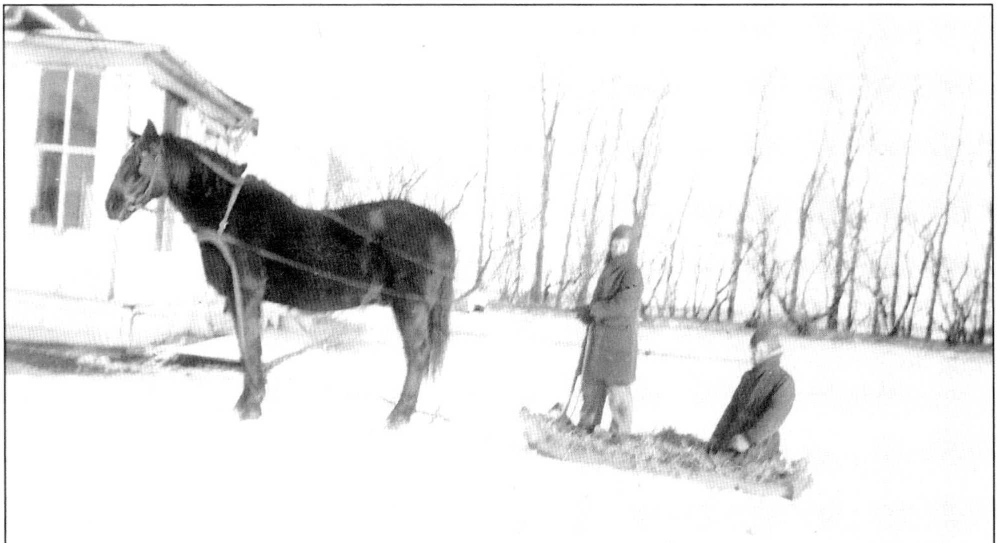

In the 1930s, you could always find something to do on a farm. These boys made a primitive sled out of wood boards and filled the sled with hay. The horse, called Diamond, was urged to pull, but it looks like he wanted his photo taken first.

Nine

Early Life in North Dakota

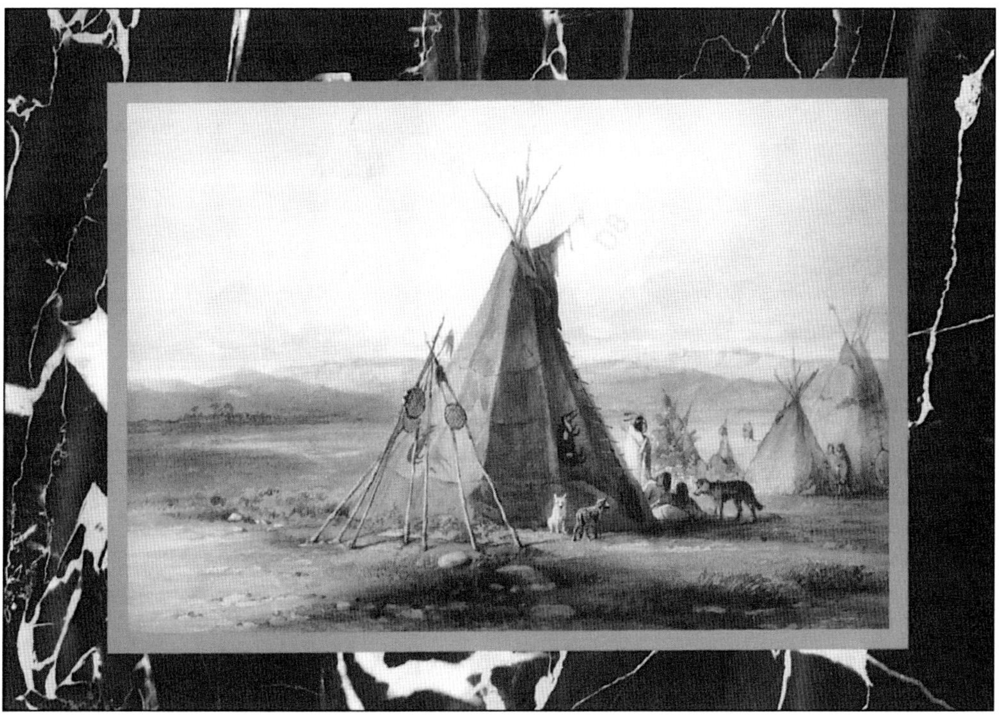

This postcard shows how North Dakota's Native Americans lived when the settlers started arriving in the 1870s. Today, the main Indian reservations are Devils Lake Sioux Indian Reservation, Standing Rock Sioux Reservation, Fort Berthold Reservation, and Turtle Mountain Pembina Chippewa Reservation.

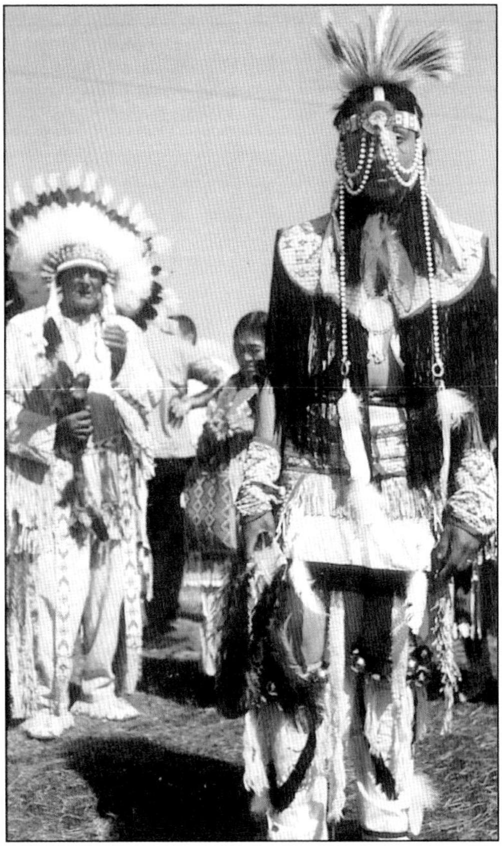

The first inhabitants of North Dakota were Native Americans. In the 1990 North Dakota census, North Dakota had 638,800 people; 25,917 of this number were Native Americans. This postcard shows Sioux Indians, who were once a fierce, nomadic people who followed buffalo herds.

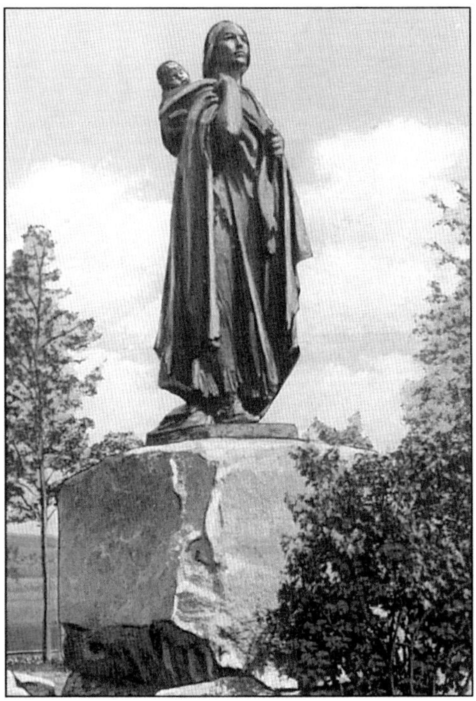

Sakakawea was the Shosone Indian woman who acted as a guide for the Lewis and Clarke expedition. Lewis and Clark spent nearly six months in North Dakota in 1804, making their winter camp at Fort Mandan.

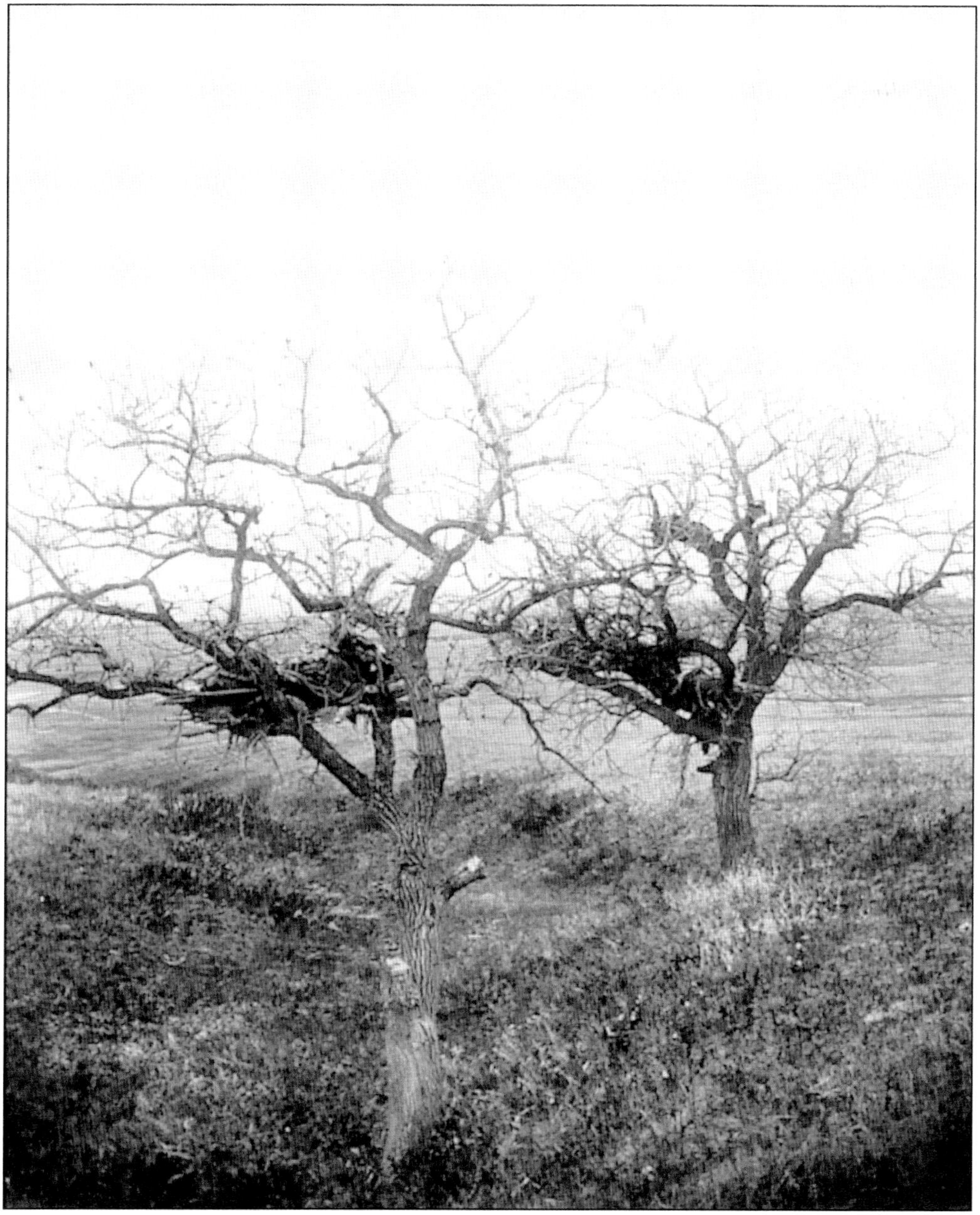

Following the Battle of Little Bighorn, many Native Americans died. They were dressed in their finest clothing and placed in the branches of strong trees. Their cherished belongings were also wrapped up with the body.

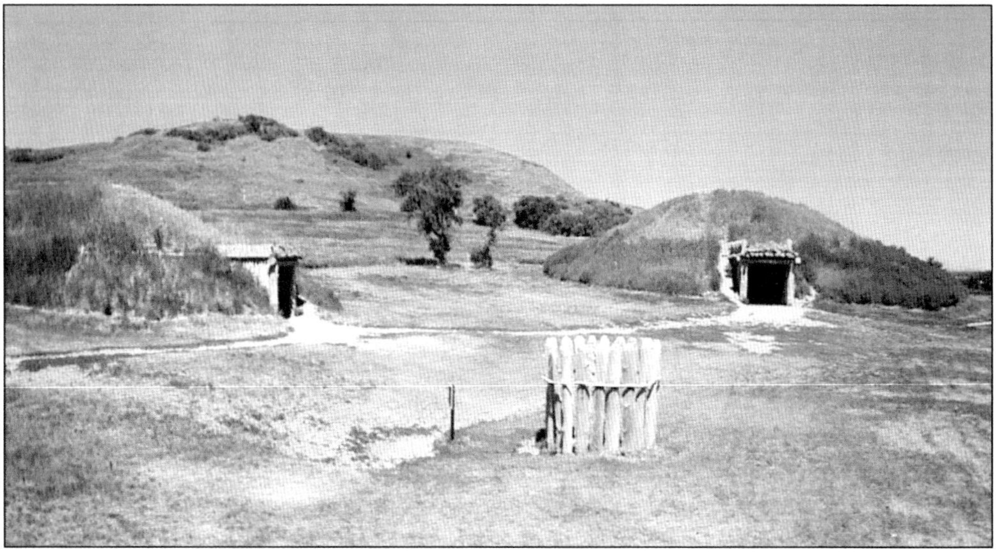

Reconstructed earth lodges were occupied by Mandan Indians, who abandoned them *c*. 1764. They are located in Fort Lincoln State Park in Mandan, North Dakota. Native Americans of North Dakota included the Mandan, Hidatsa, Arikara Nation, the Yanktonai, Siseton, Wahpeton, and other Dakota (commonly known as Sioux) Tribes. These Dakota Tribes consisted of the Pembina Chippewa, Cree, and Metis, according to the *North Dakota Blue Book*.

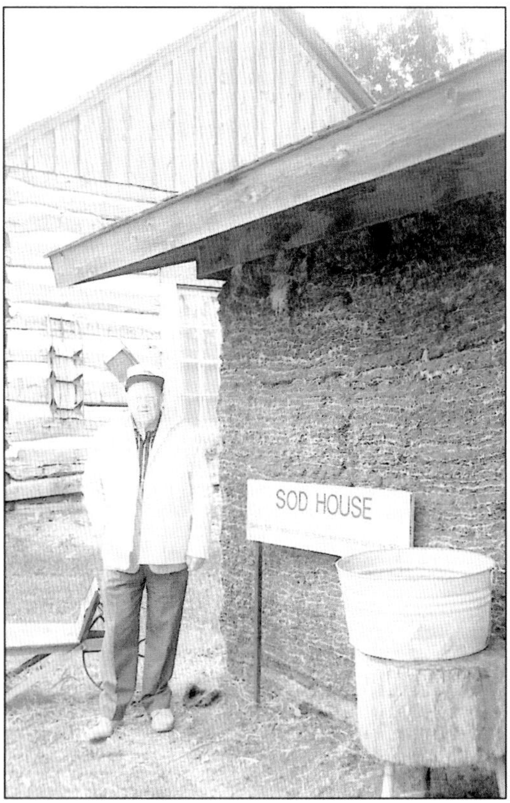

Early settlers on the open prairie built sod houses like this one. The settler might build a 14-by-16-foot sod house, laying up tiers of sod with very small windows. The walls, sometimes 2 feet thick, might be boarded on the inside and painted or whitewashed. In the background of this photograph is an original log house. These two historic houses can be seen at Bonanzaville, USA, in West Fargo, North Dakota. Bonanzaville, USA, is a pioneer village of museums. L. Aasen stands in the foreground.

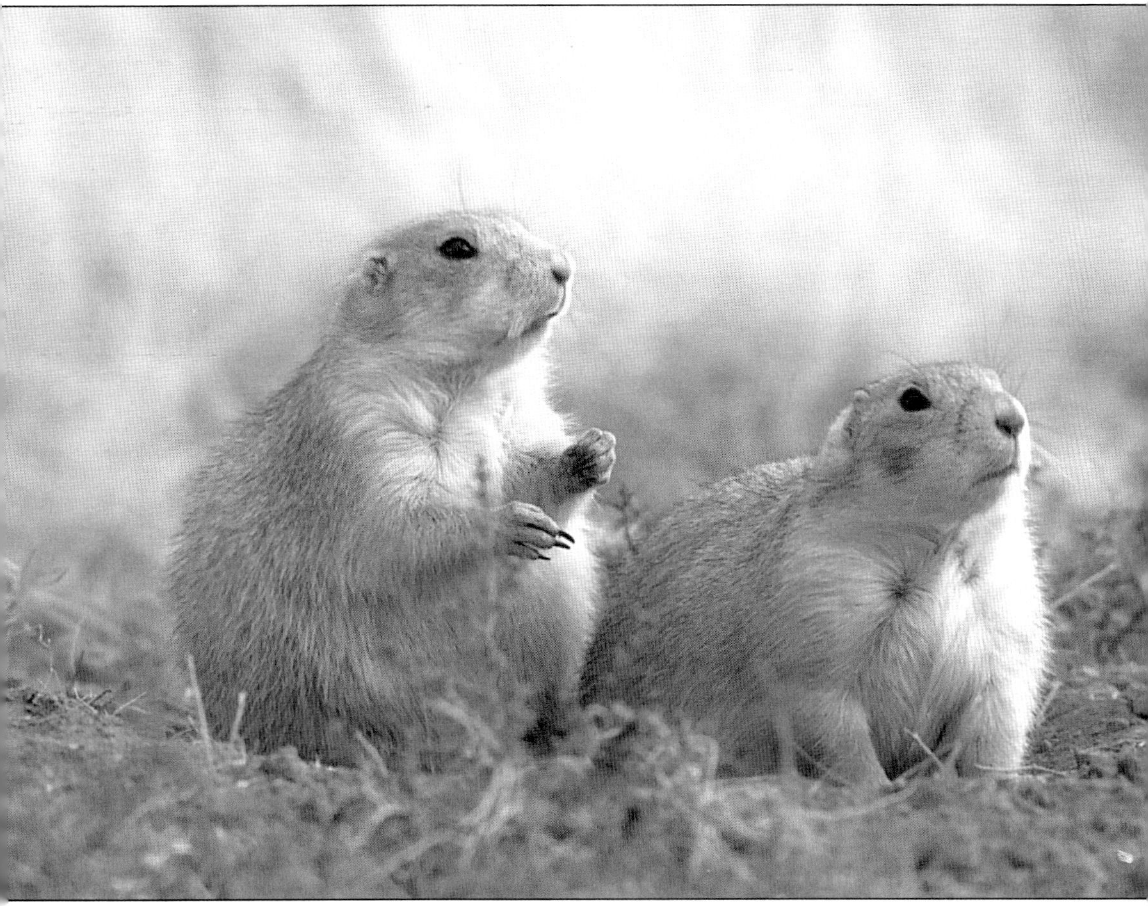

Early settlers to North Dakota were greeted by the state's famous prairie dogs, who lived in large villages. The prairie dogs post their own "sentinels," who whistle an alarm when danger approaches.

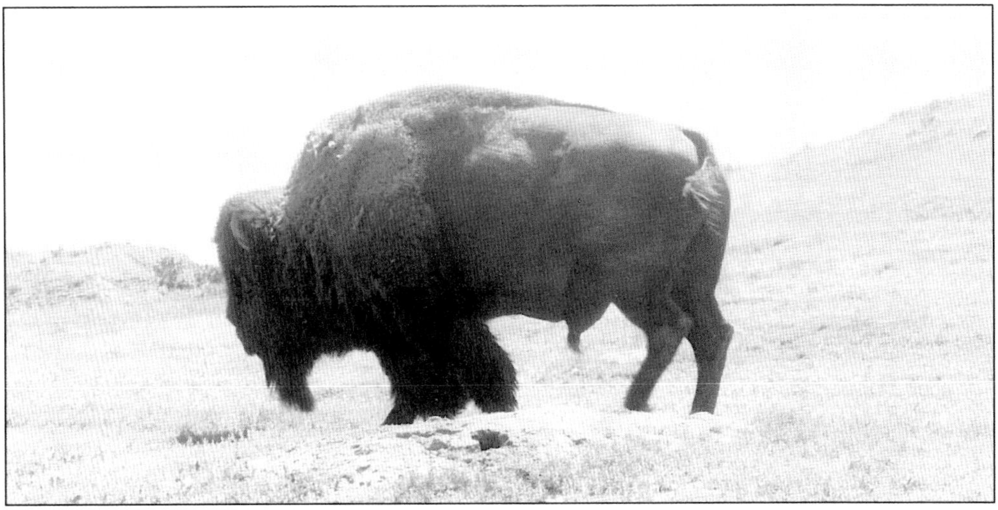

After the destruction of the buffalo herds, the harvest of buffalo bones started. The so-called "Bone Pickers" collected them from all over North Dakota and shipped them back east. The ground bones were used for fertilizer, chicken feed, or to make carbon black for refining sugar. Sugar was poured through the carbon black, which—like fine soot—helped to remove impurities in the sugar. The bone pickers got between $8 and $10 a ton. As late as 1930, farmers were still finding buffalo bones when they plowed their fields.

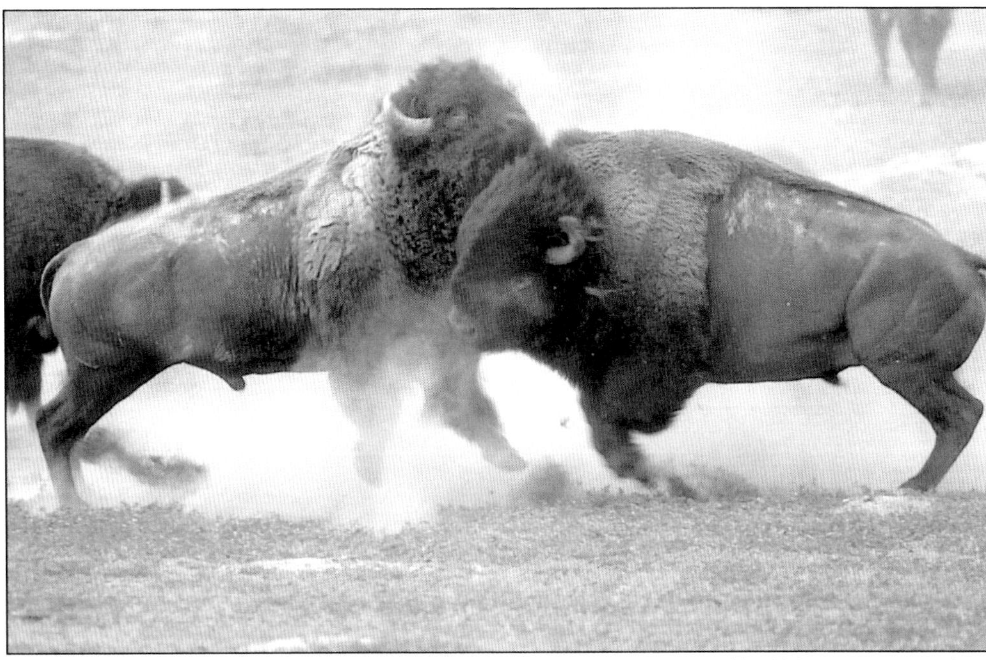

After nearly being wiped out in the early 1900s, the bison, also called buffalo, are now making a comeback in North Dakota. Today, they are raised as a tourist attraction, as well as for their meat and hides. In the Theodore Roosevelt National Park, they roam at will and watch your car with disgust as you drive by.

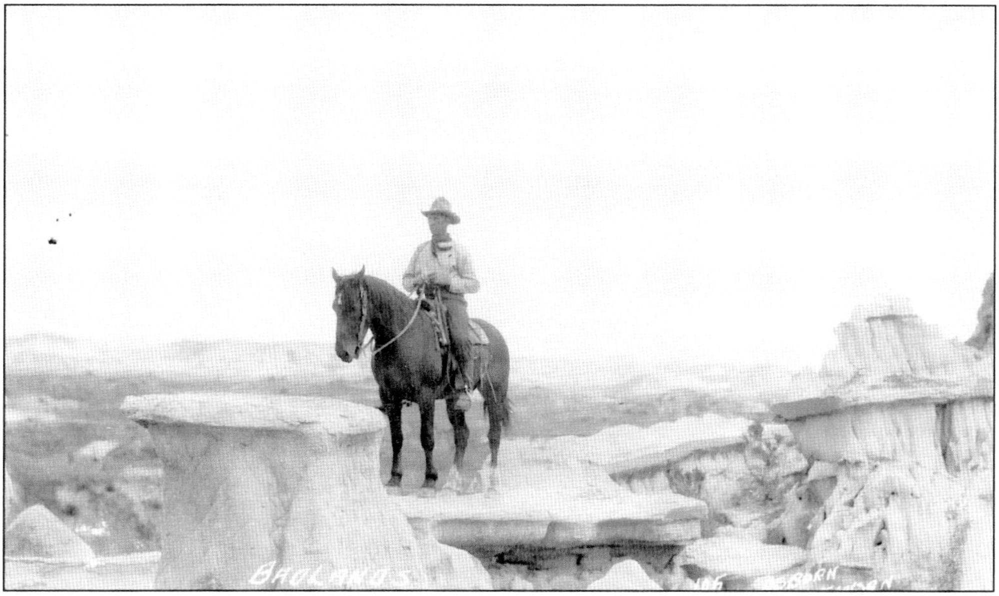

This old postcard gives a rather grim view of the Badlands, which are a beautiful, colorful part of western North Dakota. Theodore Roosevelt wrote, "the whole land is covered with a monotonous dull brown, which joined to the extraordinary shape and bizarre coloring of the water-worn buttes, gives the landscape a look of grim and forbidding desolation." However, the Badlands grew on Roosevelt and in later articles, he bragged about the beauty of the area.

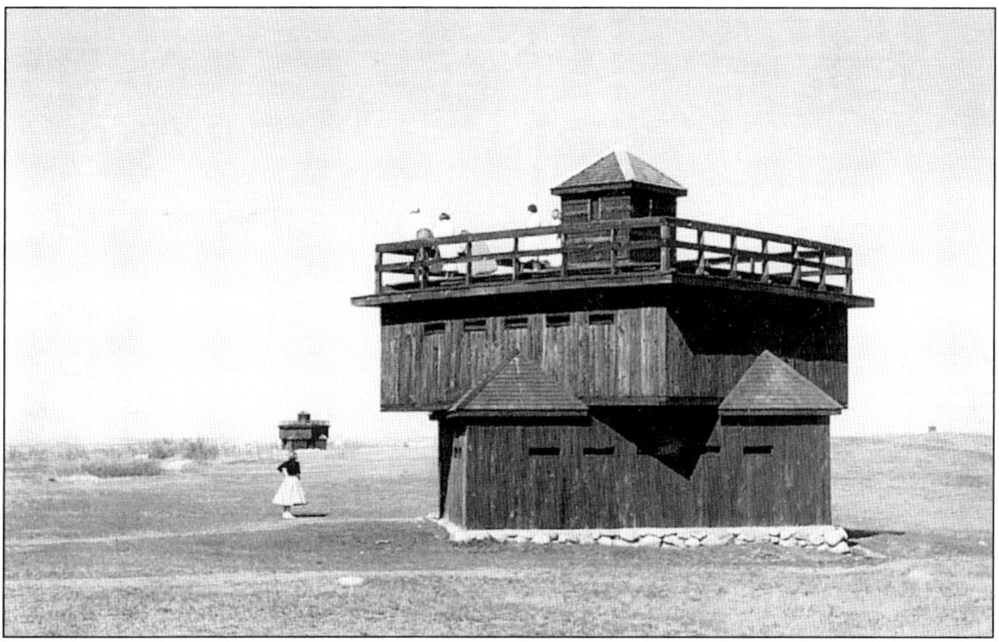

The Block House at Old Fort McKeen in Mandan, North Dakota, was built to protect the early settlers from Native Americans.

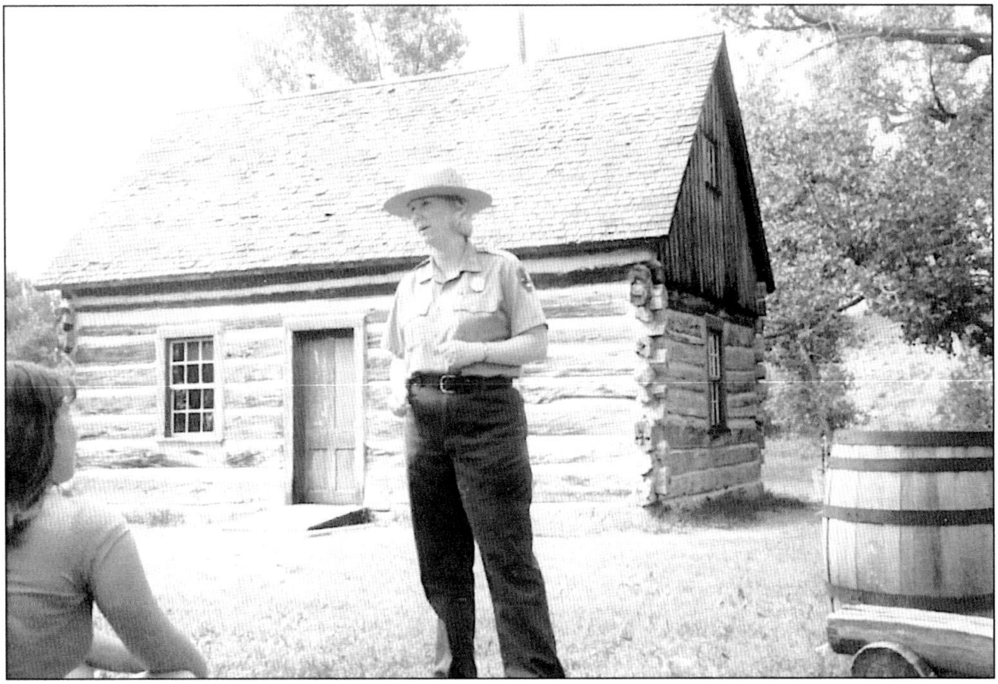

Teddy Roosevelt's famous cabin has changed location several times since it left the ranch. For a long time, it was on the capital grounds in Bismarck. It is now back at the park in Medora, North Dakota.

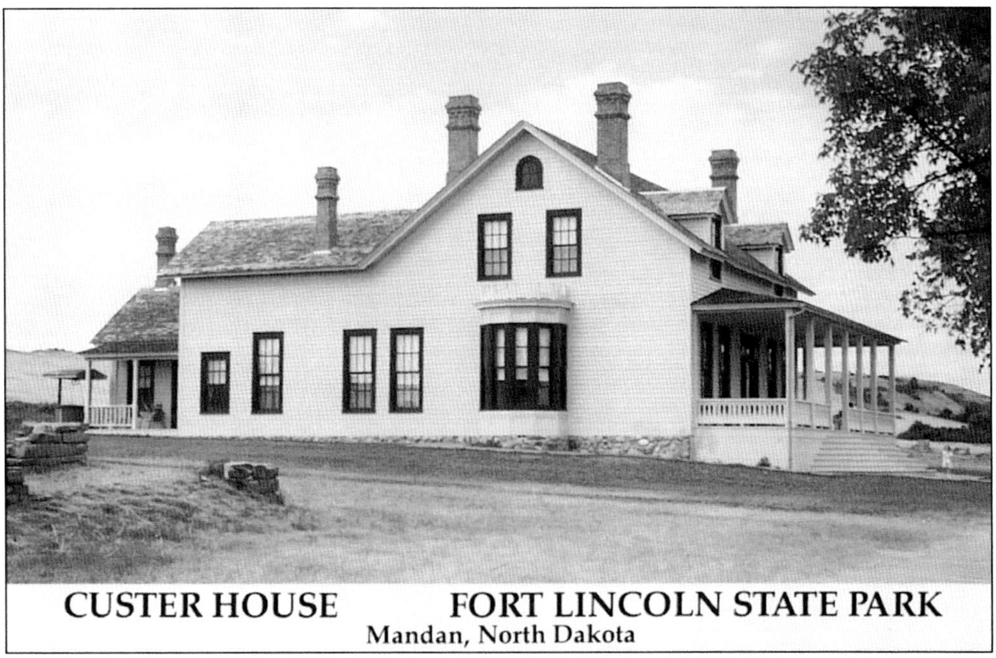

This postcard is a replica of Lt. Col. Gen. George Armstrong Custer's house in Fort Lincoln State Park near Mandan, North Dakota. General Custer and his wife, Libbie, lived in a house like this from 1874 to 1876. General Custer and 280 troopers of the Seventh Cavalry were killed in the Battle of Little Big Horn in 1876.

Ten

SNAPSHOTS OF NORTH DAKOTA 1900–1930

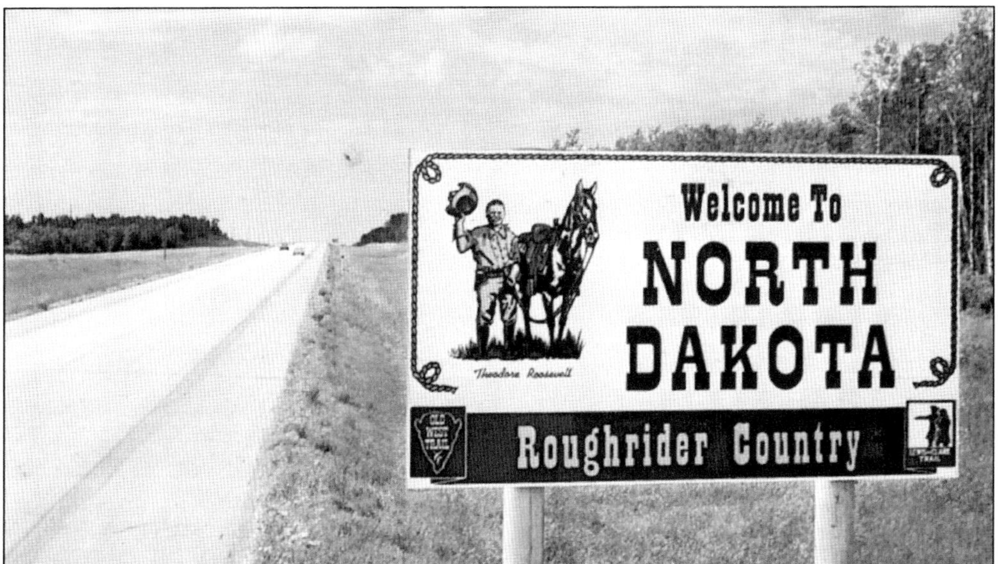

These signs greet visitors to North Dakota. It is called Roughrider Country because of the First U.S. Volunteer Cavalry, which Theodore Roosevelt organized to fight in the Spanish-American War. In 1971 and 1973, the North Dakota Legislative Assembly defeated bills intended to change the "Peace Garden State" on North Dakota license plates to "Roughrider Country."

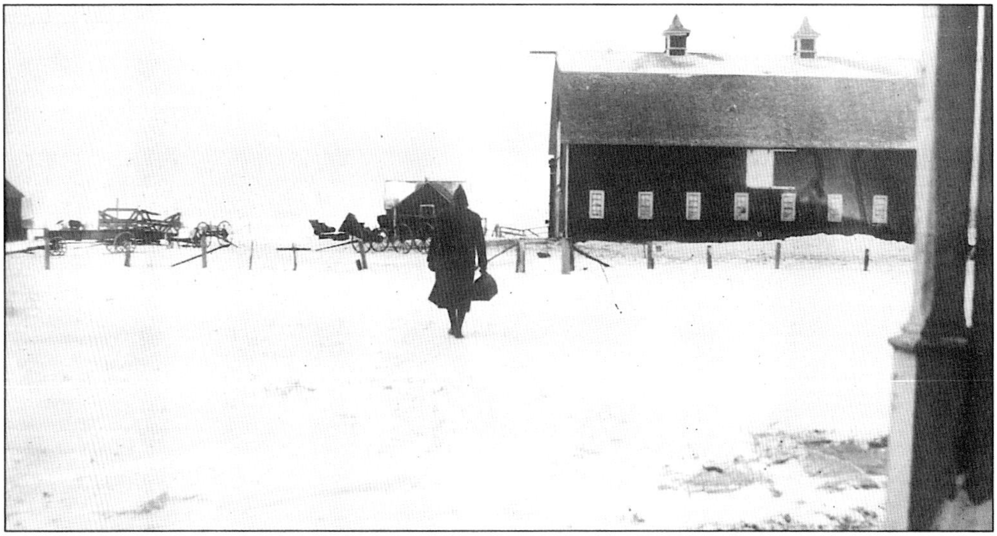

This photograph shows the author's Uncle Oliver Brenden leaving the farm near Hillsboro, North Dakota, in 1917 to go to France during World War I. He was in a lot of trench warfare, and as a result, he died a year after he got home, from mustard gas used on the battlefield.

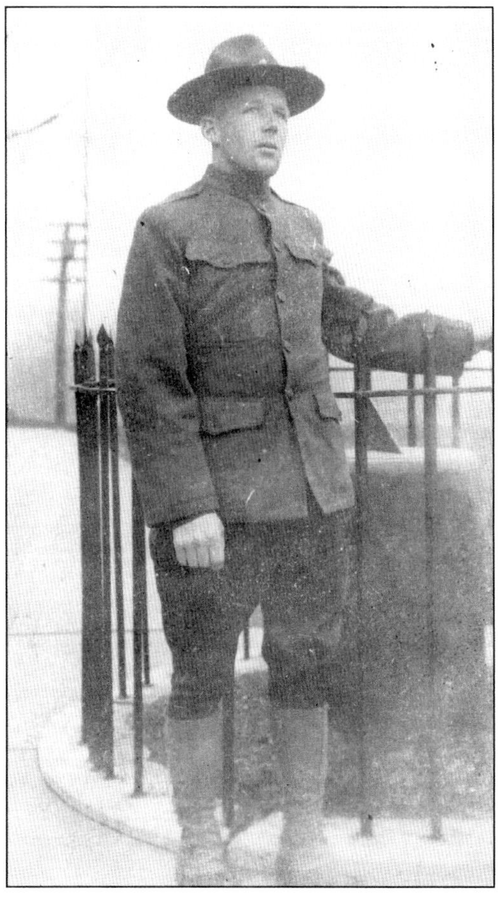

This photograph shows Nels Bergly, a World War I soldier who served in France. He sent this card from France to his friend Julia Lerfald. Like soldiers from the start of warfare, he tried to reassure Julia by writing, "I have a great time in the army so you need not worry about me at all."

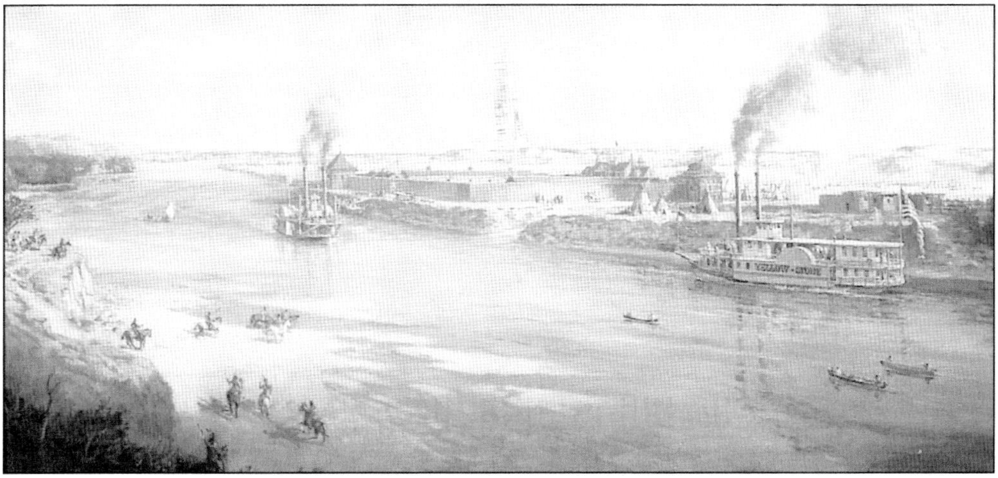

The steamboat *Yellow Stone* arrived at the Fort Union Trading Post near Williston, North Dakota, in 1835. In 1832, the *Yellow Stone* made its first trip to the upper Missouri. Steamboats were heavily used during the military engagements in the Yellowstone Valley in the 1870s. The steamboat called *Far West* served as the backup for General Terry and was navigated up the Bighorn River, laden with military supplies, before the news of Custer's defeat was received.

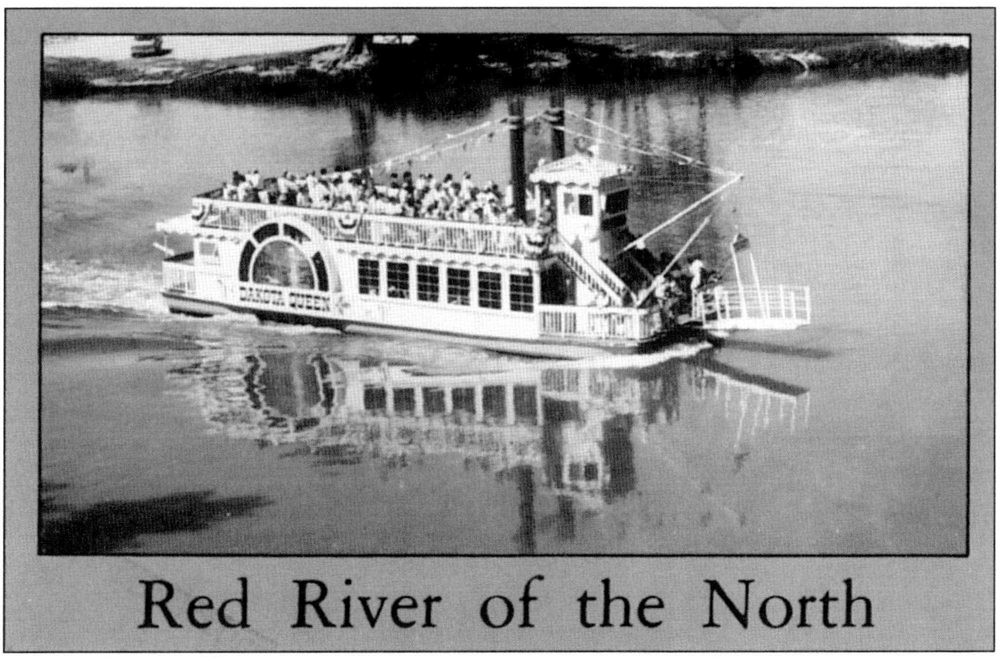

Before railroads came to North Dakota on June 6, 1872, many boats, like this one, carried freight and passengers up the Red River. Steamboating on the Red River was active from 1871 to 1878. Most of the boats were 100 feet long, with a beam from 20 to 30 feet. Their carrying capacity ranged from 90 to 200 tons. The boats generally went from Moorhead, Minnesota, to Canada.

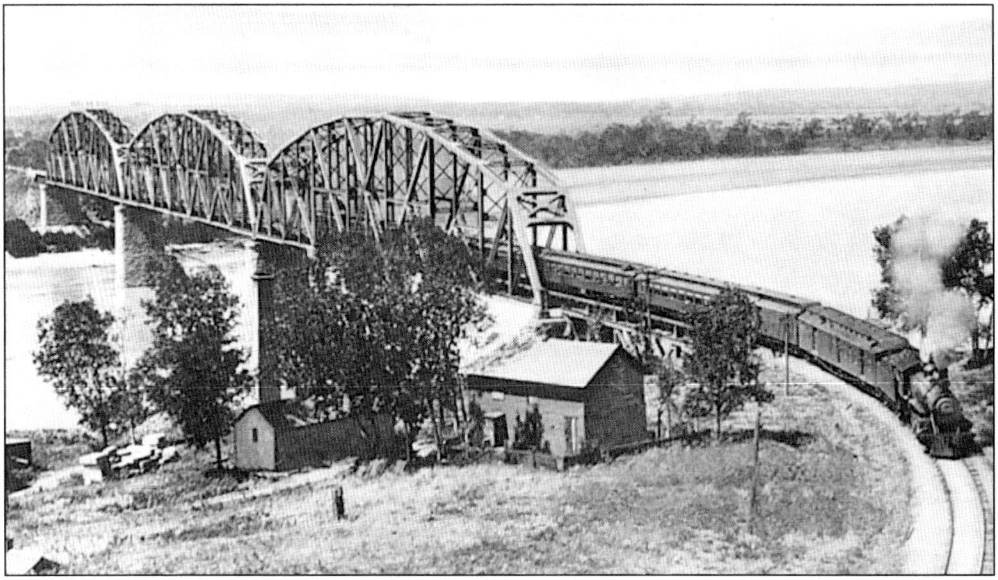

This postcard shows the Northern Pacific bridge, which crosses the Missouri River at Bismarck, North Dakota, in the 1900s. Unfortunately, professional hunters used the railroads to locate and kill entire herds of buffalo. Two or three hunters could kill up to 900 buffalo in a season. Each hunter received about $5 for the hide and meat on the buffalo.

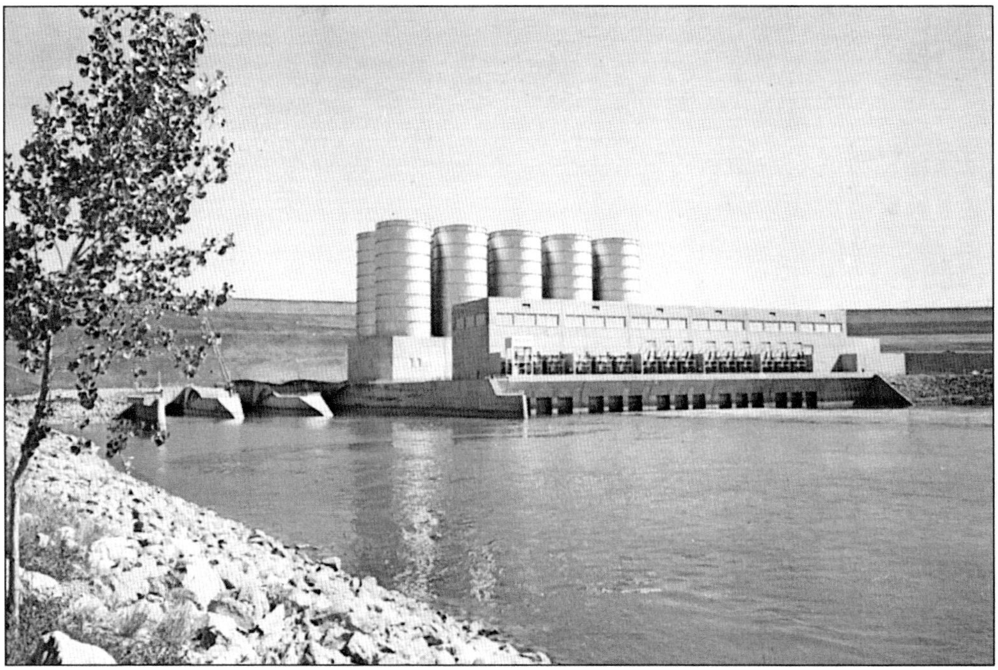

The Garrison Dam is 12,000 feet long, 210 feet high, 2,600 feet wide at the base, and 60 feet wide at the top. In all, it totals 70 million yards of earth and 1,500,000 yards of concrete. As early as 1889, North Dakotans talked of diverting the waters of the Missouri to other areas in North Dakota. Work on the dam started in 1947.

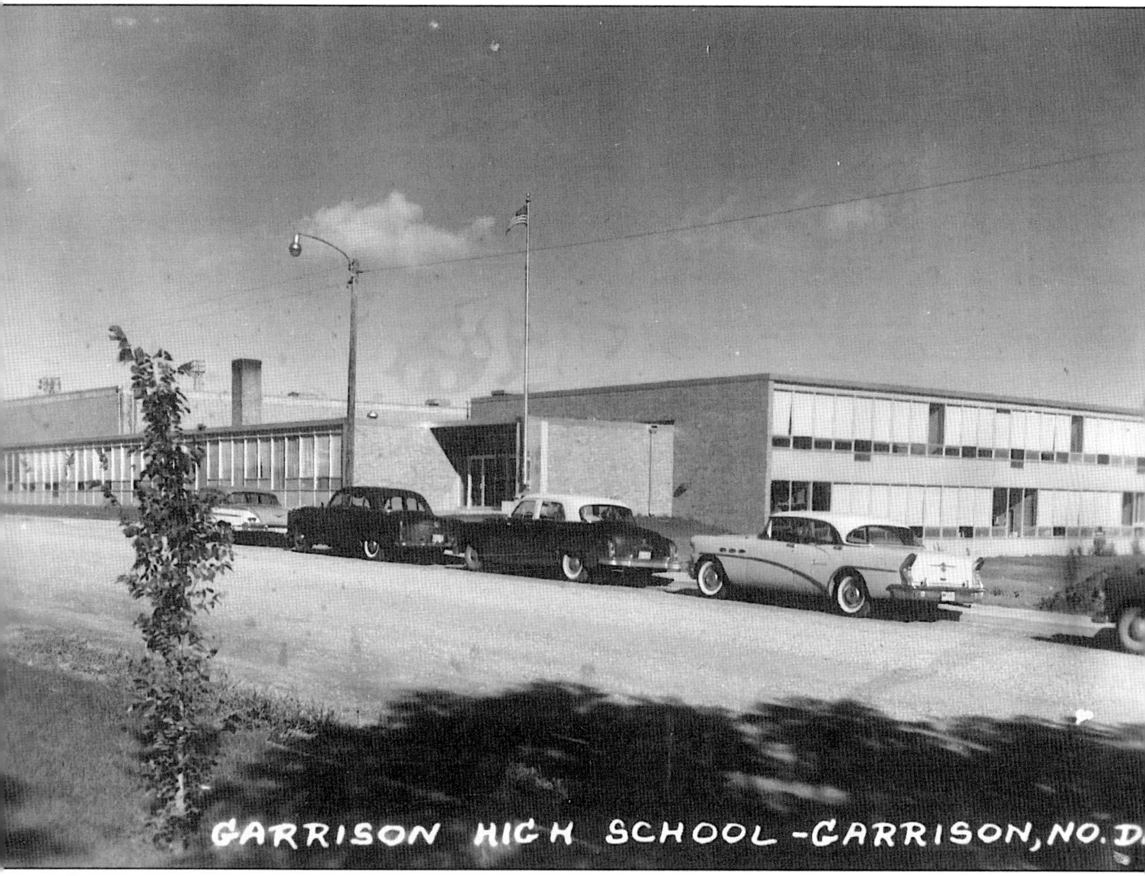

The Garrison Dam was named after Garrison, North Dakota. The dam diverts and distributes Missouri River water around the state.

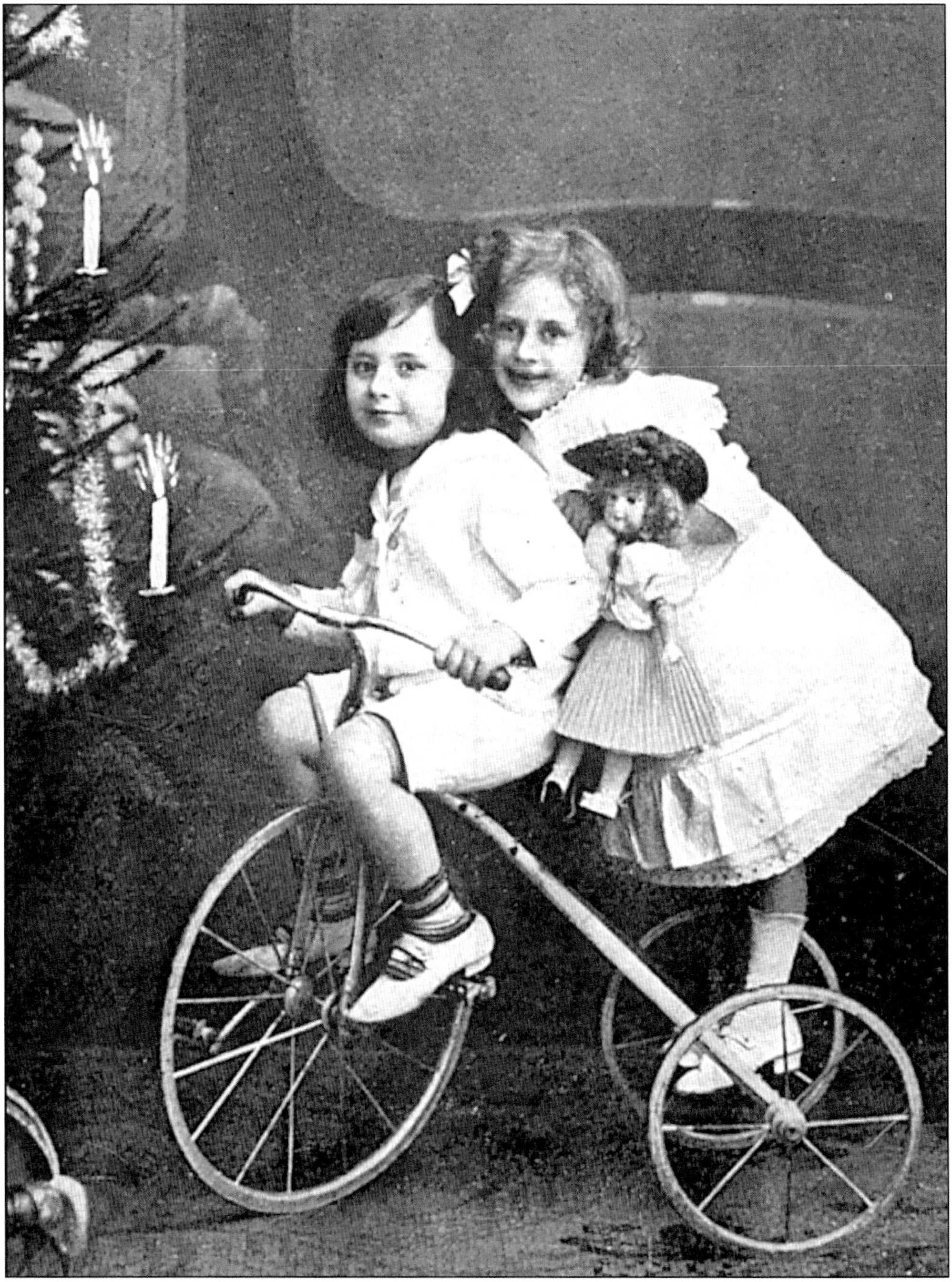

Even these pretty girls knew in 1910 that transportation has always been a challenge in North Dakota. First, there were thousands of the Red River ox carts that traveled the 500 miles between Pembina, North Dakota, and St. Paul. Their deep tracks can still be found. Next came the steamboats, which were followed by the railroads in 1872. Cars started appearing c. 1910s, and the first asphalt-surfaced state highway was the 7.5-mile stretch of U.S. Route 10 near Casselton, c. 1926. The first airplane flight was at Grand Forks in 1920. North Dakota's first commercial airline service began in 1928.

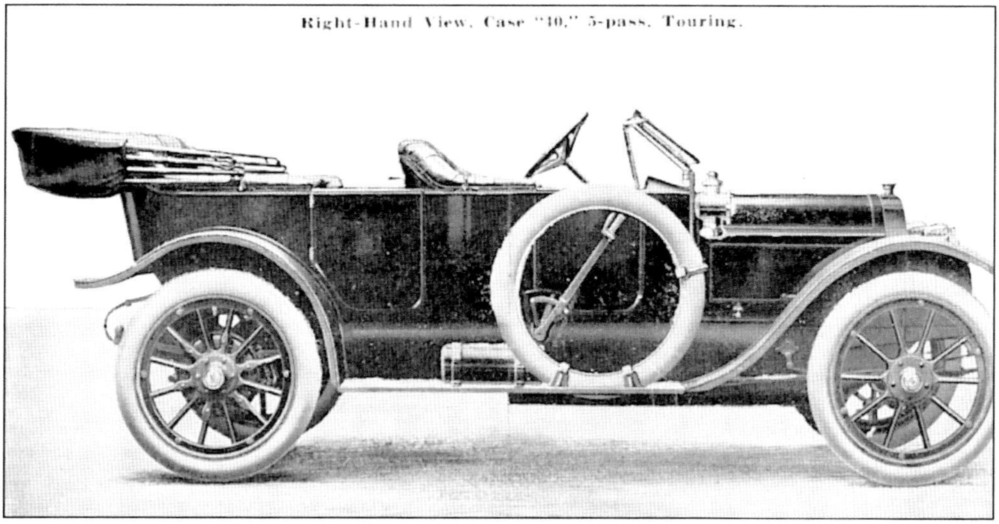

This Case, five-passenger touring car was popular between 1900 and 1920.

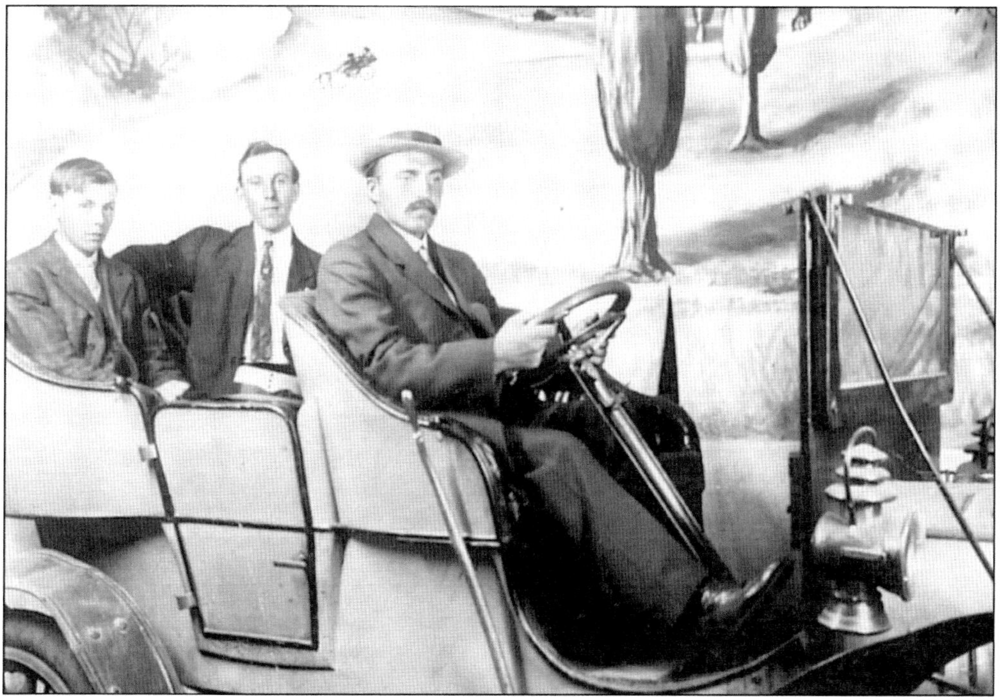

Elwyn B. Robinson in the *History of North Dakota*, writes the following: "The automobile was changing North Dakota life in the 1920s. In 1913, North Dakotans owned only 13,075 automobiles, but by 1920 they owned 92,000 and 57 percent of the state's farmers had them.

"North Dakota fell in love with the automobile. It provided an excellent means of traveling long distances over the prairies; it reduced isolation. It helped to overcome remoteness. It freed North Dakotans and gave them mobility, just as a century and a half earlier the acquisition of horses had freed the Plains Indians."

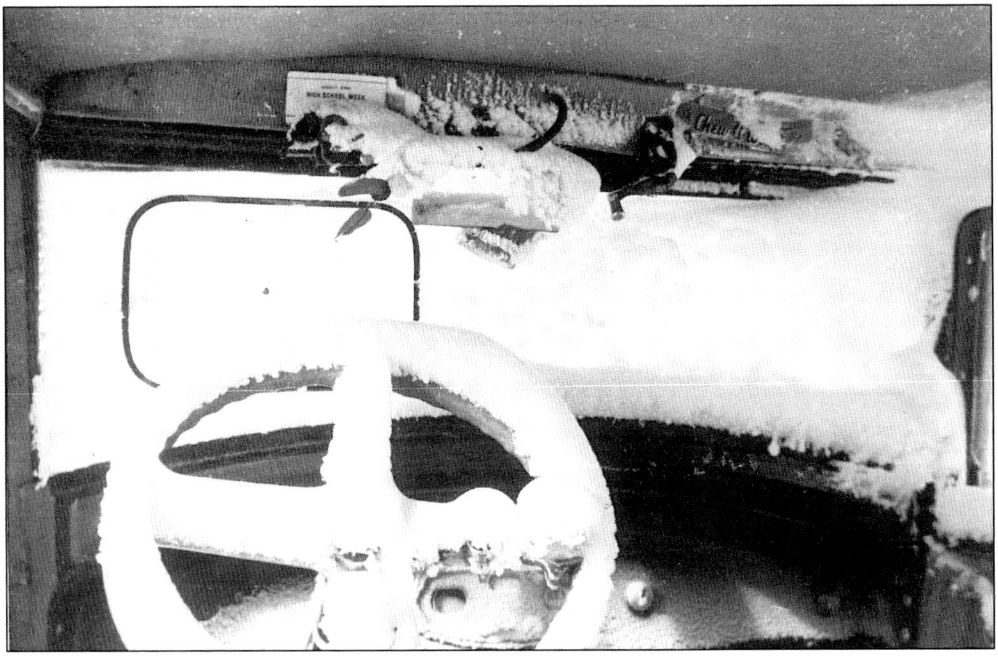

To show "snapshots" of North Dakota, snow photographs are probably required. In 1932, a strong blizzard was able to drive snow into this 1929 Whippet, which had been left near Highway 81 near Hillsboro, so children could go to school the next day.

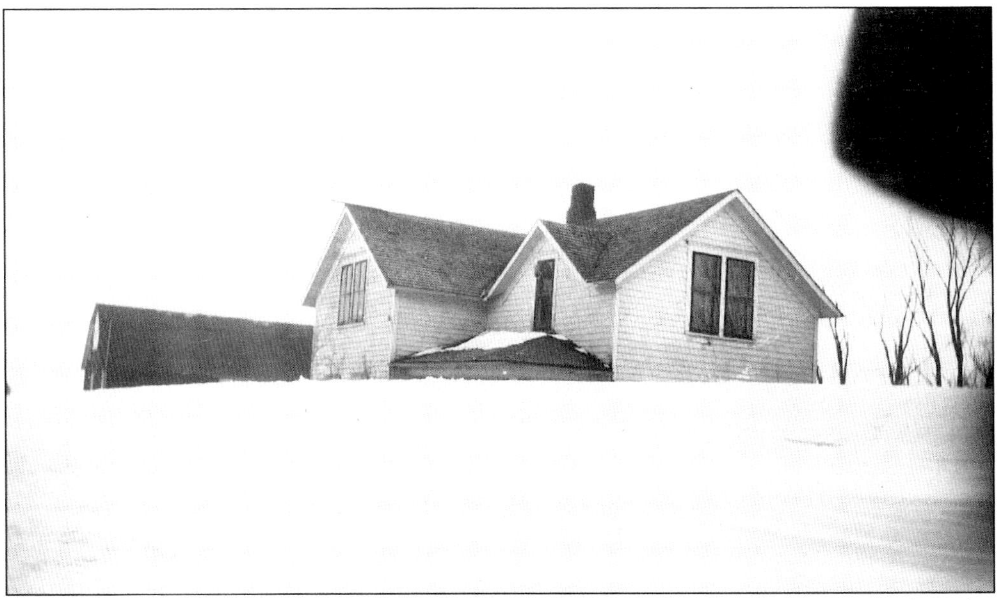

This is the Aasen farmhouse after a storm. When the author showed this photograph to his Mississippi-born wife, she thought it was a one-story house. It is a two-story house.

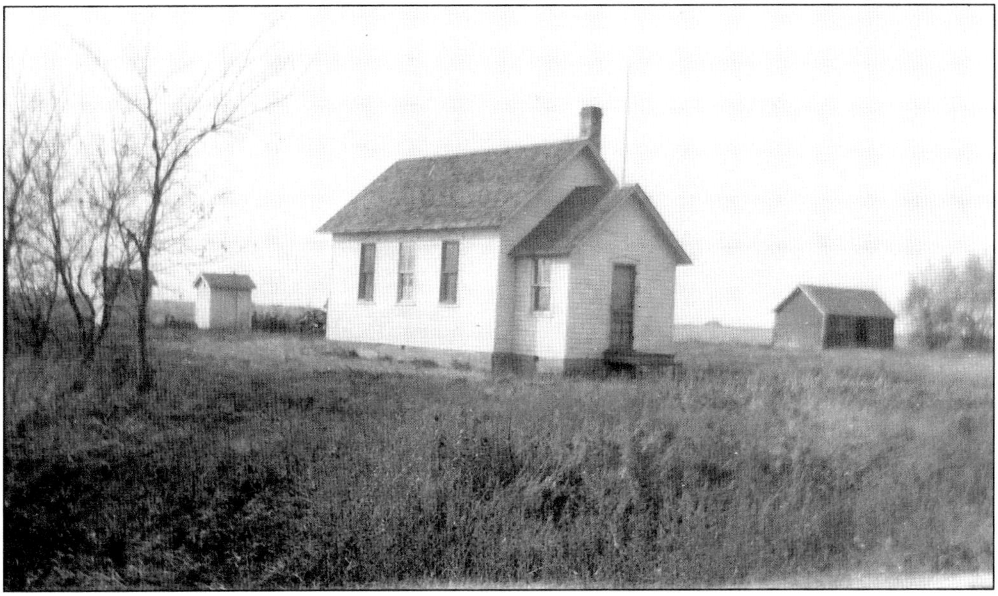

North Dakota had hundreds of one-room schoolhouses like this one in the 1900s. This is the River School 108, in Noble Township, Cass County, North Dakota. Note the two outdoor bathrooms and the shed where the teacher or the older students probably kept their horses.

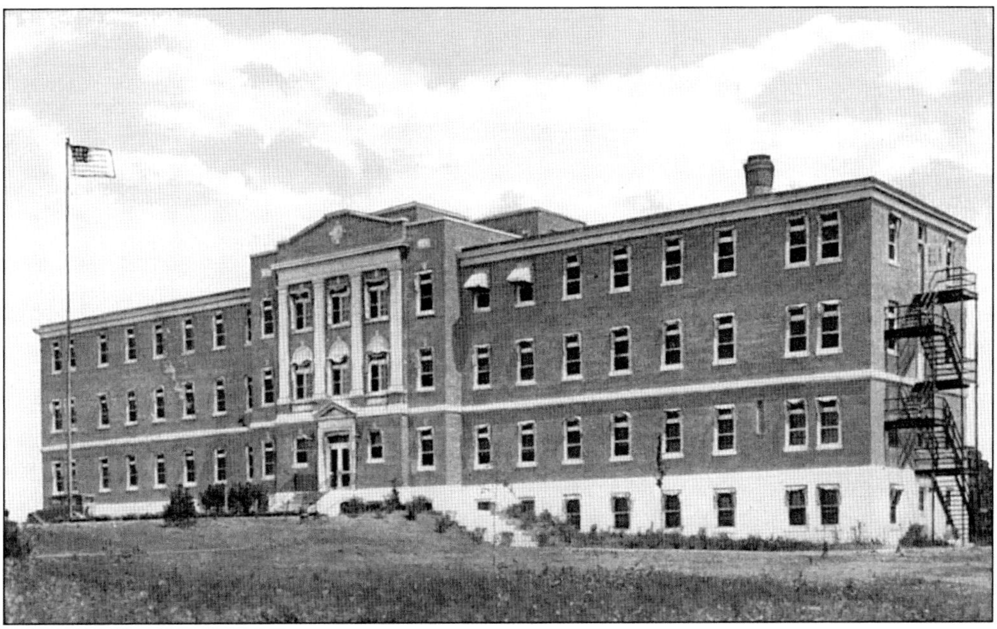

The Veterans Hospital in Fargo was built in the 1930s. It is the only hospital for veterans in the state. Today, there are about 66,000 veterans in North Dakota. The state has one home for veterans, which is located on 90 acres of land adjacent to Lisbon, North Dakota. The veterans home recently added a nursing wing.

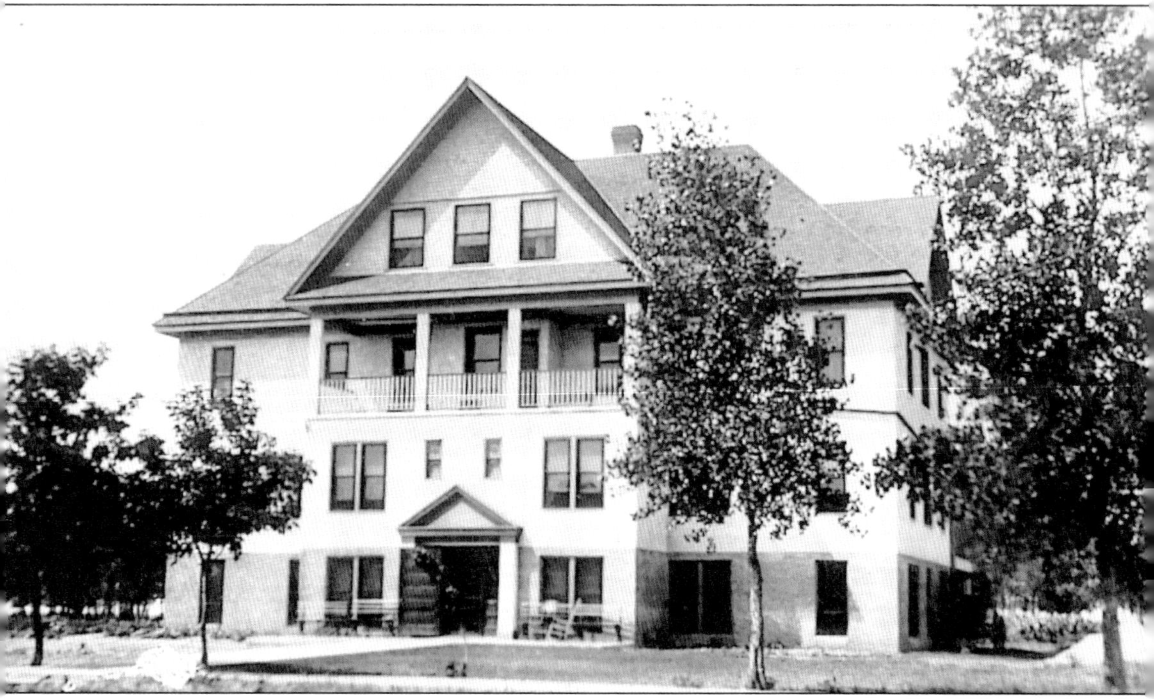

In the 1930s, Northwood, North Dakota, had an "Old People's Home." In the early 20th century, there were few "homes" of any kind for old people. Traill County did operate a "Poor Farm" for people during this period.

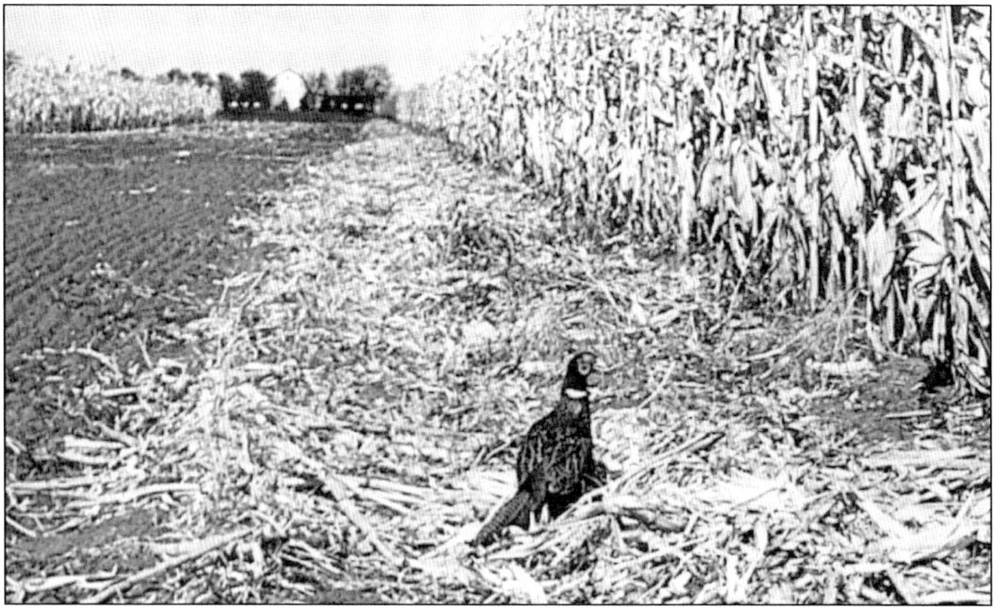

For many years, pheasant hunting in North Dakota has drawn hunters from all over the United States. The best areas for pheasant hunting are the Missouri River, its tributaries, and parts of southeastern and southwestern North Dakota. Hunters also come to North Dakota to hunt antelope, moose, elk, Hungarian partridges, grouse, prairie chickens, mourning doves, wild turkeys, ducks, coyotes, white-tailed and mule deer, and bighorn sheep.

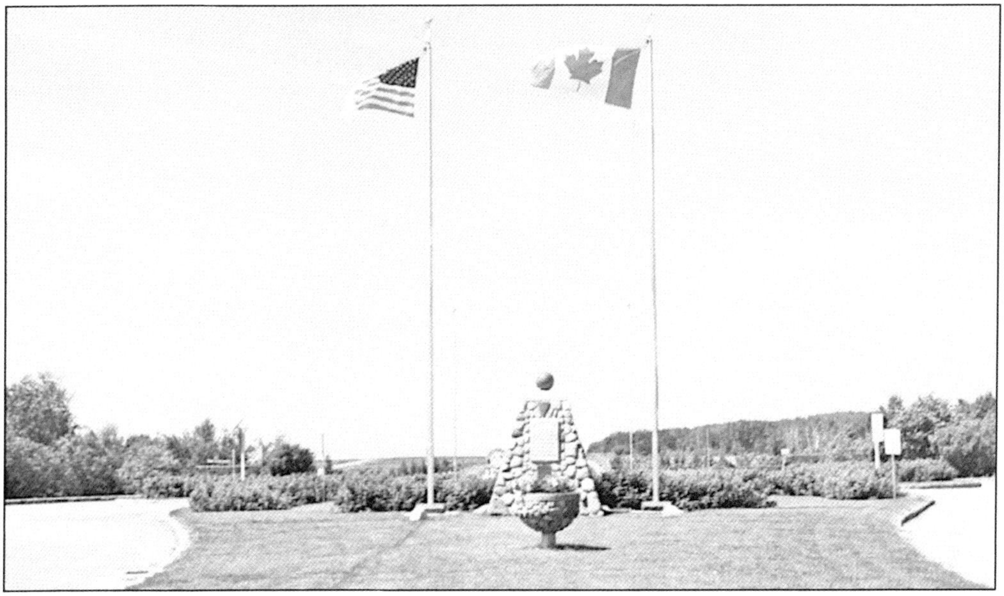

Dedicated in 1932, the International Peace Garden is in the Turtle Mountains on the border of North Dakota and Manitoba. It comprises over 2,300 acres. It commemorates the long-standing peace between the United States and Canada.

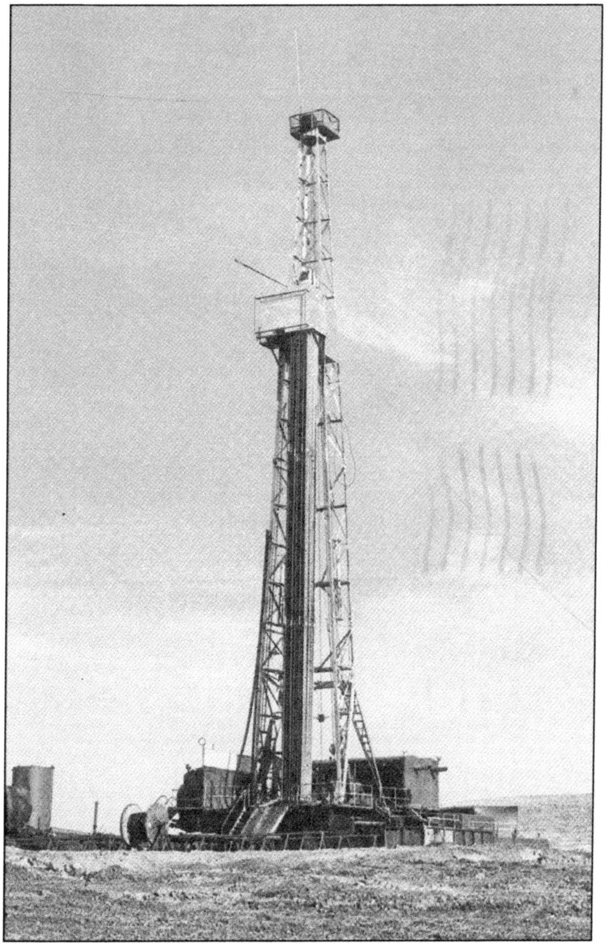

A new industry entered North Dakota in the early 1940s when oil was discovered near Tioga, North Dakota. The oil fields were not vast, but the oil was of good quality. Today, with the price of gasoline so low, few oil wells are still pumping.

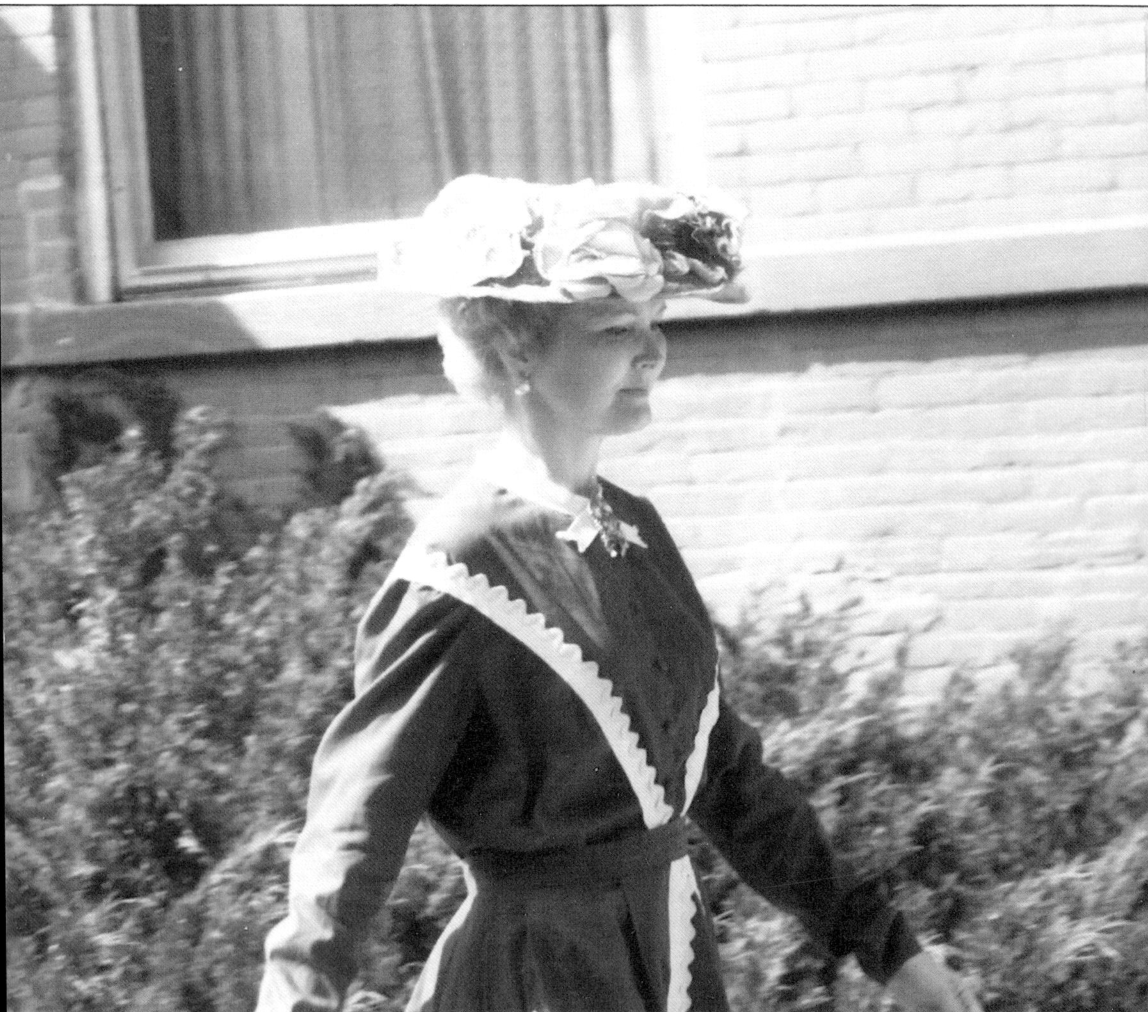

Linda Johnson, daughter of Jerry and Aagot Nysveen of Hillsboro, North Dakota, walks to the stage of a historical fashion event. Dressed for her part, she honors the past. Most towns in North Dakota now have historical museums and organizations because they realize they need to preserve the past. Linda's parents, Jerry and Aagot, have helped, with others, establish four museums in Hillsboro. They are the Pioneer Museum (old machinery), St. Olaf Chapel (old church), Plummer House Museum (first Hillsboro museum), and Centennial Museum (Native American memorabilia).

Bibliography

Geiger, Louis G. *University of Northern Plains*. Grand Forks: The University of North Dakota Press, 1958.

Jaeger, Alvin A. *North Dakota Blue Book*. Bismarck, 1995 and 1997–1999.

Lysengen, Janet Daley and Ann M. Rathke. *The Centennial Anthology of North Dakota History*; Journal of Northern Plains, State Historical Society of North Dakota, 1996.

Robinson, Elwyn B. *History of North Dakota*. Lincoln: University of Nebraska Press, 1966.